# SELF SUFFICIENCY STARTER HANDBOOK - THE ULTIMATE HOMESTEADING AND REGROWING 2-IN-1 COLLECTION

## START A SELF-SUFFICIENT LIFE STYLE, PLAN YOUR HOMESTEAD AND DISCOVER HOW TO REGROW FRESH PRODUCE FROM SCRAPS

# CONTENTS

## THE HOMESTEADING HANDBOOK

## THE REGROWER'S HANDBOOK

# THE HOMESTEADING HANDBOOK

## THE ESSENTIAL BEGINNER'S HOMESTEAD PLANNING GUIDE FOR A SELF-SUFFICIENT LIFESTYLE

# A SPECIAL GIFT TO MY READERS

Included with your purchase of this book is your free copy of
Your Homestead Planner

Follow the link below to receive your free copy:
www.kellyreedauthor.com
Or by accessing the QR code:

You can also join our Facebook community
**Homestead Living & Self Sufficiency,**
or contact me directly via kelly@kellyreedauthor.com

# INTRODUCTION

---

*"When the world wears out and society fails to satisfy, there is always the garden."*

— MINNIE AUMONIER

---

## Do You Wish You Had a Better, More Fulfilling Life?

In our modern lives, it's so common to feel as though something is missing. Sometimes we struggle to keep up with our day-to-day existence, working frantically in draining jobs, feeling as though our lives are slipping by us, and having no time to actually enjoy anything. We may feel numb, as though something has sucked all the meaning out of life; even when we *do* have downtime, all we do is bounce from one screen to another trying to figure out what will give us a sense of purpose or a flicker of happiness. Whole bookshelves of self-help books have been published in an attempt to help us improve our lives, but what if they miss a crucial element of our dissatisfaction? How can we improve our lives from within a societal structure that prioritizes cheap consumption and doesn't care how detached we feel as long as the cogs keep turning?

We tend to beat ourselves up for not being able to better our lives, but what if we're not the problem? Ever-increasing numbers of people are realizing that they want something more fulfilling for their lives, and are seeking that fulfillment by changing the way they relate to the world around them. Seeking a greater connection to nature and a more intentional way of life, people are turning to homesteading. Keep reading to discover why.

**What Is a Homestead?**

What comes to mind when you hear the word "homestead"? Maybe it conjures up images of a lost past where our ancestors worked hard to eke out a living, staying much closer to the land, the animals, and the plants that live and grow on it than the people of today. Maybe you think of an idyllic sun-drenched farm where fluffy lambs frolic in green fields, and children learn independence by fetching eggs from the chicken coop and milking cows for the cream to make ice cream. Maybe you picture somewhere far from civilization, a lone building standing amidst acres of land. Maybe you see gardens in bloom and tables full of their harvest. Or, perhaps you see solar panels and irrigation systems, closed systems providing all the electricity and water you could need. None of these ideas or images are wrong—and yet, none of them tell the whole story.

A homestead is simply a place where people make a home for themselves—the keywords being "make" and "themselves"! Homesteading is about learning to meet your needs with things you grow, gather, or otherwise produce yourself. That might mean you have a vast farm in the heart of the country, or it might mean you have a small window garden in a tiny apartment in the city. The truth is, there are many ways of homesteading, and many types of people who homestead. If you've ever wanted to make your life a little bit more sustainable, more self-sufficient, more organic, or even just a little bit more independent, then homesteading has something to offer you.

**Who Should Read This Book?**

If you were curious enough to pick this book up, it's for you! Maybe you already know that you're interested and you're hoping to find a great book to guide you through the process. Or, maybe you came across this book and it sparked something in you, and you'd like to follow that spark and see where it leads. This book is meant to impart knowledge and distill a broad topic down to its most essential parts. However, it will also help you to imagine a new way of living and give you the confidence to pursue that new lifestyle. If anything on this list applies to you, you are one of the many people that I wrote this book for:

- You're a city-dweller who longs for a more rural lifestyle.
- You want to reduce your environmental impact.
- You want to be less dependent on others for your food, water, and power.
- You're tired of expensive power and water bills.
- You dislike that your food is highly processed and exposed to chemicals and pesticides.
- You wish you could spend more time connecting to nature, experiencing the benefits of outdoor life, and feeling confident and satisfied that you can take care of yourself.
- You want more control over your life in general.
- You're planning to start a life off the grid and you want to make the best choices possible.
- You can't go off-grid at this point in your life, but you'd like to make small changes toward a more self-sufficient lifestyle.

If you identified with any of those statements, then this book can help you on your way to building a better, more rewarding way of life.

**Who Wrote This, and What Do They Know About Homesteading?**

My name is Kelly Reed, and my husband Robert and I have been homesteading since 2009. Over a decade of experience with off-grid living has given us a wealth of knowledge and expertise, but it wasn't always like that! When we started, we were totally new to all of this, just like you. We spent a lot of time and energy looking through resources that promised to help us plan and prepare. We found that there were plenty of resources—in fact, there were almost too many—but it was difficult to navigate such an overwhelming amount of information. Sometimes, these sources seemed to contradict one another, and many also offered an idealized idea of what homesteading life was like, which set us up for a rude awakening. This confusion meant that we went through a lot of frustration and pain, not to mention losing a lot of time and money when we made uninformed or misguided choices. Through a lot of trial and error, we've learned the best way to do things—but we don't want rude awakenings or trial and error for you. That's why I've written this book. I've only included the things I believe you need to know so you won't have to sift through tons of irrelevant content. Reading this, you'll get the benefit of all of the years I spent testing my research and honing my knowledge, and I can't wait to share it with you.

**Getting Started on Your Homestead Journey**

There are many ways you could go about starting your homesteading life. You could jump right in, figuring things out as you go along. That may sound exciting and appealing; however, it could be costly if you make uninformed decisions or expensive mistakes. A large enough error might even lead you to regret your decision altogether. On the other hand, you could spend a long time planning by reading, researching, and consulting experts. However, after days, weeks, or months of wading through the enormous amount of information out there, you might feel no closer to having a solid plan. In fact, you might feel frustrated and stuck, and end up never actually getting your dreams off the ground. Neither of these situations is ideal.

A better option is to find a thorough, unbiased guide that will give you the right information and practical solutions—that is exactly why this book exists. We've done the hard part for you; this book compiles all the basics that you need to know to get started while dispelling common myths and giving you a *real* idea of what the lifestyle is like. It will empower you to make well-informed decisions and give you what you need to get started, whether you're hoping to start a garden in your apartment window box or build a self-sustaining farm from the ground up. Here are some of the things you can expect to learn in the coming chapters:

- what homesteading is
- all the different ways it can be beneficial and how to incorporate those things into your daily life, even if you don't live in the country or want to go off-grid
- what to expect on your homesteading journey
- how to save time and money by avoiding common pitfalls and mistakes
- the laws, regulations, and other requirements related to homesteading
- the best places in the United States for homesteaders and/or off-grid living
- how to operate your own utilities, including renewable water and energy systems
- how to prepare for medical emergencies and other disasters

- what to expect, and how to prepare for homestead maintenance
- how to budget, and especially how to homestead on a small budget
- the differences in the types of properties, and which is best for you
- the importance of community, and how to find (and be) good neighbors

Reading this book will not only give you tons of great information and practical tips—it will invigorate your imagination and open your eyes to the many possibilities of homesteading. And, best of all, it will give you the confidence and information you need to make the right choices for you. Now, let's get started!

# 1

# THE HOMESTEADING SPECTRUM

E arlier, I asked you what it is that you picture when you hear the word "homestead." Hopefully, you're already beginning to expand your ideas of what that can be, and to understand that this way of life is a spectrum along which there is something for almost everyone, no matter their lifestyle or location.

*Homesteading life exists on a spectrum.*

However, some popular perceptions aren't actually true. Some people, for example, believe that homesteading means going without modern conveniences like electricity. A quick search online reveals a number of homesteading blogs, proving that many homesteaders have not only electricity but the internet as well. Below, we'll dispel some other common myths and misconceptions.

## Myths and Misconceptions About Homesteading

*Myth: Homesteading requires a large amount of land.*

It's not the space that makes a homesteader—it's what you do with that space. You don't need a large amount of land or even *any* land. You can actually do this anywhere, and it can be scaled up or down to fit within the space available to you. Some people may choose to own acres of land where they grow crops and raise livestock. Others may choose to own smaller amounts of land or to start out by leasing land in order to gain skills and experience before becoming landowners themselves. And some may focus on other ways of being self-sufficient, such as making their own clothes and cooking all their own meals from scratch using foods bought locally. It's all about how you approach your life; there are many ways of increasing the sustainability of your lifestyle that have nothing to do with size.

*Myth: Homesteading means you're living on free land.*

This idea probably comes from a time in American history when the federal government had a lot of land that it had seized or purchased, and wanted to encourage Americans to settle on that land. To achieve this goal, several laws—collectively called the Homestead Acts—were passed in the late 1800s and early 1900s. These laws allowed people to move onto parcels of land, where they would live, farm, and otherwise care for the land. If they did this for five years, the government would grant them the deed to that land.

As appealing as the idea of free land in exchange for labor and care sounds, the last Homestead Act was passed over a century ago in 1916, and it isn't nearly as easy to find free land nowadays. There are still some places in the U.S. running programs that give people land for free or for extremely reduced prices, so if it's your dream to live on free land, don't despair—it can be possible to make that happen. However, no one should feel like they're not truly homesteading if they aren't living on free land.

*Myth: Homesteading requires special expertise or prior farm experience.*

While planning and knowledge are always good to have, you don't need any special skills to get started and you don't have to have a background in farming. In fact, historical homesteaders (which we discussed earlier) came from all different walks of life and learned as they went. Modern homesteading is no different; the most important thing you need is the passion to start a new way of life. That passion is what will drive you to learn and to try new challenges, which will help you grow and learn. Start small, work hard, and you'll soon find your knowledge and skills growing exponentially.

*Myth: Homesteaders all live "off the grid," and homesteading is all about preparing for doomsday or some other apocalyptic future.*

It's a common misconception that all homesteaders live "off the grid," meaning that they are not connected to any public utilities such as water and electricity. While many *do* live off the grid, this is a matter of opinion and preference. If you are able to live off the grid and that's what you want, then you'll find resources in this book to help you do that. But if you're not interested in a life off the grid or if it's not feasible for you at the moment, it is absolutely not a requirement.

This misconception goes hand in hand with another, which is that people who homestead and/or live off the grid do so because they are concerned about a future where "the grid" fails and we are all left to fend for ourselves. But while this lifestyle will certainly make you more independent and able to provide for yourself, most people don't seek it out because they're worried about future disasters. Instead, they're drawn to the do-it-yourself lifestyle, and enjoy the autonomy that comes from knowing how to build, cook, and otherwise create their homes and lives on their own terms.

*Myth: Homesteading means you're completely self-sufficient.*

Again, there are very few rules about this way of life, and as with other parts of it, the self-sufficiency that people practice exists along a spectrum. Just as some live totally off the grid, some may be absolutely self-sufficient. More common, however, are those people who value and appreciate community. It is rare for anyone to never need help from anyone else, whether that help is in the form of exchanging goods and services, giving and receiving advice, or sharing knowledge. Your community might be your local network or the broader community across the country, but either way, that community helps you thrive. It also allows people to pursue their own particular interests. One person might be an excellent gardener, another might be great at sewing, and a third be excellent at dealing with solar energy. Before our modern monetary system, people negotiated excesses and shortages through barter and trading, using other people's proficiencies to make up for their own shortcomings, and vice versa. Homesteading follows this philosophy.

*Myth: Homesteaders live far away from other people, surrounded by dangerous wilderness.*

As we've just discussed, there's a lot of community in homesteading. This includes many people who have neighbors within walking distance. And as will be discussed later in this book, there are many ways to reduce the risks of living in the country, whether it be receiving proper training, securing communication lines, knowing how to contact and access emergency services, maintaining your stock of living necessities, or having basic first aid knowledge. Safety is less dependent on your environment and situation than it is on being prepared for what that situation and environment might generate. For some, this approach to life brings an increased sense of safety and security because they feel more informed and prepared to take care of themselves in a variety of situations.

*Myth: Homesteading isn't enough to support yourself or earn an income.*

Actually, there are all sorts of ways that you can earn income in this lifestyle. Some people make money directly from their homestead, by selling either goods (things they've grown and/or made) or services (skills they've acquired and can share with others). Some work part-time or have seasonal jobs near where they live, and others work remotely via the internet. Some even share their life via blogs, which can be monetized. There is a myriad of possibilities, and because of their can-do spirit, homesteaders are imaginative and innovative, and they apply those traits to money-making. Plus, many of the costs associated with more conventional lifestyles are eliminated by a more sustainable way of living. By growing your own food, making your own clothes, and producing your own power, you can greatly reduce your cost of living.

*Myth: Homesteading is very difficult and too time-consuming for you to have other jobs or hobbies.*

To be completely honest, this life is unquestionably difficult at times. This book would not be giving you the unbiased and clear-eyed overview it promised if it claimed otherwise. Especially at the beginning of your journey, you may struggle to learn new skills, to adapt to a new way of life, or to balance incorporating these new ventures with the more modern elements of your life. But many, *many* people have come before you, and their choices illustrate the variety of ways to structure your life so that it works for you. Homesteaders have full-time jobs, they volunteer, they pursue hobbies, they raise families. At times, of course, there are setbacks, failures, and frustrations. Persevering through these things, and learning that you can, is a big part of what makes this life so rewarding.

*Myth: Homesteading is very simple, and with minimal effort, you can create an idyllic paradise.*

While some fear this undertaking is too difficult, others have an idealized view of it, picturing the enjoyment of the end product without considering the effort required to achieve those results. A homestead is not the garden of Eden—it takes work. This does not mean, however, that it is unattainable, or will require the sacrifice of your whole life. You will succeed by starting where you are and finding the right balance—and, in return, you will get closer to nature, become more aware of the world around you, know what goes into your food and clothes, and in general create a healthier, more holistic life for yourself. For those who truly love it, the effort is more than worth those rewards.

*Myth: There is one true way to be a homesteader.*

It should be evident by this point that there are exceptions to almost any "rule" that you might have come across. In fact, there is really only one constant: all homesteaders hope to become more self-sufficient. If you hope for that and you have the will to see that hope through, then you are in the right place. Homesteading is not about doing any one thing. It is about creating a life where you have the means and skills to meet your needs; it means regaining some of the self-sustaining skills that have been lost over generations and reclaiming a role in your own subsistence, rather than being merely a detached consumer; it means valuing not just the end product, but the process that created it; it is about building a more intentional life for yourself.

## Different Types of Homesteading

While there is no one true way, most homesteads can be loosely grouped into one of several categories. These categories are based on two main factors: location and scale. In other words, where will you make your home, and how big will your operation be?

### *Apartment Homesteading*

This is homesteading on the smallest scale, for those who live in urban environments, rent their homes, and/or own no outdoor space. Apartment homesteading is all about making the most of the space you have. It often involves a good mix of self-sufficiency and modern conveniences. Those who practice it focus on ways they can modify conventional apartment living to be more self-sustaining. If this sounds like you, here are some ways you can get started:

- **Look for ways to reuse items and materials.** This could be switching from disposable items (like paper towels) to ones that can be used many times (such as a cloth towel), or keeping items that can be used more than once (like glass bottles and jars). It could mean shopping at thrift stores rather than buying new clothes.

- **You could also try looking for tutorials that teach you how to repurpose items that you no longer use into something you need.** Get creative—imagination is an important part of this!
- **Make your own things.** This can be as complex as learning to sew your own clothes, or as simple as nailing together some boards to make a basic shelf. You could learn to carve, to knit, to weave, to make your own cleaning and beauty projects, or all of the above.
- **Start a garden.** There are any number of ways to grow a garden, even if you have no outside space. You could have a container garden that sits on your windowsill, or your balcony, if you have one. You could see if there's garden space available on your building rooftop—if there's not, you could ask the landlord if you can start one. Some neighborhoods also have community gardens, where you will be given your own allotment where you can plant and cultivate vegetables, fruits, and herbs.
- **Cook and preserve your own food.** If you're used to eating a lot of restaurant food and takeout food, start by learning some basic cooking skills. If you already know the basics, try going deeper to learn to cook completely from scratch. And to make the food you're growing in your garden last longer, you can also learn how to can, pickle, dry, and otherwise preserve that food so it can feed you for months to come.

*Backyard Homesteading*

A step up from apartment homesteading, this takes place in an urban or suburban environment where you have your own yard that you can use to grow food and raise small livestock. It still usually involves a mixture of traditional living with the more conventional modern lifestyle. Backyard homesteaders make the most of their land by planning carefully, which allows them to grow lots of different plants in different seasons and for different purposes. This can be surprisingly effective and is usually limited only by your planning skills and your imagination (and occasionally, your homeowner's association—be sure to check the rules and incorporate them in your plans). If you're considering backyard homesteading, here are some ideas to get you started:

- **Raise livestock.** It might seem strange to think of chickens or goats in the suburbs, but given the right conditions, it's totally doable. Raising hens to provide fresh eggs is a great first step in raising livestock. If you have a family, feeding the flock and gathering the eggs are good ways to involve your children and help them learn independence.
- **Upgrade your garden.** Many homeowners plant trees, flowers, and shrubs in their yards, but that space can also be used to grow edible plants. You can plant nut bushes or fruit trees. Utilize planting techniques like companion planting or intercropping (both methods of growing different types of plants in the same space) to

make the most of the area that you have. Again, get creative!

- **Learn to fix things that break.** Owning a home means that you're responsible when things go wrong. Instead of calling a plumber, an electrician, or another type of handyman when something breaks, learn to do your own repairs. You can still consult professionals for big tasks, but by educating yourself about how to do small repairs, you can work your way up to more complex jobs and find more independence.

Preserve your own food, make your own things, and lean into reusable materials on a larger scale than you could in an apartment. More room means you can try things on a bigger scale. Use your basement to store canned and preserved goods. Hang your clothes to dry on a clothesline rather than using a dryer. Set up a basic carpentry shop in your garage or spare room. Thinking creatively is key to having a thriving suburban homestead.

*Small- to Large-Scale Homesteading*

This is probably the most well-known type of homesteading. These are often in rural locations and on larger areas of land, though the size can vary wildly. The smaller end of the spectrum might be a few acres while the larger end might be more than a hundred. The biggest difference created by scale will be exactly how self-sufficient you can be. If you want to raise large livestock like cattle, you'll need enough land to support them. If you want to grow their food yourself, rather than purchase it, then you'll need enough acreage to grow both livestock feed and whatever food you need. If your goal is to homestead on a large scale someday, these are some aspirations you might begin working toward:

- **Expand the type of livestock you raise.** If you have enough room, this might include raising cattle for meat or cows for milk or sheep for wool. It also might include building beehives to harvest your own honey or raising enough chickens that you will have a surplus of eggs to sell for profit.
- **Plant and harvest crops.** If your property is of a smaller size, you might have a large garden (or possibly several), some fruit trees or bushes, and potentially a greenhouse or two. If your farm is larger, you might plant things on a larger scale, with orchards of fruit trees and fields of crops. Again, at this point, you might no longer be growing food just for yourself, but also to sell for profit, or to exchange with others in return for their goods or services.
- **Build your own house.** Take a cue from early homesteaders and start with just a parcel of land. It's not necessary to build your own house to be a homesteader, of course, but for many people, being involved in the planning and construction of their home from the ground up is one more way to be intentional about how they live. Plus, being involved in the building of your house means that you understand how it is put together and are that much more equipped to maintain and repair it.

- **Become completely self-sufficient.** If absolute self-sufficiency is your long-term goal, then this is the choice for you. With enough time, planning, and land, you can create a system that supports you completely, providing shelter, food, clothing, water, and power without dependency on any external institutions. Homesteads like this take a *lot* of work, including setting up and maintaining your own power grid and water filtration system, but the effort is worth it for those that long for this level of autonomy.

Looking at these three groups, is there one that speaks to you, one that inspires you? The point of presenting these categories is not to make you feel that you have to categorize your own efforts but to illustrate the range of options available. As you begin to plan, remember that your self-sufficiency doesn't have to be extreme or total. Start small and look for ways to modify your current lifestyle. Ask yourself: What can I grow? What can I make? What skills can I learn? As you start to answer those questions, the next section will help you create some initial goals.

## Setting Homesteading Goals

Once you've gotten started and you're planning your first goals, ask yourself two questions: What is my eventual objective? And are these SMART goals?

When thinking about your eventual objective, try to picture the perfect life; what does it look like? You'll want to keep this picture in mind to be sure that the plans you make now will move you toward that objective. Knowing your end game will help you prioritize your goals and plan accordingly. It will also help you to not get distracted by what other people are doing. Staying focused on your goals and values despite what others are doing is key to constructing a life that will satisfy and support you.

Now, with these goals in mind, you can ask yourself if these are SMART goals. SMART is an acronym invented by consultant George T. Doran in the 1980s; it stands for Specific, Measurable, Attainable, Relevant, and Time-bound. These five principles help to make sure that goals are concrete and achievable rather than vague and overly ambitious. Here's a further breakdown of how each concept affects your goal-setting:

Specific: Specific goals name exactly what it is you hope to achieve. They are not ambiguous or conceptual. They help you focus on particular steps that, when taken together, will lead you to your goal. For example, instead of saying, "I will become more self-sufficient with my food," say "I will learn to grow vegetables in my garden that I can eat."

Measurable: Measurable goals have an endpoint after which you can definitively say that you have achieved that goal. This gives you the ability to know how close or far you are to achieving your goal and keeps you from abandoning goals because you're struggling to recognize how far you've progressed. Instead of saying, "I will learn to grow vegetables that I can eat," say "I will learn to grow tomatoes, beans, and kale."

Attainable: Attainable goals are goals that you can actually accomplish. This means that you have to consider your current skill levels and limitations when setting a goal. If you're an accomplished carpenter, making a table might be attainable, but if you've never picked up a hammer, you'll want to start with something smaller. If you've never gardened before and your goal is to grow tomatoes, beans, and kale, start by setting a goal of growing one of those vegetables.

Relevant: Relevant goals are related to both your lifestyle and your long-term plans. This is where it is really handy to know your eventual objectives. If you hope to someday work and live on a large-scale farm, then food goals that help you on your way to being completely self-sufficient are relevant. If you don't currently live on a farm and don't plan to in the future, then food goals that aim toward sustainability through other means (a local food co-op, perhaps, or a mix of farmer's market, home-grown, and store-bought food) might make more sense for you.

Time-bound: Setting a time limit for your goals not only gives you the motivation to achieve them but also makes it easier to measure your progress. If you know you want to achieve a goal within a certain period of time, you can break down everything you need to do and create an action plan for achieving that goal. For example, instead of saying, "I will learn to grow tomatoes, beans, and kale," say "I will learn to grow tomatoes, beans, and kale by the end of this year."

**Next Steps**

By now, you should have a good idea of what homesteading is and isn't, as well as the different ways that it can be done. With all that information, you can start to dream of your new life and what it will look like. In the rest of this book, you will learn more about how homesteading works and how it can work for you. Once you have a thorough understanding of what it requires and what it has to offer, you can use SMART goals to help you start to move toward that vision.

# 2

# IS HOMESTEADING LEGAL?

If you've done your own research online, you might be frustrated by the lack of clear information about the legality of homesteading. As we've established, though some people might live off the grid, homesteading and off-grid living are not the same thing. However, online sources often confuse the terms or use them interchangeably. This only adds to the difficulty in understanding what is and isn't legal. Further complicating matters is the fact that each state has its own laws and regulations regarding both homesteading and off-grid living. But don't be discouraged! This book exists to inform and guide your decisions, and that includes helping you understand what is and isn't legal. If you plan to buy land, build a house, set up your own water and electricity, raise livestock, or grow your own food, understanding the laws discussed below will be especially important. We'll walk you through them one by one.

**Camping on Your Property**

It may seem strange since you own the land on which you would be camping, but in a lot of places, there is a limit to how long you can camp—usually two weeks. After that two weeks is up, you must either move into a more permanent abode or move off the property. This includes camping in camper vans and some trailers. If you were hoping to camp on the property while you built your house, you can apply for a special permit to do so, but be aware that it can be very difficult to procure one of these permits. As with everything on this list, it is wise to double-check the exact rules of your local municipality, but know that it is unlikely you can just pitch a tent and call it a day. Eventually, you will need a permanent shelter to stay within the law.

**Minimum Square Footage Laws for Houses**

There are quite a few rules that govern building a house, no matter where you build it. Anytime someone builds a new structure, the plans for that structure must be approved by the local government. To start, there is a minimum required square footage. In other words, if your planned house is too small, you won't be granted building permits. The minimum frequently falls between 500 and 1,000 square feet, meaning that many micro-houses or "tiny houses" might not be approved.

**Minimum Square Footage Laws for Land**

In addition to regulations on the size of houses themselves, there is also a minimum on the size of land you can buy (or sell). This minimum varies by location and environment, meaning that lots in the city are often allowed to be smaller than lots in the country. Local governments put these regulations in place to keep rural areas from becoming too densely populated. It is common for lot sizes in rural areas to have a minimum of five to ten acres, although in some places the minimum can be as high as 20 or even 40 acres. For both minimum house and land square footage, exceptions called "variances" can be granted to allow for smaller structures or lots, but these exceptions are very rare, and it is best not to plan on getting one.

**Building Codes**

Once you start building your house, you must follow national and international building codes. It is important to follow these codes because your building will be inspected by the local authorities to be sure it complies. It is also important because these codes are designed to ensure that structures are safe. If you're intimidated by the idea of keeping track of construction and being sure you are following code, you can hire a building contractor, whose job involves making sure you adhere to the codes.

**Water Utility Regulations**

The first rule with water is that you *must* have it! If your building plans don't include access to clean water, they will not be approved. Normally, this would be done by connecting to city- or county-run water lines; in some places, connecting to this network is required. Those wishing to live off the grid will look for locations where they are allowed to use alternatives to the municipal water supply, such as a well dug on the property or use of a natural spring. Another alternative is to collect and purify rainwater, but this method of getting water is frequently illegal even in locations where other alternatives are allowed.

## Power Utility Regulations

Laws in most places do not allow people to live completely without electricity. This is generally because electricity is required to meet certain safety standards. As with water, some places will require citizens to be hooked up to the local electrical network. As a general rule, the closer you are to a town or city, the more likely it is that you will be required to connect to the power grid. In places where you are allowed to generate your own electricity, you can consider different options, such as solar panels, wind turbines, or thermal wells. If you do generate your own electricity, you might be allowed to sell any excess electricity you generate to the county or city, which it will then sell to other residents. Some states also incentivize the use of renewable energy with tax cuts. If you do opt for an alternative method of power generation, it is also important to be sure that it is installed and maintained correctly.

## Septic System Regulations

One aspect of living "on the grid" that is often taken for granted is septic waste disposal. It is obviously illegal to dump septic waste, so if you're not planning to be hooked up to the local sewer system, you'll need to establish your own septic system. This involves testing the ground's absorption rate, getting the appropriate permits, and procuring and burying a septic tank. Often, you will be required to have the system installed by a professional. There are some alternatives to using a traditional septic system, such as using a chemical toilet (like those used in RVs) or a composting toilet. However, these are only legal in some situations, and will also need to be approved before being put to use.

### Raising Livestock and Growing Food

If you are planning to keep animals on your land, you must be sure that your property is zoned for agriculture. There are generally fewer regulations on growing food, especially fruits and vegetables. However, for both livestock and crops, if you intend to sell any of what you raise or grow, then you must procure a permit. Your land and any relevant facilities will be inspected before the permit is issued. With grain, in particular, it is important to determine if your operation will be considered a commercial farm, as it might then be subject to certain farming regulations. A related issue is game hunting, which also requires a permit (even if you're hunting on your own land) and the type of animal you can hunt may be restricted by location or season.

### Paying Taxes

While many people choose to homestead because they want more control over their lives, there is one area where you will always be subject to local and federal jurisdiction, and that is taxes. No matter how independent you are, if you own property, you must pay property taxes, and if you make money, you must pay income taxes. It is always possible that you will qualify for certain tax incentives and exemptions, however, so it may be wise to consult a tax expert during your planning.

## Choosing Where to Homestead

You may have noticed a common theme in all of the above information—the laws change depending on where you live. It is always important to double-check local rules and regulations, but if you're planning to relocate, then you have a chance to pick which state is the best place for you. The next section of this chapter is dedicated to helping you determine that.

### A Brief Overview of U.S. Climate Zones

In addition to local laws, another very important factor to consider when relocating is what the weather will be like in your future home. Climate is one of the most important things to consider when planning for any lifestyle, but it is especially important when you plan to be working outdoors, caring for livestock and plants, and generally more exposed to weather and elements of nature. Specific needs might also be highly influenced by climate, such as how much sun you can expect to get if you plan to rely on solar energy. There is no one correct climate, as people can thrive in all sorts of environments, and some people are particularly suited to even the most extreme climates. However, many people find that mild, variable climates are ideal for homesteads, given their diverse seasons and lack of severe temperatures.

The continental U.S. is typically divided into these five climate regions:

*The Northeast:* Known for its seasons, especially its epic fall foliage, the Northeast encompasses the states of Maine, Vermont, New Hampshire, Massachusetts, Rhode Island,

Connecticut, New York, New Jersey, and Pennsylvania. The climate here is varied and diverse, with chilly winters and semi-humid summers. Generally, the farther north you travel, the colder the winters; the farther south, the more humid the summers.

*The Southeast:* Containing the greatest number of states, the Southeast includes Kentucky, Tennessee, Virginia, West Virginia, Delaware, Maryland, North Carolina, South Carolina, Mississippi, Alabama, Georgia, Florida, Louisiana, and Arkansas. The Southeast is considered subtropical and can be quite humid. The winters are usually mild and the summers can be very hot.

*The Midwest:* Spanning the middle of the country, the Midwest is made up of Ohio, Indiana, Illinois, Michigan, Minnesota, Wisconsin, Iowa, Missouri, North Dakota, South Dakota, Nebraska, and Kansas. The summers here are often similar to those in the Southeast, hot and humid, but the winters get much colder. Snow and subzero temperatures are common.

*The Southwest:* Containing only four states—Oklahoma, Texas, Arizona, and New Mexico—the Southwest still spans a good amount of land. This area of the country contains a lot of deserts, which means the temperatures tend to be extreme. The climate in coastal areas, influenced by the currents from the Pacific Ocean, has more moderate temperatures that stay consistent throughout the year.

*The West:* This region includes states along the Pacific coast and in the northwest corner of the country, and is composed of California, Nevada, Washington, Oregon, Idaho, Montana,

Wyoming, Colorado, and Utah. Summers here are often dry and cool, and winters also tend to be mild. The further south you go, the dryer the climate gets; likewise, the further north you travel, the better the weather becomes.

*Hawaii & Alaska:* Because they are not physically connected to the rest of the U.S., both these states have distinct climates from any other regions. Hawaii has a tropical climate, though local weather can vary quite a bit depending on altitude and land features. Alaska, because of its large landmass, is made up of many different climate zones. Most of Alaska's population lives in the southern and eastern parts of the state, which are milder in climate compared to the further, northern reaches of the state.

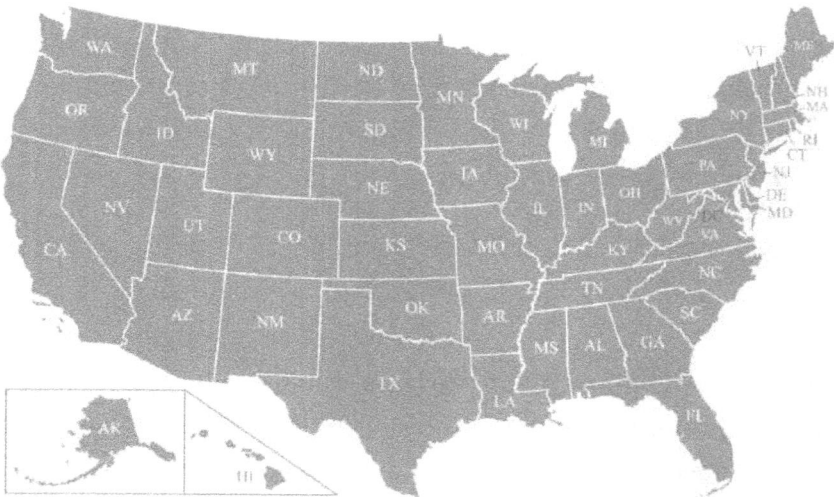

## The Best U.S. States for Homesteading

As with all the choices you'll make in this endeavor, it is important to remember that the best state for your homestead is the one where you can build the life you want—even if that's not the place that the majority of others choose. However, several states jump to the top of consideration because of their suitability for homesteading and living off the grid. To make things simple, we've done the legwork for you, compiling and cross-referencing research into the handy list below.

Some key things to be aware of as you consider these options are land prices, cost of living, local laws and building codes, taxes (property, income, and sales), and, as we just discussed, climate. If your budget allows, it can be a good idea to visit any prospective states, specifically the area where you might like to live. Look around, talk to locals, and get a feel for what living there might be like. A state may appeal to you on paper, but leave you underwhelmed in reality. Alternatively, a state may have stricter laws, harsher weather, or other potential negatives, but you might decide these things are worth it if you really love the idea of living there. The key is to know both what you want and what a state has to offer, so you can choose a location that is the best fit for you.

### Top Choices

#### *Missouri*

Missouri comes up frequently when researching homestead-friendly states. This midwestern state has varied landscapes and allows you to experience all four seasons without also experiencing the extremes of some other places. It has a mild winter that doesn't last too long, with the last frost happening in April or early May. This works well for growing crops, as does the average of 40 inches of rainfall per year. Missouri authorities are supportive of off-grid living, and their laws reflect that: you are not required to connect to a septic system, you're allowed to collect rainwater, and there are not many strict zoning regulations or building codes. Fishing is legal in many of Missouri's lakes, as well.

Missouri has a long history of farming, and most of the nearly 95,000 farms there are smaller and family-owned. This translates into quite a few communities focused on self-sufficiency, as well as a high amount of things like farmer's markets or "U-Pick" farms. You can declare your home a homestead after living on it for 40 consecutive months, and once declared, you can claim up to a $15,000 exemption on it. Other positives for the state include moderate taxes (both sales and property), incentives for using solar power, and an abundance of rural countryside. However, it is important to note that Missouri has high state income taxes, and land prices can be expensive. It is also good to be aware that droughts and other natural disasters do sometimes occur.

### Oregon

This state in the far northwest of the country is known for its gorgeous scenery and prolific farmer's markets. Oregon is a great place to move if you like the idea of a lot of community, either through lots of close neighbors or as part of a town dedicated to homesteading. In fact, some communities in

Oregon have taken this to a whole new level, with large off-grid communes like Three Rivers and Breitenbush Hot Springs even becoming tourist attractions. There is a lot of diversity in Oregon landscapes, with deserts, forests, and beaches in different parts of the state. Farmland is usually inexpensive and, especially in the rainier parts of the state, very fertile.

Oregon offers homestead exemptions of up to $40,000 for single people and $50,000 for married couples. Within the city limits, you are allowed to protect up to one city block, while outside those limits, you can cover up to 160 acres. There are a lot of natural resources, such as high-quality timber, as well as a lot of public land for recreation, with very few restrictions on hunting and fishing. Other benefits of living in Oregon include no state sales tax, average property taxes, rebates for solar power, and programs for farmers like grants and educational opportunities. However, Oregon does have a high cost of living and fairly high income taxes.

### Tennessee

Tennessee is a great option if you're on a budget and hoping to keep costs low. They have a lot to offer financially, including a cost of living that's 10% below the U.S. average and very low property taxes. The laws and regulations in this state are also appealing, with minimal building codes in a lot of counties and low restrictions on activities like rainwater collecting and raw milk herd-sharing. Tennessee also offers a rural homesteading land grant and hosts the annual Great Appalachian Homesteading Conference. The state protects property from being seized by creditors in the case of a financial crisis and allows exemptions of up to $5,000.

Tennessee also has a lot of natural beauty and great natural resources, including many opportunities to hunt and fish. The weather is temperate and the growing season lasts around nine months. The land is great for growing crops, especially in the middle and western parts of the state. Tennessee's main drawbacks are weather-related, given the occasionally cold winters and the possibility of tornados and flooding.

### Idaho

Idaho is great for agriculture, having a reputation for some of the most fertile soil in the U.S. This explains why around 15% of the population are farmers. It also boasts beautiful rolling green hills and mountains. Its population density offers a good balance, as the population is sparse enough to allow you space and privacy without feeling truly isolated from other people. Both living costs and land costs are low, and natural disasters are rare. The laws in Idaho offer support for growing crops, raising livestock, and even homeschooling your children, as well as giving declared homesteaders who own their property financial protection up to $100,000, and exemptions in property taxes. This explains why there are over 60,000 homesteads in the state.

Idaho's other advantages include outdoor recreational possibilities (such as skiing, whitewater rafting, fishing, and hunting), a low crime rate, and tax incentives for solar power. The state is becoming more popular, though, so there is potential for a population boom that would drive up prices; other potential negatives include harsh winters, high income taxes, and occasional floods, wildfires, and earthquakes.

### North Carolina

North Carolina might be less popular for those who want to farm lots of crops, but it offers great opportunities for other types of homesteading. Its mountains are well-suited to raising goats and there are lots of wild foods, such as berries or mushrooms, for those who are interested in foraging for food. The western part of the state is particularly popular among homesteaders, with major communities in the Saluda and Black Mountain regions that continue to grow.

North Carolina offers solar power rebates, low property taxes and laws that are conducive to homestead and off-grid lifestyles. Its growing season is a good length and the climate is moderate. The state also gives declared homesteaders good protection under the law, which might offset some of the negatives, such as high sales and income taxes and high land prices.

### Wyoming

Unlike Oregon and North Carolina, which offer a lot of community, or Idaho, which offers a good balance between privacy and community, Wyoming is a great state for those who really value solitude. The broad horizon and extensive space mean great views and, combined with the low population density, a chance to withdraw more completely from modern life.

Wyoming has a lot of resources for both farming and ranching, and the land—good for both growing crops and raising livestock—isn't too expensive. With a low cost of living, low property and sales taxes, and no state income tax, Wyoming is also appealing to those on a budget. Additionally, exemptions for homesteaders protect up to $40,000. The state boasts an average of 114 sunny days per year, which is higher than states known for their sunshine, like California. Wyoming is not for everyone, however, because of the severe winters, short growing season, and lack of rain (which can occasionally lead to wildfires).

**Other States to Consider**

The above states may be the most appealing to homesteaders for their laws, climate, and land, but they are not the only options. Read on to discover other states that still have a lot to offer.

*Alabama* — Alabama's cost of living is low and the cost of land also tends to be low. It has some of the lowest property taxes in the U.S. and therefore is ideal for large land purchases. The state gets 56 inches of rain per year and there are no restrictions on collecting rainwater. Some places in Alabama have no building codes at the county level. However, Alabama can be quite hot and occasionally has hurricanes or tornadoes.

*Alaska* — Alaska is similar to Wyoming in that it will appeal to those who wish to have a lot of privacy and solitude. In fact, some parts of Alaska can only be reached by plane. However, there are parts of Alaska, especially further south, that have more established communities. Alaska also has a low level of regulation and generally permissive laws. The trade-off for this is an extreme climate, especially in the north of the state, where some regions are inside the Arctic Circle.

*Arizona* — This state in the Southwest is warm all year and gets the most sunshine of all U.S. states, which makes it ideal for those who want to use solar power. The land is also very cheap and the growing season is long. However, much of the land is desert which can make growing food a challenge, especially as Arizona can have droughts. Locations near fresh water are ideal, as this allows you to drill for a well and get the water you need from there.

*Arkansas* — Arkansas has a lot of positives including an unlimited homestead exemption, low to moderate land prices, low property taxes, and a low cost of living. Known for the grandeur of the Ozarks, the state also has 9,700 miles of streams and 600,000 acres of lakes. With such expansive wilderness, this is another state that's great for those who want a little more seclusion and those who intend to rely on natural resources. The climate is mild and the growing season is long, lasting 200 days. It can be harder to find land here, though, because of competition with bigger agriculture corporations, and the income and sales taxes are high.

*Colorado* — Flexible zoning codes and local municipal support of green and sustainable housing are two of the big draws in Colorado. Some counties have no building codes, the most well-known of these being Delta, Custer, and Montezuma counties (but note that the state itself still has building codes that must be followed). Colorado is also a great place for renewable energy sources, with plenty of wind and sunshine for both solar and wind-powered electricity.

*Hawaii* — Hawaii's weather and tropical climate have made it a famously nice place to live, but lesser-known is the fact that outside of cities, many Hawaiian residents already live off the grid. The state gets a lot of both sunshine and rain, which means its soil is great for growing things. Wind and solar energy are both good options, and there is no restriction on rainwater collection. The state does have some restrictive regulations, however, as well as a high cost of living.

*Indiana* — The southern portion of Indiana is especially popular among homesteaders as it has a low population density, a good growing season, and warmer weather. Land can be expensive in Indiana, but taxes and living costs are generally low. There is a tradition of farming in Indiana with the majority of its 56,000 farms being smaller scale and owned by families. Indiana also has a lot of green space; unfortunately, it also has frequent floods and tornadoes.

*Iowa* — The combination of great land and lower living costs makes Iowa a favorite among farmers. Low property taxes and a 100% exemption on homesteads up to 40 acres in rural areas also make it appealing. If you choose to install solar panels, the cost of that is exempt from sales tax, and you're also eligible for a tax credit. It is worth being aware that Iowa, like some other states, can have higher farmland costs because of its popularity with farmers. It also has higher state taxes and residents sometimes have to deal with tornados, floods, and long winters.

*Maine* — Maine has many homestead-friendly laws and zoning regulations as well as many natural resources such as timber, water, and rock. There is a lot of open land and prices are good, especially in more rural regions. Many people admire Maine's landscapes and the variety between the inland and coastal areas. The growing season is unfortunately short, but other benefits, such as low property taxes, still draw homesteaders to the state.

*Michigan* — While Michigan is a relatively expensive state to live in and has stricter regulations than many other states, it also has quite a lot to offer. It has good soil and right-to-farm laws, meaning farmers are protected against nuisance complaints from neighbors so long as they follow approved farming practices. This might be why Michigan has over 47,000 farms of varying sizes. The state also has Lake Michigan, in which residents are allowed to fish for trout and salmon. The growing season is around 140 days long, though it is common practice to extend the growing period by building greenhouses.

*Montana* — With its wide, sweeping plains and prairies, Montana is great for livestock and wind energy. Outside of those grasslands, you can find timber and other natural resources. The land is affordable and the cost of living is decent. Montana's growing season is short, though, making it another state where people tend to build greenhouses. With a sparse population, Montana is another option for those looking for space and privacy.

*Ohio* — Ohio is very amenable to off-grid lifestyles, with many counties having such relaxed laws and zoning codes that they don't even have a dedicated permit office. Other points in Ohio's favor include inexpensive land costs, low property taxes, low cost of living, lots of natural resources, and a five-month growing period.

*Texas* — Most parts of Texas have a long growing season and the land can be very reasonably priced, especially in less populated areas. Additionally, Texas offers a lot of timber and rock, which residents can use for construction. Something to be aware of, however, is that Texas contains many desert regions, which means a scarcity of water sources. This can make farming more difficult and cuts down on opportunities to hunt or fish.

*Virginia* — While Virginia's high population may make it a poor fit for those seeking solitude, the state has many positives if you're looking for a less remote lifestyle. It has good soil quality and a very long growing season. Unfortunately, cost of living, income tax, and land prices tend to be high, but property taxes are low and the climate is mild. The higher population also means a higher density of education and work opportunities if you're interested in a way of life that balances community with independence.

**Next!**

As you can see, there's a lot to think about if you're considering moving for your homestead! Once you've found the best place for it, the next two chapters have everything you need to get started setting up your utilities, planning a garden, and raising livestock.

# 3

# HOMESTEAD UTILITIES

This chapter will walk you through some of the most important aspects of setting up your homestead: how you will take care of your water, power, and waste needs. All three are crucial systems not only because they are everyday necessities, but as we established in the last chapter, most homes are legally required to have access to water, functioning electricity, and an appropriate place to dispose of sewage.

## Water Systems

Many factors will affect the type of water system that you choose to use. You must consider the type of property you own, the average rainfall in your area, and the natural water sources available (or not) on your land. If you're buying a property, it will be important to find out what sort of water resources exist on the property through the seller/real estate agent as well as your own testing and research.

Your household's average water consumption and budget will also influence your choices. Keep in mind that having a garden or livestock will increase your water consumption; if your budget is tight, learning to reduce water usage where you can is very helpful in keeping water costs low. It's a good idea to have multiple water supplies in the event that one fails, especially if living off the grid. Below are some of the most common water systems that homesteaders use:

### City Water ("on the grid")

This one is pretty self-explanatory. If you're not interested in living off the grid, you can connect your home to the local municipal water supply. This method has the least amount of control, but also the least amount of responsibility. If you're living in a town or city, you may even be required to use this water supply, but this requirement becomes less likely as your location gets more remote.

### Well Water

Most people are familiar with the basic function of a well. It is essentially a hole dug down from the surface that allows you to access underground water. Wells are expensive to establish, but once set up, they don't require much maintenance and they're one of the most reliable ways to get water. If you're buying a rural property that has already been inhabited, you may be lucky enough to find a place that already has a well. This can make your life easier, but always be sure to have the well water tested before you buy. The Environmental Protection Agency has a list of recommended substances to test for in water, including bacteria, nitrates, pH levels, dissolved solids, tannins, chloride, and copper, as well as water hardness. This testing should be done by a lab that is certified at the state level; you can usually get information on which labs to use from your local health department. (You should also continue to test your water every year or two to monitor its levels.)

## WATER WELL CONSTRUCTION

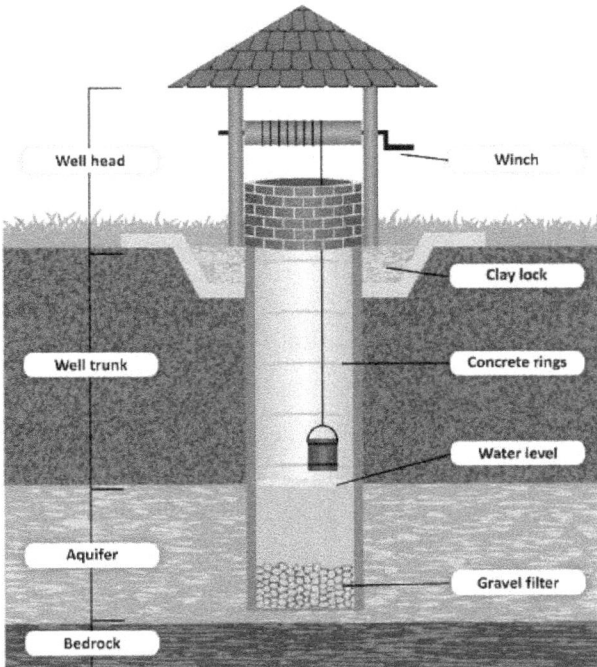

Well head

Winch

Clay lock

Well trunk

Concrete rings

Water level

Aquifer

Gravel filter

Bedrock

If you don't already have a well on your property, you'll have to drill one. Wells come in a variety of depths; shallower wells are cheaper and easier to draw from, while deeper wells have less risk of contamination, but are more expensive. Once the well is dug, a pump draws the water up from the ground. (You can draw the water up with a dipper or bucket, but that method is very slow because of the limited amount of water that can be transported at one time.) It is standard to use electrical pumps nowadays, although some people do prefer a manual pump, or at least have one set up in case of a power failure.

Before digging a well, check to be sure you'll have the rights to any water you find. Even if it's on your property, if the water connects to other properties in the area, you may not have full irrigation rights. Lastly, if your area is known for seismic activity or other activity that destabilizes the ground (such as drilling or fracking), a well might not be the best choice. But there are plenty of other options to consider:

### Natural Water Sources

This refers to any naturally occurring sources of water, such as a pond, creek, or river. Obviously, you can only use a natural water source if you have one on your land (and even then, be sure you check with the local laws—sometimes owning land does not mean you own the rights to the water on that land). It is also good to be aware that many creeks or streams dry up in the summer. Until you have spent a few years on a property, don't trust the claim that any body of water is year-round.

Each of these water supplies has its own advantages and drawbacks. A creek or river is not only a water source but could also be used for a hydro-power system (more on this later). Running water also tends to be purer than still water because the movement through rocks and sand acts as a filter system. A pond, however, can be duplicated with DIY efforts. Some homesteads even use a man-made reservoir to collect rainwater runoff.

Springs, which are essentially naturally occurring wells, are great because they bring water up from deep underground, which can then be diverted into your home's system.

### Rainwater Collection

Obviously, rainwater collection works best in climates that see a lot of rainfall. As noted above, many people will use man-made reservoirs to collect rainwater, usually by redirecting runoff from their roof. Rainwater is free and it can be easy and fairly inexpensive to set up a system to collect it. However, because this supply is dependent upon the weather, it can be advisable not to make this your primary water access. This will depend on how much rain you can expect to get and your capacity to store excess rain for use on dry days. And, as noted in the previous chapter, sometimes rainwater collection is illegal, so be sure to check that with your local laws.

If you do plan to use your roof runoff, it's important to know that the material of your roof makes a big difference. Water that has been collected from an asphalt roof, for example, can be *very* contaminated, suited to watering plants but not drinking. Tile and slate roofs are considered much better, and metal roofs are considered ideal for collecting rainwater runoff.

### Water Storage and Delivery

In addition to collecting water via whichever methods are available to and fitting for you, you'll need a way to store any excess, as well as a way to deliver that water to all the places that you need it. For the first, people commonly use cisterns, and for the second, you'll most likely need a pump.

*Cisterns*

A cistern is merely a tank specifically for water. These can be either above or below ground and are usually made of plastic, which is inexpensive, light when empty, and resistant to microbial growth. Above-ground cisterns tend to be smaller and easier to move, and sometimes double as containers for water transportation. Those below ground are often made of more durable material and are more expensive. If you live in a colder climate, it is best to have an underground cistern placed below the frost line, so that it will not freeze. If you have the opportunity, you can place a cistern so that your water pressure is aided by gravity.

*Water Pumps*

As just mentioned, some systems rely on gravity for their water pressure. This is called a "gravity-fed" system, and it depends on placing your water tank higher than your home so that gravity pulls the water down into your pipes. (This same principle is used in on-grid water sources, such as water towers.) This is only possible in some situations, and you may still need a pump to get water from your source into your cistern. Your other option is to rely primarily on a water pump, which can be stronger and more consistent but will require power. How much power will depend on your water consumption, as that will determine the amount of water you need to move on average. Some homesteaders use solar power for their water pumps, and we'll discuss solar power in more depth in the next section on electricity.

## Water Purification and Filtration

Another thing that you need no matter which water source you choose (unless you're staying connected to the grid) is a way to filter and purify your water. You may see these terms used interchangeably, but filtration is used to mean getting rid of physical contaminants while purification is used to mean the removal of chemical contaminants, such as bacteria and other biological hazards. There may be times when you'll need to use very stringent filtration and purification methods for your water, such as water for bathing and drinking. There are other times when less exacting methods, or even no methods, will be needed, such as for watering your garden. There are laws around the purity of drinking water and you're responsible for testing your water at least twice a year (in the spring and fall) to make sure it is safe.

There are two basic types of filtration systems: inline and gravity-fed. Again, gravity-fed systems rely on the force of gravity to move water: the water is placed in the top of a container with a filter at the bottom, and gravity pulls it through that filter to another, clean container underneath. Gravity-fed filters can be used even without regular plumbing. Inline filters, on the other hand, are placed in your plumbing, meaning that the water is filtered as it enters your home.

It can be wise to employ multiple filtration and purification systems, especially if you have reason to believe your water sources might be contaminated. (Surface water, for instance, is particularly vulnerable to contamination, and can be unsafe to drink even if it tests okay.) Having one system that filters out particles and other physical contaminants and a second to remove biological hazards can be the safest way to go. It is also a good idea to have a backup method of water purification in the event that your main system is offline. Below are some of the different ways you can filter and purify your water.

*Filters*

You can buy filters and you can also make your own. Simple DIY filters, such as creating a membrane filter by straining water through a piece of cloth, are great to have on hand for emergency use, but are obviously too small in scale to filter all the water for your household needs. More involved processes include pumping your water through a carbon (bio) or ceramic filter.

*Biofilters*

*In a biofilter, water moves through three layers to filter your water.*

Biofilters are slightly more complex filters that can still be made at home. They involve three layers of filtration: gravel, sand, and charcoal. The gravel and sand work to screen out physical contaminants while the charcoal gets rid of chemical contaminants. (However, biofilters do not remove heavy metal or bacteria from your water, so be sure to keep that in mind when planning.) Gravel and sand are obviously quite easy to procure, and the charcoal can be made from waste wood gathered from your property. Make sure you clean these materials before putting them into your filter by rinsing them in a bucket of water. Swirl the water around until it gets cloudy, then drain it out and replace it with fresh water. Repeat until the water stays clear. In addition to cleaning all the elements before you put the filter together, this type of filter should be taken apart to clean the vessel and replace the filtering components yearly.

*Ceramic Filters*

Ceramic filters use the porous nature of clay to screen out impurities. You can still put these together yourself, although unless you are especially good at pottery, you'll need to buy the ceramic filters. If you're particular about the taste of your water, or you'd like an extra level of purification, you can get ceramic filters with cores made from activated charcoal or silver. This method, therefore, has more upfront costs (you need about two filters per person in your household just for drinking water purposes), but the filters can last up to a decade. Another potential drawback is that water filters very slowly through these systems, so it can take a while for water to be available after filters have been replaced.

*Chemical Purification*

This method adds chemicals to your water to destroy impurities. Generally, chlorine-based bleach is used. (Usually, when people talk about chlorine, they are referring to bleach with a chlorine base, though there are other bleaches with different chemical makeups.) As you might guess, one of the bigger downsides of this is the taste it gives your water. The power of this method of disinfection is determined by variables such as the temperature, pH, and clarity of the water. This is an easy and fast way to purify water, especially in an emergency. Some people also purify with iodine, but given iodine's light sensitivity, the potential for iodine allergies, and the fact that it is not safe for pregnant women, I don't personally recommend it.

*UV (Sunlight) Purification*

*UV light bulbs emit frequencies that destroy contaminants in water.*

You can purify water using actual sunlight or specially-made UV light bulbs. The frequencies in UV light can destroy the cell structures of contaminants in your water. This method of purification does not remove sediment or other debris from your water, and it is only effective against certain chemical contaminants, so it is best to pair this method with another process. It's also very important that there is nothing between the UV light and the water—even things that look clear to us can block UV rays. It is best for water to be uncovered so the light can hit it directly, but if you must cover your water, you'll need to do so with specially-made plastic that is designed to let UV rays pass through it.

There are two commonly used types of UV light bulbs: low pressure/high output (LPHO) and medium pressure/high output (MPHO). LPHOs are more energy-efficient, but less powerful and therefore require more units or more time to disinfect the same amount of water. MPHOs, on the other hand, are more powerful but less energy efficient. There are also low pressure/low output (LPLO) bulbs, but they are not as frequently used because they are much less powerful. Essentially, you'll always be trading off power for energy efficiency, and which you choose should be based on the volume of water you expect to disinfect and whether or not speed and power are more important to you than saving energy.

*Distillation*

Mimicking the natural water cycle, distillation works by heating water until it evaporates and then condensing the steam into water in a new, clean container. The heat of this process will kill bacteria and other microorganisms, while the evaporation leaves behind physical impurities like sediment and particles. Because of this, distillation is a very effective way of disinfecting your water. Technically, you can use distillation anywhere that you have a heat source and a way to collect the condensing water, including your kitchen. The smallest water distillers are actually made to sit on your counter or table, and they distill just a small amount of water at a time.

However, in order to be practical as a method for purifying all your water, you'll need a bigger operation. You can either have a distillation point installed in your plumbing system, or you can purchase a large (usually called "commercial") distiller. The in-system distiller purifies water as you need it, which means you are never distilling more water than you need. However, it does have an upfront cost of up to $1,000 for purchase and installation. A commercial distiller will have the capacity to distill around 75 gallons of water each day, a much higher volume of water than a countertop distiller, but it will use a proportionately higher amount of energy. Some people use a solar water distiller in order to distill a larger amount of water while using less energy. This involves placing water under glass or plastic with access to sunlight, which will then heat the water to evaporation. This method of distillation obviously is best suited if you live somewhere warm with strong, direct sunlight.

*Boiling*

As noted above, heating water will kill bacteria and microorganisms, so boiling your water will disinfect it. The water must be kept at a rolling boil for at least a minute. Notably, you'll want to pair a method of filtration with boiling, as on its own it will not remove physical contaminants. While not practical as a main source of purification, boiling is very handy for purifying small amounts of water quickly, or if you find your other methods of purification unavailable. It is also easy to do and, as long as you have a pan and a source of heat such as your kitchen stove, it's free.

Now that we've covered the most common water systems for homesteaders, let's take a look at the options for electricity.

**Power Systems**

When you're accustomed to living on the power grid, you might take power for granted because it's always on and available. But if you're going to generate your own power, you suddenly have to consider all the things in your home that require electricity, from the lights to the Wi-Fi router to your hairdryer. The first step when moving to your own power system is to consider how you might slim down your electricity usage. Just like with water, the less electricity you consume, the more your budget will thank you. Look for small tasks that you can do manually, and if you're building a new home, make sure to consider ways the design and construction can reduce your energy footprint.

*Solar Energy*

If you live in a climate that gets a lot of sun, solar energy can be a great option. Solar energy is very efficient, and once installed, it requires only a small amount of maintenance. However, you'll need solar panels to collect the sun's energy, an inverter that converts that energy, and batteries to store it. The price of this system and the cost to have it professionally installed is high, so you'll want to be sure you'll get enough sunny days to pay off this investment. Solar energy is also an option for heating your water, which is important if you don't want to take exclusively cold showers. (We'll discuss more heating options a little later in this chapter.)

*Wind Energy*

This is another source of power that depends on your climate. You should be able to look up the wind resource map for your area to find out what sort of wind your homestead will get. Wind energy isn't quite as efficient as solar energy, but if you live somewhere that is windy and overcast, it can work much better than a solar panel. The main costs for wind energy are the tower and turbine. It's important to have these somewhere relatively unobstructed; the higher the better, so if you have hills on your property, you might consider setting them up there. Because the towers are quite tall, you may struggle to be approved for them, especially if you live in less rural areas. Something to consider with wind energy is that the energy is generated by the mechanical process of turning the turbine, so the components will wear down over time and eventually need to be replaced.

If you're located in a climate that gets a decent amount of both sun and wind, but you're not sure either is enough to fully power your household, you could consider a hybrid system that uses both.

*Geothermal Energy*

As the components of its name indicate (geo = earth, thermal = heat), this form of power is dependent on heat obtained from the ground. This system works by pumping water through a pipe system that is buried underground. In the winter, the water in the pipes is heated by the warmth underground and then carried up to your heating pump, where that warmth is transferred to air that will be circulated throughout the house. Because it extracts heat from the ground, which is relatively warm, rather than from the winter air, which is very cold, this system is extremely efficient, with an input-output ratio of four to one. Unfortunately, you must have a professional install a geothermal heat pump, so the upfront costs are high. This type of energy system works especially well to heat and cool your home. It is less common than wind or solar energy, but as technology advances, it is becoming more common over time.

*Hydroelectricity*

This form of energy is only an option for those who have a source of running water, but if that's true for you, it's a great way to generate energy. These systems work by placing a mechanical component, usually a turbine, into the water and generating power from the turning of that component. Running water is much more constant than wind or sun, so the supply of energy from a micro-hydro system is more regular and therefore dependable than those systems. Hydroelectric systems need to be consciously designed and constructed so that they don't disrupt the natural environment of the water source, most likely requiring professional installation, and like wind turbines, they will require routine maintenance and upkeep.

*Generator*

Many people are familiar with generators, and some may even already own them as a backup power source for when there are disruptions to grid power. Generators can also be used as a backup for your renewable energy sources, and are especially recommended for any areas that are prone to tornadoes or other weather that might knock out power. Generators can run on gas, diesel, propane, or occasionally other fuels. When choosing a generator, it's important to get the right size if you want it to be able to power your whole household in the event of a failure from your primary power source.

**Energy Storage**

It might be strange to think of storing energy the way that you would food or water, but when you're generating your own power, any amount you can store in the present could end up helping you in the future. One method of storing power is using your local public power utility. Most utilities will store your power for you (and if you're sure you won't need the extra power, many will also buy it). This, of course, means that you would have to remain connected to the power grid. The other option is to store your excess energy in batteries. Batteries designed to store power like this come with a high upfront cost, but should last at least five years, and even longer if you care for them properly.

**Waste Disposal**

Setting up your own waste system might seem intimidating at first, but don't let that deter you. Dealing with waste is a problem many homesteaders have confronted and solved, and there are a wide variety of options available. Whether you're prioritizing ease and comfort or sustainability and simplicity, there is a waste disposal system that is right for you.

*Regular Plumbing System to a Septic Tank or System*

This method is both common and easy to get approved by your local authorities. Your inside system would consist of toilets and pipes, just like most regular plumbing systems. The waste from this system then drains into a tank or septic field on your property. Once in the tank, solid waste will move to the bottom to be broken down by bacteria, while the water will evaporate out through a specially designed pipe. Regular maintenance of a septic tank involves having it pumped out every few years. This will remove the solids at the bottom that haven't broken down (called sludge) as well as the grease and fat that has floated to the top (called scum). Pumping empties out the tank so it is ready to start the process over again. It is important to be aware of how the weather affects septic systems, especially in cold climates. If there's a risk of freezing (which can crack pipes and tanks), then it is best to have an underground system or one that is very well-insulated.

## Septic Tank Diagram

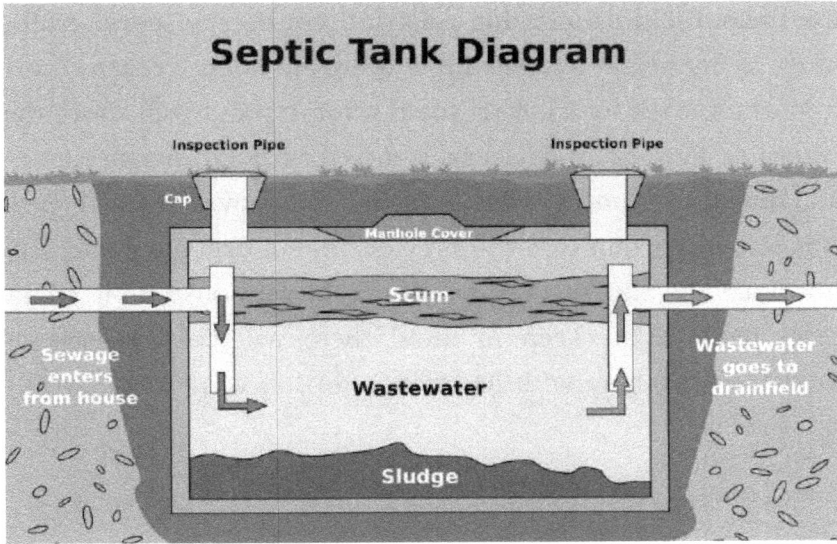

*DIY Septic System*

This is similar to the above, but you would do all the design and installation work yourself. As homeowners, you are already responsible for getting the correct permits and following all codes, so some people prefer to take the task on themselves rather than pay someone to do it. While this requires a lot of research and hard work, it also means you thoroughly understand your septic system and are fully equipped to take care of maintenance or any problems that arise.

*Outhouse or Pit Latrine*

On the other end of the spectrum is an outhouse, which is essentially a hole dug in the ground with a cover or seat over it and a small shelter around it. You're probably familiar with the idea of outhouses historically before indoor plumbing was developed, but many living on homesteads or off the grid still use them. Building a latrine does not require any special skills, but it is important to keep a few things in mind. Perhaps most important is the location, as you'll want to put it well above the waterline (especially if you have a well), a good distance away and downhill from any water sources, and above the flood level. It is also important that you only dispose of organic waste, and not pour any sort of chemicals into the outhouse, as it might react badly. Also, keep in mind there will be a release of methane gas (along with its strong odor) as your waste breaks down.

*Honey Bucket*

The honey bucket is essentially the small, portable version of an outhouse, consisting of a plastic bag inside a container, topped with a seat. This method is not highly recommended, because once the bag is full you have to dispose of the waste yourself, either by emptying the bags into a hole you dig or finding a local waste center that accepts human waste. However, it will work if you find yourself in need of a portable toilet alternative, and it can be handy to keep as a backup since it is small and easily stored.

*Compost Toilet*

This method of waste disposal will appeal to anyone who wants to do more with waste than simply get rid of it. Like an outhouse, the construction of a composting toilet is fairly simple. A container, usually a bucket, is placed under a specially-made toilet seat. After using the toilet, you add a layer of sawdust to soak up the moisture. There are also versions with electric or hand-turned cranks that speed up the composting process. Once the container is full, it can be added to your compost pile. This method not only keeps your compost pile full but also saves water because it does not involve flushing. Most compost toilets also have vent hoses that keep the toilet from smelling. Compost toilets are only legal in some states, however, so be sure to check your local laws.

*Incinerator Toilet*

An incinerator toilet is powered by either propane or electricity, and it does just what its name implies—it burns your waste. If you don't want to compost your waste or dig a hole, but you'd prefer not to have a full septic system, this can be a good option for you. While you will save water, you will be required to buy paper liners for the toilet bowl. A downside of these toilets is the amount of energy that they use. Whether your model runs on propane or electricity, a steady supply of power is needed. For this reason, some manufacturers of incinerator toilets recommend not using solar power or other methods of power that can be inconsistent or unpredictable with their products.

*Lagoons*

Septic systems work by filtering waste through the soil, but in some places, the soil will not work well for this purpose. In that case, you might need a lagoon instead. A lagoon works by collecting your wastewater in a (usually man-made) depression in the ground, where it can then be broken down by microbes. Even if your soil is fine, a lagoon can be a cheaper alternative to a septic system. However, not all areas allow for lagoons, and some people will be put off by having an uncovered pool of waste on their property.

*Greywater Systems*

Wastewater is actually broken into two different types, greywater and blackwater. Most of what we think of as waste is usually blackwater, meaning it is contaminated by human waste. However, a significant portion of wastewater is actually greywater, which is water that has gone through the system—think showers, sinks, washing machines, etc.—but is not contaminated by human waste. This water can be reused for certain tasks where the purity of the water doesn't need to be held to strict standards, such as watering your garden or flushing your toilet.

If you'd like to divert greywater so that it can be reused like this, there are several methods of doing so. Some people simply collect used water in buckets by hand to be reused, while others install plumbing that reroutes their greywater. Most frequently, this plumbing will take water draining from places like your washing machine and bathtub, and redirect it to one of two places: your garden irrigation system to water your plants, or your bathroom plumbing to be used to flush your toilets. In general, by using greywater instead of freshwater to flush toilets, you can reduce your water consumption by around a third. However, if you intend to use greywater in your garden, be sure that any cleaners you are using (like soap, shampoo, and laundry detergent) do *not* have any chemicals in them that will harm your plants.

## Trash Removal

If you're located in an urban or suburban environment, you're likely going to continue to use the municipal trash services provided by the local government. However, if you're somewhere more rural, you might be in charge of your own garbage removal. This is another area where learning to reduce and reuse will come in handy. Everything that you can avoid (like plastic bags) or reuse (like containers) is something that you don't have to haul when you get rid of your trash. Next, be sure you're separating out things you can compost and recycle into separate bins from your regular trash. (I'd recommend a smaller compost bin so it can be easily transferred to your compost pile when full without too much trouble.) Recyclables can be taken to your nearest recycling center—check with your local authorities for locations and guidelines on what can be recycled. Everything that's left will need to be taken to the nearest landfill, with the exception of anything that contains hazardous materials—again, check local regulations.

## Heating

Last in our exploration of utilities, but certainly not the least important (just ask anyone who's ever spent the winter in a drafty farmhouse!), heating is perhaps the utility most affected by lifestyle and planning. The amount of energy you exert heating your house is directly related to your house's space and insulation. A larger house means more space that must be heated, and a drafty house with lots of leaks where hot air can escape and cold air can sneak in will require more energy to heat. So if you're planning to build a house, be sure to include proper insulation and sealants, and consider eliminating square footage that you don't need. If you're working with a house that already exists, it could be worth the time and effort to check for drafts and seal and insulate where you can, as best you can. Gaps can be filled with sealants or foam; thin windows can be reinforced with plastic sheeting or covered with heavy shades; empty rooms can be closed off. You can also consider an exterior windbreak to block north winds. All of this can help make whichever of the below methods you choose that much more efficient.

*Wood-Burning Stoves*

Unlike fireplaces, which are open to the air through the chimney and therefore tend to be inefficient, wood stoves can work well to heat your house. Their upfront cost is reasonable, and depending on your land, you might have access to all the firewood you need. If not, firewood is relatively inexpensive and easy to get. If you'd like to make your wood stove work even better, you can keep a few weeks' worth of firewood inside, allowing it to warm up first and therefore take less energy to burn. You'll need a method, such as fans, to circulate the hot air they create. Most importantly, this method of heating needs constant supervision and maintenance.

*Propane Heaters*

These types of heaters can be portable or they can be built-in. Since they run on propane, they don't require electricity. However, you *will* need to be sure they are properly ventilated, including possibly opening a window at times to manage the fumes. Propane degrades very slowly, which means it can be stored for a long time—however because tanks are pressurized, they must be stored carefully and appropriately. A lot of propane heaters will have thermostats, which makes regulating the temperature (and therefore the amount of energy you use) very easy.

*Solar Heat*

There are two ways to heat your home with solar energy— passive and active. Passive solar heating means you take advantage of the heat naturally created by the sun's rays. This could be as simple as having wide, south-facing windows that let in a lot of warm sunshine, or it could be a more complex setup involving thermal walls or water tanks to amplify the sun's warmth. Even a wall made of dark material or painted in a dark color can help to absorb and then radiate heat from sunlight.

Active solar energy is more in line with general solar power systems. There are methods to collect warmth from the sun and then redistribute that through the rest of the house. A common way of doing this is to place water in conductive containers, such as glass or copper, and then pipe that water throughout the house once the water is hot. If you've ever lived in a house with radiant heat, the concept is very similar—but in this case, it is not a water heater but the sun that is heating the water.

*Biomass System*

When biological materials begin to decompose and break down, that process creates heat. Biomass systems work by placing metal pipes inside of piles of compost and other degradable waste. Those pipes absorb the heat from the pile and then redistribute it to other locations. This type of system probably cannot generate enough heat for your entire household, but it can be a handy and environmentally-friendly way to complement your main source of heat. You'll already be generating the waste—you might as well use it!

**Next!**

Hopefully, by this point, you've got a good grasp on what types of systems you might like to try in your own homestead. As I'll keep reminding you, there are *so* many options available, and so many ways to implement those options to fit a variety of lifestyles. Now that you know what choices are available for your utilities, the next chapter will walk you through another huge part of homesteading—growing food and raising livestock.

# 4

# FARMING AND RAISING ANIMALS

A big part of creating a more independent life for yourself through homesteading is gaining the ability to feed yourself. Imagine never having to make another grocery run, and never wondering what, exactly, is in the food that you eat. With some hard work and careful planning, you can make that happen—and this chapter will help you!

For your first step down this sustainable food path, I recommend planting a garden. While some people eventually run large farms with acres of crops that they sell for a profit, for most homesteaders, planting fruits and vegetables is all about providing for their families. For this purpose, a large garden will be more than enough. The key is to choose what you plant carefully; always consider the nutritional value of your garden's yield. Everyone needs protein, carbohydrates, and fats in their diet, as well as vitamins and minerals. The goal is to grow enough variety that you can get a balanced diet from your harvest and to accomplish this, planning is essential.

## Planning Your Garden

Careful planning before you begin your garden can save you a lot of time and money, not only by avoiding costly mistakes but also by helping you optimize your space so that your garden is as productive as possible. The first thing to consider is the location. You need somewhere with ample access to sunlight and water—beyond that, you can tailor your garden to fit your situation and needs. You can either start with a location and let its characteristics dictate how you'll set your garden up, or you can make a list of your ideal garden traits and look for a space that will fit them. If you don't have land or a yard, you can start with a container garden, such as a vertical garden, potted plants, or window boxes.

Once you know where your garden will be, you should collect some data. Measure the area and if possible draw a plan of where you'll be putting each of your plants. Also, track how much sunlight the area gets, and if you're planting in the ground, testing the soil is a good idea. Dig a small hole and examine the soil you take out of it; the best soil is porous and not too hard, able to be crumbled by hand into smaller bits that keep shape under pressure. Test the compactness of your soil by pushing a thin wire down into the earth—you should be able to get about a foot down before the wire bends. You can also look for what lives in the soil as an indication of its health—earthworms are a particularly good sign. Lastly, you can get a testing kit that will tell you the pH balance of your soil. Different plants will do best in different acidities, but generally, you want a pH between 6 and 7.5.

Once you've gathered all of this data, move on to supplies. I recommend making a list of all the supplies you'll need to get started—some possibilities are stakes, a watering system, a book for your notes, and containers if you're planting a container garden (though you can also make containers yourself). Especially when you start your garden, before things start to grow, you'll want to be *very* organized so that you know where you've planted each plant.

When it comes to planning the actual contents of your garden, a number of things will determine which plants are most appropriate. Consider your climate, as certain plants can only grow in certain climate zones. The amount of space you have is also an important factor, as some plants require a lot of space while others do not. Beans, for instance, usually need half a foot or less between plants; large gourds, on the other hand, can need as much as four feet.

Also be aware that certain plants grow well with each other, while others do not. For example, basil helps tomatoes and peppers grow by keeping away insects, while mint, chives, and garlic will keep slugs and aphids off your lettuce. On the other hand, keeping tomatoes and corn apart will stop them from sharing diseases common to both plants, and keeping lettuce away from parsley will stop the latter from crowding the former. These are just a few common examples, so be sure to research the specific interactions of the plants you're considering before purchasing seeds or seedlings. Another thing to be aware of is plant height. Taller plants should be placed farthest from the direction of the sun so that they don't block the light from other plants.

Timing is also an important factor of planning, especially if you intend to preserve what you harvest. Make sure you space out your harvest times. It's best to do all this planning in winter or early spring so that once the weather is warm enough, you can jump right into planting. While you're waiting for the weather, you can start seedlings inside.

*Garden Irrigation Systems*

If you're going to have a large garden, you might need to create a dedicated watering system. There are three basic types of irrigation systems that you can use to water your plants: soaking, dripping, and spraying.

Soaking uses a specially constructed hose that has many tiny holes in its surface that allow the water to seep out slowly. The hose lays beside your plants and the water seeping out saturates the ground around their roots.

Dripping follows a similar principle, but instead of tiny holes all over the surface of the hose, the holes are a little larger and set at intervals. You line up these holes to deliver water directly to specific plants.

Spraying utilizes sprinklers to deliver water over large areas.

Each system has its own benefits. Determine which to use based on the area that you need to cover, the amount of control you'd like over where the water goes, and the specific needs of your plants. For example, you might like a soaking irrigation system for plants that need frequent watering but whose leaves need to stay dry, versus a spraying system that will cover all parts of the plants with water. Or you might choose a dripping irrigation system if you only want to water certain plants at a time. You can also combine any of these systems with regular garden hoses, using the regular hose as a connector for spaces between plants where you don't want to waste water.

*Raised Beds*

A raised bed garden elevates the area where you're planting, whether through containers or built-up mounds of earth. This type of garden can have several benefits, including the ability to choose the type of soil you use, and bringing up the height of your plants so they are easier to tend and harvest. It can also keep the roots of your plants away from potential contaminants in the ground. The drawbacks of raised beds are their cost and the higher level of exposure, meaning your soil will be more susceptible to heat, cold, and dryness. You also need rows between the beds to walk through, so if you don't have a lot of space, this option might not be for you.

Designing a raised bed garden involves a lot of personal preference, but the average dimensions are 12 to 18 inches tall by 3 to 4 feet wide (length can be whatever works for you). If boxing in your beds, you can use wood (be sure any treatments on the wood are natural), concrete blocks, or metal. You may have seen old tires used as planters, but I don't recommend that; over time, the chemicals in the rubber can seep into your beds and harm your plants (and you, when you eat them).

*Aquaponics*

One of the more creative ways to grow food in a small space, aquaponics is the pairing of aquaculture and hydroponics. By combining these two things, you're creating an ecosystem where fish waste nourishes the plants and the plants' use of this waste keeps the water clean. Not only is this less work for you, but it also helps you avoid using commercial fertilizers that can have harmful chemicals in them. Because an aquaponic system raises fish *and* grows plants, it is a great way to provide a lot of food with a good variety of nutrients without needing much space. You can grow almost any type of plant with an aquaponics system, but some plants are particularly well-suited to it, and a few will give you a hard time. Tomatoes, peppers, lettuce, cabbage, cauliflower, ginger, basil, and strawberries will all thrive in this setting. You'll want to avoid blueberries (they tend to need a lower pH than other plants), chrysanthemums (these need a higher pH), and mint (which will grow well, but so quickly that it can choke out other plants).

You can make a simple aquaponics system by adding plants on floating mats to the top of a fish tank, or you can make a more elaborate system containing multiple containers and more hardy plant support. Aquaponics allows you to start small and build up your system as you become more experienced. Whatever the size of your setup, you'll need a pumping system that will help circulate the water between the fish tank and the plant beds. You'll also need a growing medium for your plants and the bacteria you'll add to help maintain balance. Aquaponics does not use soil, but rather materials such as sand, clay balls, and gravel.

*An illustration of a basic aquaponics system*

The plants and fish you choose for your system will depend on your location, the size of your tanks, and what type of temperature exposure you can expect. You want to place the system somewhere that gets a lot of sun, but you might also want a screen or other material to shade the fish tank from direct sunlight so it doesn't get too hot. Since you won't be able to move things once they're running without a lot of work, make sure you're completely confident of your location before you start to build. And because the system needs to be carefully calibrated and all the chemicals in the water balanced, you'll want to do more research and consult experts if you're planning to set the system up yourself.

*Having a Root Cellar*

Once you have all this delicious food grown and harvested, you're going to need somewhere to keep it. A root cellar is a great way to store food off the grid without the need for refrigeration. Root cellars work by taking advantage of the naturally cooler temperatures underground. The temperature of the soil at ten feet underground is generally around 50 to 60 degrees Fahrenheit, and the earth around and above your root cellar will cocoon it, acting as natural insulation to keep the temperature stable.

Your root cellar can be as small or large as you'd like. The smallest of root cellars are just containers that you bury. This method is simple and easy, and only takes the time you need to dig a hole. However, it is obviously more suited to storing foods that you want to keep for later, but won't necessarily need to access regularly. The container should be made of material that is waterproof and strong enough not to collapse or degrade over time, so metal and plastic are your best bet.

For larger root cellars, if you're lucky enough to have a dry, unheated basement with space to share, you can convert part of it into an indoor root cellar. Otherwise, you'll need to dig somewhere on your property. You first have to dig out space, then reinforce the floor and walls. A concrete floor is best if your budget can handle it; if not, you can use stones or wooden planks. It's important to have a floor to give yourself a level space that can support weight, insulate the temperature, and discourage burrowing animals from trying to get into your cellar. You can use stones, bricks, or masonry blocks for the walls, though the latter two are a bit more expensive. Finish off your cellar by capping it with a concrete slab if you can, and making sure your door and other access points seal well to keep out unwanted pests.

Once you have your root cellar constructed, you have to add a way for the air to circulate. Some of the foods you store will release ethylene gas as they ripen, and you need to have ways for that gas to escape and for fresh air to come in. At this point, you also need to decide what foods you'd like to store, as this will determine exactly how your root cellar functions. Foods with a long shelf life often do better in a dry environment, while fresh produce needs some moisture. If you plan to store both in your cellar, you should either create separate sections or seal your dry foods in airtight containers. You also should keep any items that might rust, such as cans, in sealed containers.

It's a good idea to outfit your root cellar with shelves, as that will allow you to keep your food off the floor and store your foods at different elevations to cater to their needs. For instance, you can keep foods most likely to produce ethylene gas on the top shelves, as the gas will rise and stay away from other foods. The space closer to the floor will be cooler, so you can keep any foods that need a little extra chill on your bottom shelves.

The last thing to remember about storing your foods is to know and track their expiration dates so that you can eat foods before they go bad. With a little bit of organization, you can have a system that keeps you consuming ripe food and replacing it with fresh food. You should also routinely look over the cellar to be sure all your seals are intact, you have no rodent problems, and the temperature and humidity are where you want them.

*Foods to Stock Up On*

The best foods to keep on hand, whether purchased or grown, are foods that have a lot of nutritional value and will last for a long time. While certainly not extensive, here is a list of foods with a long shelf life to get you started:

- brown rice
- oatmeal
- granola
- beans
- nuts (dried, unshelled, unsalted; in particular, pecans, pistachios, and sunflower seeds)
- peanut butter
- canned fish (in particular, mackerel, sardines, and tuna)
- beef jerky
- apple sauce
- dried fruit
- honey
- powdered milk
- oil (specifically coconut oil)
- spices

These will obviously be supplemented by what you grow yourself. In terms of meat, rabbits and poultry will not take too long to raise to adulthood (two to three years) and poultry will provide you with eggs in the meantime. For crops, winter squash and beans can be harvested the first year they're grown. Some other staples that will take longer but are worth space in your long-term plans include corn, potatoes, apples, and wheat if you intend to eventually be completely self-sufficient.

**Livestock**

Raising animals can be a huge part of your food self-sufficiency. Whether you dream of a farm full of different kinds of animals or just a few chickens in a tiny yard, adding livestock to your homestead can have many benefits. Your animals can be a source of fresh and organic meat, eggs, and milk. With milk, you can also make dairy products like butter, yogurt, cheese, and even ice cream. Grazing animals will also help keep your grass short, and animal waste can be used as a fertilizer for your garden. Caring for animals can be a great way to involve your whole family in the process of homesteading. And, if you intend to breed your animals, you can add those offspring to your own livestock, sell them for profit, or trade them to someone else within the homesteading community for other things you need.

This next section will take you through some of the most common animals you might want to keep, and the pros and cons of each. Something to keep in mind, no matter what type of animal you plan on raising, is that all livestock require regular health checkups. When you first get your animals, you should be sure they have had all required vaccinations and blood tests and have been dewormed. The specifics of these will vary by animal and location. For example, most mammals will need vaccinations for tetanus and rabies, and many states require birds to be tested for *Salmonella* and avian influenza. Your large animal veterinarian can let you know what type of regular care your animals need, and if you're new to the area and don't have a veterinarian yet, you can ask your local homesteading community for recommendations.

### *Chickens*

Chickens obviously have the advantage of being quite small, and therefore easy to raise in a lot of different environments. If you plan to raise chickens in an urban environment, however, be sure to check the local laws. Many cities will allow you to have chickens but not roosters. Chickens can live free-range (allowed to roam as they please), in a coop with a yard, or in specially designed chicken cages. Even if you choose to cage your chickens, it is good to have enough room for them to move around a little. Each chicken should have a minimum of two square feet and enough height that they can easily walk around upright. About six hens will be enough to have eggs for the average family. You can also raise chickens for their meat. You can either keep a different set of chickens specifically for this purpose, or you can raise female chicks to lay eggs and male chicks for their meat.

For the healthiest chickens (and therefore the best amount of eggs), feed them both grain and protein-rich chicken feed. They will also eat your leftover food, grass, and bugs that they find while grazing. In fact, chickens are great at eliminating pests. They will peck away at your garden, so be sure to keep them separate from that—unless you are just starting your garden, in which case you can let them loose to tear up the ground, making your job of planting even easier. In the same way, you can let them into your compost pile, where they will tear up most organic material, helping it to decompose faster (as well as sometimes adding their own waste to the pile).

How often chickens lay eggs is dependent on a number of factors, including nutrition and weather, but the most prominent factor is the amount of daylight they receive. Usually, chickens will lay an egg daily during spring, summer, and fall, when there is a longer period from dawn until dusk. Once the hours of light per day dip below twelve, chickens are likely to stop laying. This is not true for all chickens but will be the case for the majority. If you really want to extend the laying season, it might be possible by introducing artificial daylight into your chicken's habitat, but be sure to talk to a professional about the potential impact that this may have on your chickens' health before deciding to do so.

### Geese and Ducks

Both geese and duck eggs are larger than chicken eggs, though they also tend to stop laying once the weather gets colder and there is less daylight. Geese require a bit more space than chickens, given that they prefer to roam and graze for their food. You can also feed them grain at night. One warning about geese is that they're very popular with foxes, so they need to be kept inside a shelter at night. Rats, though perhaps not as big of a threat, can also be a problem, so be sure that your enclosure for your geese is rat-proof.

Ducks are susceptible to an even larger number of predators, including skunks, raccoons, coyotes, owls, hawks, snakes, and even cats and dogs. It is important that your duck shelter is off the ground just a little, not only so it is more secure from these many predators, but also so it stays dry. Also, ensure that their shelter contains enough soft materials (such as straw) for the ducks to make nests.

You might think ducks need water because we associate them with it so strongly, but ducks only need enough water to drink. However, having a source of water to swim in will make your ducks happier, so if you're able to provide that, you should! Ducks can be fed from a feeder, as long as you're sure to keep their food and water separate. They are also happy to eat weeds and bugs if you have the space to let them roam during the day. In fact, they will eat bugs off of your garden, and won't damage the plants as chickens would; just wait until after your plants are tall enough that the ducks won't accidentally step on them.

If you are planning to raise ducks and chickens together, you have to be careful with your male ducks (drakes) and female chickens. Drakes are not discriminant and can try to mate with chickens, but the two are not compatible, and your hens may be injured. However, if you have enough female ducks (usually three per every male), then the drake should be satisfied by mating with the other ducks and leave your chickens alone.

### Rabbits

While they, unfortunately, don't lay eggs, rabbits have a lot of other advantages, particularly if you're new to livestock. They are fairly docile and don't make a lot of noise, and they are easy to breed yourself if that's an interest. Rabbits are happy to consume garden leftovers and any other greens that you don't want, and raising rabbits can also help your garden grow, as their waste has good fertilizing properties.

Rabbit meat is also very healthy for you, as it is quite lean and nutritious. If you're planning to butcher your animals yourself, rabbits have a much nicer learning curve than some other animals, especially those with feathers. You can also use the rabbit hides to make things, and certain breeds (like the Angora) have fur that you can shave and make into yarn. You can use the things you make from pelts and yarn around your own house, or you can sell them for additional income.

### Pigs

If you're planning to be food independent while also having bacon, you'll need to raise pigs. Some people prefer to breed their own pigs, thereby supplying their own stock, while others would rather buy piglets each year and then raise them to adulthood. The choice is up to you. When buying pigs, be sure the farm or breeder has a good reputation for healthy animals. While it may be tempting to go for chubby piglets, that can actually be an indication that the adult pig will carry a lot of lard. It's also good to know that the longer a pig has been nursed, the healthier it will be.

Pigs will eat leftovers from both your table and your garden. This helps keep the cost of feeding them low, although it is good to be sure they get some grain. If you have the room, you can supply this yourself by raising a small amount of corn. You can also give your pigs mineral and protein supplements to keep them healthy. Pigs will not overeat and can be fed from a feeder, meaning a large amount of their care can be automated.

When saving scraps for your pigs, be sure to separate out anything that could harm them, such as paper, plastic, or anything with chemicals.

For living space, you can get your pigs a hog house or build them a shed. Make sure that the floor of this space is high enough off the ground that it will stay dry, and that sunlight can get in to help keep it fresh. It is also good to keep in mind that when piglets are very small they can slip through many spaces, so plan your pen accordingly. The smaller the space, the less exercise the pigs will get—and therefore the quicker they will grow. But you will want to find the right balance because cramped spaces can become unsanitary and allow parasites to grow on the pigs.

When harvesting pigs for meat, you can do it all yourself, have someone else do the entire process (from slaughter through curing and smoking), or you can have someone slaughter and dress them before returning the meat to you to do your own curing and smoking. You can check with neighbors, breeders, or feed suppliers for recommendations about where to get your pigs slaughtered.

### Sheep

As their diet consists mainly of grass, sheep are fairly inexpensive to raise after the initial cost of purchase. Depending on the quality of your land, you will need about an acre of land for every two to three ewes (plus lambs). If you have the room on your property, you can start them at one spot and move them once they've eaten most of the grass. (Always graze sheep after cows, never cows after sheep, as the sheep will have eaten too much for the cows to find food.)

It is best to look for a breed that is native to your area. Starting with a small number of ewes is recommended. If you want to breed your ewes, you can add a ram, or you could look into borrowing a ram for breeding. You can expect each ewe to have one or two lambs on average.

### Goats

Goats are great for those who are just starting out with livestock. They take up less land and need less food than cows, but they still can provide both milk and meat. Goats will eat all kinds of plants, including herbs, trees, and bushes, which means you can let them graze for a large portion of their diet and they can be helpful in clearing land, eating the brush that you would otherwise have to pull up. They don't require a lot of supervision, though they are known to be smart enough to escape their pens if given the chance. Therefore, it's important that you be sure their enclosure is escape-proof.

For many people, goat milk is easier on the stomach than cow milk. It is a preferred alternative among those with digestion problems, including young children, older people, and people with ulcers. The American Dairy Goat Association has guides on eight different breeds of dairy goats; among those, Nubian goats are often considered the best. They are great milk producers, and their milk has a high amount of both butterfat and protein.

Goats are a good source of lean red meat. Traditionally, cows have been a bigger source of red meat in the United States, but goat meat production has been growing since the early 1990s. Some of the main meat goat breeds are Spanish (wild) goats, Boer goats, Kiko goats, Myotonic (fainting) goats, Savanna goats, and Texmaster goats. Generally, the Boer breed, brought to the U.S. from South Africa, is considered to have the best meat.

### Cows

The largest animal on this list, cows are also the largest commitment in terms of both money and time. Dairy cows must be milked multiple times every day, and both dairy cows and beef cattle require a significant amount of food and land. However, cows also offer a big return on investment, from meat to dairy products to offspring that you can sell or trade. There are hundreds of different breeds of cattle, but these are some of the most popular that you might consider for your farm:

*Angus* — This breed and the beef it produces are very well known in the United States. If you're planning to raise beef cattle, this is definitely one to consider—especially if you plan to sell what you raise, given the breed's well-known brand.

*Hereford* — These cows are mainly raised for beef, though they are sometimes also used as dairy cows. They are found all over the world because of their ability to adapt to a variety of climates, so if you're hoping to raise cattle but are worried about their suitability to your local weather, you may want to look into these.

*Charolais* — As you might guess from the name, this type of cow was first found in France. These cows are well-known for the quality of their meat as well as their hides and are often cross-bred with other breeds.

*Galloway* — A breed from Scotland, these cows have distinct fluffy coats. They are one of the oldest breeds of cattle and another strong beef breed.

*Limousin* — Another French breed that is now raised in many places, the Limousin is generally bred for its meat. However, they also make great work cows.

*Simmental* — This Swiss breed has been in the United States for over 200 years, and while it is often used for dairy production in other places, here it is more commonly known as a beef breed. The Simmental is a fast grower and is one of the larger breeds of cows.

*Shorthorn* — The Shorthorn breed was actually created to fulfill both dairy and beef needs, so they are a great choice if you want flexibility, or if you're yet not sure whether beef or dairy is right for you. Some breeders have cultivated a specialty for either dairy or beef Shorthorns, though, so be sure to discuss this with your breeder before you buy from them.

*Holstein Friesian* — These cows produce the highest volume of milk among all the breeds. If your household consumes a lot of dairy products or if you're hoping to make and sell them, this breed is a great choice.

*Brahman* — This breed is ancient and is well-known for its hardiness. It is very resistant to diseases, parasites, and overheating, is able to withstand extreme climates, and can also survive long periods with little food.

*Scottish Highland* — Hailing from Scotland, obviously, you might have seen this long-haired cow on postcards featuring the Scottish Highlands that gave it its name. Like the Brahman, the Scottish Highland cow is also very robust. It is less susceptible to disease and is able to thrive in both hot and cold climate zones.

### Bees

Bees may not be the first thing you think of when you think of livestock, but beekeeping is a growing interest among home-steaders and the general population. The obvious benefit is the ability to make your own honey, but you can also get the satisfaction of knowing that your bees are contributing to the local ecosystem through their hard work pollinating local flowers. Consuming local honey is also thought to help with allergies.

As with all these animals, it is important to do your research, especially since improper handling of bees can lead to the very unpleasant experience of being stung. There are a lot of resources for learning about bees, including many local beekeeping organizations. Local organizations are particularly good for beekeeping because the specifics of your location will influence how to best care for your bees.

Spring is the best time to start a hive, so plan ahead and do your research the year before. You'll then be in good shape to place your bee order in the winter. You can start with a standard package of bees, or you can start with what's called a nucleus colony. A nucleus colony comes with a queen who will lay eggs, worker bees, other bees of various ages, and food. This setup means you are not starting the hives from scratch, so your bees have a better chance to thrive. It also allows your hive to grow quickly. You'll want to feed your bees with sugar water in the beginning, to help them get acclimated; you won't need to do this forever, though, because as they become familiar with the area and more flowers begin to bloom for them to feed on, they will stop drinking the sugar water.

It is difficult to move a hive once it's established, so be sure to place it somewhere safe and easy to access. You'll want to periodically check in with your hive by opening it, and for this, you'll need a specific set of tools: protective clothing (leather gloves, a veil, and/or a jacket), a smoker, a bee brush, a frame lifter, a multipurpose hive tool, and a set of regular pliers. You can purchase these new or used, but if you get used equipment, make sure you clean it thoroughly before introducing your own bees. Always start your smoker *before* opening your hive, as this helps to discourage the bees from stinging. The best way to tell if your hive is healthy is to look at the queen; if she's laying eggs, then she is happy, and a happy and healthy queen means the rest of the hive will be happy and healthy, as well.

**Next!**

After establishing your location, utilities, crops, and livestock, your homestead will be shaping up pretty well! You're informed about how to raise livestock and grow food, how to heat and power your home, how to dispose of waste, and how to provide yourself with water. If you can get all those things lined up, you'll have a good solid foundation on which to build your homesteading dreams. In the next few chapters, we'll look at how to prepare yourself for both exceptional situations, like medical emergencies, and day-to-day life, like standard homestead maintenance.

# 5

# MEDICAL CARE

While it is important for everyone everywhere to be prepared for medical emergencies, it is particularly crucial if you're planning to live in a more remote area. It's a good idea to know how to treat minor injuries yourself and to know what to do in the case of major injuries or other life-threatening situations. Due to travel time, terrain, and other impediments, access to emergency services and medical care can be limited in rural areas. This chapter will describe both preventative measures that you can take to avert disasters before they happen and methods to deal with those that are unpreventable.

There are two categories that most emergencies fall into: those that jeopardize your home, such as a tornado or flood, and those that don't, such as medical problems. The best mindset is to do everything you can to prepare for both kinds on your own, but have systems in place to utilize whatever outside resources might be available. Below are some tips to be as ready as possible for whatever life throws at you.

**Preparing for a Crisis**

*Be aware of your surroundings.*

This is not just a call for in-the-moment awareness, though you should have that, too. You need to be aware of what might happen—weather, accidents, natural hazards, etc.—as well as what services are available to help you. There will be dangers that are particular to your area. Look into the history of your location and talk to long-time residents. Find out what threats might exist from local wildlife, and learn about those animals' behavioral cues and what to do if you encounter them. Know how far away traditional means of medical help such as hospitals are, and how long it will take an ambulance or other transportation to get you there. Essentially, map out what potential perils exist, and then make plans for what you will do if they happen.

*Remote doesn't mean disconnected.*

Communication is vital for homesteaders for a variety of reasons. Weather alerts via a weather radio or from a website that tracks your local weather can help you know trouble is coming in time to brace for it. A standard radio tuned to a local news station can also warn you of potential disasters. Even if you plan to take care of minor injuries yourself, be sure to keep contact information for emergency services. Have several backup means of communication, such as a landline as well as a cell phone. If you live somewhere with bad cell reception, consider investing in a satellite phone. And very importantly, test all your communication methods routinely. You want to fix any problems that arise *before* an emergency, not during one.

*Remember your community.*

Even if you're living quite far from city limits, most people will still have some type of neighbors—if the lot you're looking to homestead on is so remote that you have nobody to turn to when calamity strikes, you might want to keep looking. Just as you should have contact information for emergency services, you should also gather contact information for any neighbors close enough to help you in an emergency. Don't only call them if something goes wrong, though—foster a relationship with them. Be willing to help them when they need it, which will build camaraderie and trust. Being there for one another is not just a sentimental idea for homesteaders—it's a way to guarantee everyone's survival.

*Put together emergency kits.*

Whether dealing with a small misfortune or a huge catastrophe, the last thing you want to be doing is running around collecting items that you need. The idea of a first aid kit is familiar to most people, but you should also pack bags that you can grab at a moment's notice. Fill these with essentials such as emergency cash, copies of important documents, a battery-powered or hand-crank radio, flashlights, extra batteries, a power bank for charging cell phones and other small electronics, matches (in a waterproof container), a whistle, wipes, soap, basic tools, small amounts of non-perishable food, bottled water, a can opener, eating utensils, maps, hand sanitizer, and medical supplies, including any medications you need. You might include additional things specific to your household, such as pet supplies, baby supplies, etc. Having these bags on hand will give you peace of mind, and make you less likely to panic when you need a clear state of mind.

*Discuss your plans.*

It is important to plan for any and all scenarios, but it is equally important that everyone in your household knows what those plans are. Routine discussion will help keep things fresh in everyone's minds and make sure that you are adapting to any changed circumstances. Be sure that you have a designated place where everyone will meet in the event that you must leave your home. You might even have several different points, in the case of different situations. You can also keep other emergency supplies at your meeting point, such as more food, blankets, extra clothes, larger containers of water, a fire extinguisher, a temporary shelter such as a tent, etc.

*Level up your skills.*

There are a number of courses you can take that will help you be more prepared and useful in an emergency, including first aid, CPR, wilderness survival, and wilderness first responder classes. If you're unable to find a course near you, try checking online. These will teach you to assess a situation and know how to proceed. You'll learn to treat small injuries and what to do to mitigate the damage from larger ones. Not only will these courses increase your expertise, but they will help you keep a level head in a time of crisis. It might be cliché to say that knowledge is power, but it's cliché because it's true. When you know what is happening and what can fix it, you will be empowered to act swiftly and decisively.

## Common Injuries

The best way to minimize injuries is to anticipate them. If you assume that you will not get hurt, injuries will take you by surprise, and you'll be left with no clear way to handle them. However, if you assume that it's likely you will get hurt, not only will you be ready when it happens, but you'll also be training yourself to stay cognizant of potential harm. Here are some frequent injuries to be aware of and prepared for:

*Blisters* — Blisters are one of the most common skin irritations. Friction, exposure to extreme heat or cold, and allergic reactions to plants or insect bites all can cause blisters. Common sense can save you from many of these. Wear proper clothing that fits well and is appropriate to the weather, make sure your skin is covered when handling unfamiliar plants or other substances, and use bug repellent.

*Cuts* — Even in every day, non-homesteading life, we risk being cut all the time. Knives, garden tools, power tools, and even scissors can cut you if you're not careful. On a homestead, there are additional risks, such as using an axe or putting up barbed wire. Reduce your risk by wearing protective gear and always using the right tool for the task.

*Muscle Injuries* — Life on a homestead can involve significantly more physical activity than most other lifestyles. You'll find yourself lugging a lot of heavy things! This can be particularly stressful on your neck and back. Practice correct lifting and carrying posture, and never lift or carry something heavier than you can manage.

*Heat Exhaustion* — With increased physical exertion can come overheating, and you need to be especially mindful of this if you live in a warm environment. While it may seem more efficient to keep going, in reality, pushing past your limits can make you faint or dizzy. Take regular breaks and drink a lot of water whenever working in heat.

*Accidents with Machinery* — Chances are that if you live and work on a farm, at some point you'll need to use machinery such as a tractor or chainsaw. Due to the nature of these machines, injuries resulting from their misuse are often serious or even fatal. While there is no way to be completely accident-proof, many of these injuries happen because machinery is operated carelessly or in a way that it was not made to operate. Always be sure you follow all safety protocols and wear the proper safety gear, and keep all of your machinery well-maintained in good, working order.

*Hunting Injuries* — Obviously, hunting weapons can cause very serious or even fatal injuries. If you are going to be using a gun or other hunting weapon, the first step to safety is making sure that you are properly trained and certified. Always be sure to keep guns locked away from children and other untrained individuals. When you are hunting, wear the correct high visibility clothing, and be aware of your surroundings at all times to prevent accidental shootings.

**First Aid Kit Checklist**

You can obviously buy a first aid kit fairly easily, but you might want to make your own so that you can be sure it meets your specific needs. Try to get in the habit of replacing anything that you use right away, and go through your kit regularly (at least every six months) to replace anything you've missed or any of the medicines that have expired. Here's a basic list of what to keep in your first aid kit:

- Bandages, including one or two boxes of band-aids in assorted sizes, absorbent wound dressings, cloth tape, rolled gauze, a roller bandage, triangular bandages, and sterile gauze pads in assorted sizes
- An instant cold pack
- Antiseptic wipes
- Antibiotic and hydrocortisone ointments
- Aspirin
- A non-mercury, non-glass oral thermometer
- Tweezers
- Non-latex gloves
- A CPR mask
- An emergency (Mylar) blanket

Some other things that might be good to keep in or near your first aid kit are prescription medications or medications that you regularly take and important medical information such as the doctor's phone number, family contact numbers, health insurance information, and family member blood types.

**Next!**

While the information in this chapter may seem daunting, remember that part of being ready for emergency situations is considering and preparing for all possibilities. Not only will it keep you safe, but it will also help ease your mind. Knowing that you have the skills and resources to take care of yourself and your family in a crisis might even give you the confidence you never had when you were relying on others to do that for you.

# 6

# HOMESTEAD MAINTENANCE

With homesteading, freedom and responsibility go hand in hand. You're in charge of things! Which means… you're in charge of things. And that includes all of the equipment that you'll use to make your homestead work. The last few chapters gave you an idea of the various systems, machines, gadgets, and tools that come together to keep a homestead running. This chapter is about maintaining all those things. As we briefly touched on when discussing accidents and medical emergencies, it is very important to make sure that everything is in good shape and working properly. Not only does that keep things safe, but it also improves productivity and helps you avoid unnecessary delays.

## Organization

The first step to maintenance is to keep everything organized and to put things away when you're done with them. Tools that get left in random places will go missing or get damaged much more easily. My tip for keeping things neat and tidy is to group tools by type and have a designated container or area for each group. It doesn't matter how you categorize them—it could be by function (cutting, fastening, etc.), by application (plumbing, electrical, etc.), by size, or even by color if you want! All that matters is that you'll be able to remember where they go and why.

I also suggest keeping a list or chart with all of your more complex tools or gadgets that need regular maintenance, such as oil changes or filter changes. Record what you should check, how often, when you last serviced it, and the specifics of any part (such as batteries) that will need regular replacement. Keep this list somewhere easy to access near your tools so that you'll remember to update it as necessary.

**Cleaning and Storage**

This is common sense, but worth stressing anyway: keeping things clean is essential to keeping them in good working order. This is especially true for seasonal equipment that will be stored for large portions of the year. When you use something for the last time before putting it away for the season, make sure you *thoroughly* clean it. It should also be totally dry before being stored, as moisture can make things rust, rot, or grow mildew. Things that are used frequently should be cleaned and put away in the same spot after every use. Making sure equipment is stored somewhere away from bugs, dirt, and dust is important, especially if that equipment is used to handle food in any way.

**Tool Maintenance**

There are four big things that taking care of your tools prevents: dullness, rust, wear and tear, and stiffness. The first two are fairly straightforward. Sharp and rust-free tools are easier to use and work better, which also means they are safer. Some tools can be sharpened at home and others are best left to professionals—you should be able to get that done at a hardware store. Rust is easy to remove yourself with a little elbow grease and some steel wool, sandpaper, a wire brush, or a rust remover.

Wear and tear are often less about proactive maintenance and more about proper use, but you can help keep wooden tools in good shape by applying wood butter or oil to prevent drying, cracks, and splinters. As for stiffness, grease and oil are your friends. Grease in the gears of machines keeps them running well, and oil can be applied to any stuck joints, hinges, or other moving parts. Remember to be aware of how you use the tools and make absolutely sure that any grease applied to tools that might be used for or around food is non-toxic.

**Vehicle and Machine Maintenance**

As I suggested above, keep detailed records of your maintenance schedule for any complex machinery, including vehicles. Regularly inspect tires, hoses, and wiring, and change out batteries and fluids. Look for leaks, loose wires, and damage. Every time you finish using a vehicle, make sure the headlights and other parts of the vehicle that use battery power are turned off. This small habit can save you the immense frustration of an unexpected dead battery. Also, be mindful of how weather can affect vehicles. Heat and cold can alter the air pressure in your tires and gas can freeze if a vehicle is not frequently used in wintertime, so empty the gas tanks of any equipment you don't intend to use throughout the winter.

**Maintenance Checklist**

You can break your maintenance list into two categories: things to check often, and things that you should check a few times throughout the year.

Things to Check Often:

- Anything broken or worn out. This may seem obvious, but it is important to repair small problems as they happen to avoid the chance of them snowballing and becoming much bigger problems. Some common issues you'll want to fix right away are:
- Broken or blown light bulbs
- Water leaks
- Rusted metal
- Broken windows or other glass
- Chipped or peeling paint
- Cracked putty
- Traps or other forms of pest control. As with broken things, make sure to solve this problem right away, before it grows and you run the risk of infestation.
- Anywhere that water might leak. In addition to fixing leaks quickly, it is important to do regular checks to look for leakage. Catching a leak early can be the

difference between a minor inconvenience and a huge catastrophe.

- Your main electrical panel. There are a few things you should do here:
- Look for signs of moisture, such as watermarks or rust.
- Check all your breakers, turning them on and off to test that they're working.
- Tighten any loose fuses.
- Check for heat or the scent of burning. (If either of these is present, call your electrician ASAP.)
- Your emergency cash fund. This isn't necessarily a thing to do, but it is something to maintain. You should always have a bit of money stashed away for unexpected expenses, and if you spend any of that money, replace it as soon as you can.

Things to Check a Few Times a Year:

- Doors and windows. The biggest thing to look for here is drafts. Ensure that when they're closed, everything is sealed tight. You should also examine door and window frames for warping or instability, which could be a sign of bigger problems.
- Walls. It's likely you will notice most damage to your walls when it occurs, but it can never hurt to take a few hours once or twice a year and do a thorough check. If you find cracks or holes, fill them and make note of where they are so you can make sure they don't increase. You should also look for water stains.

- Ceilings. Similar to walls, but you also need to check for sagging or changes in shape.
- Paint. Both interior and exterior paints provide a barrier between raw materials and everyday wear or, in the case of exteriors, weather. Repaint any blistered, cracked, or peeling areas.
- Pipes and fixtures. Make sure none of your taps are leaking. If you find a leak, try replacing the washer— that usually solves the problem. Check all seals on things like tile and grout, especially around areas like the toilet and the bathtub. Thoroughly investigate anywhere the seal might be broken as water leaks in these spaces can lead to mold, which can get out of hand if left unchecked.
- Roof(s). Look for damage, including loose shingles, warping, bubbling, or other indications of structural problems. Keep your roof clear of branches and other things that might have fallen onto it.
- Chimney(s). For wood-burning chimneys, call a chimney sweep annually to clean them out and routinely check for damage in the bricks or mortar. If you have a gas appliance in your chimney, have a qualified technician inspect it yearly.
- Steps, stairs, railings, etc. Check the security of *all* of your steps, both indoor and outdoor. Discovering a wobbly railing or unsteady step through a routine check is vastly preferable to discovering it when it breaks or comes loose under your foot.
- Gutters and drains. Keep an eye on these all year round, but be sure to check and clean them of leaves and other

obstructions before you expect periods of heavy rain. Drains can become loose over time and may need to be reset, so check this as well.

- Exterior wooden surfaces. Test the seal on your outdoor wood by dripping water on it. The water should bead up. If it soaks into the wood, then the seal needs to be redone. Be sure to sand the wood down before resealing it. Also, inspect any wood for signs of insect infestation or decay.
- Garages, barns, workshops, etc. Check anything from the above list that also applies to these structures— walls, ceilings, wood, paint, etc.
- Paved areas and/or driveways. Look for worn parts or cracks. Repair any uneven areas, especially if they are routinely driven on or if their slope might direct rainwater toward your house or other structures.

**Next!**

As we've made our way through the book, I've frequently reminded you that planning is essential to homesteading because careful planning can save you time, money, and headaches. Proper maintenance is an extension of that and is essential to making your homestead run smoothly. It will help you avoid costly repairs and delay-causing breakdowns while also just making your life easier. There is another essential organizational tool for your homesteading journey that we have yet to discuss, and that's your budget. The next chapter will take a deep dive into what a budget does, how to make one, and how to tighten it when you don't have a lot of funds.

# 7

# HOMESTEAD BUDGETING

**W**hy Is Budgeting Important?

You're probably familiar with budgeting, no matter your background. A budget is a good tool for anyone running a household of any kind. However, homesteading has a particular set of pros and cons when it comes to budgeting; there are many expenses that you likely aren't used to budgeting for, especially if you are working on a large scale with many additional vehicles or machines to maintain. Not only are these expenses unfamiliar to those used to urban or suburban living, but that equipment can be vital to the function and well-being of your household. Because of this, you need to be able to take care of these unexpected expenses in a timely manner. This means that you must have a cushion in your budget, so that one or two negative events don't mean severe setbacks or the collapse of your entire enterprise.

Another thing to consider about homesteading life is that it goes in seasons. There will be particular costs associated with each season (planting costs in spring, harvesting costs in fall, etc.), so your budget needs to be more than a predetermined monthly calculation of expenses and income. Similarly, your income likely won't be a set amount that you receive at a set interval. You might have a large amount of money come in at once, but you need to make that money last for a long time. A budget will help you know when you can spend money and when you need to save that money for later on in the year.

Right now, you might be working for an employer who is responsible for taking taxes out of your paycheck and paying them to the government. Much of your income in homesteading will not be for an employer—in fact, you might be employing other people. This means that you also need to adjust your budget to account for the taxes that you'll have to pay. And if you are transitioning from being employed to working for yourself, you have to account for the cost of that transition. You might be hoping to eventually make your homestead the main source of your income, but it will take time for you to turn a profit. This can be years, so it is very, very important to go into that endeavor with a solid budget, where you know what money you'll have coming in, how you'll be spending it, and generally how you'll survive until you are able to sustain yourself.

On the positive side, you'll find you have a lot more control over all areas of your life. This gives you the flexibility to choose less expensive options rather than being locked into whatever utility or service has the monopoly over your area. It also means you might be doing or making a lot of things yourself, eliminating the need to pay for them. All of this impacts your bottom line, and it's important to not just cross your fingers and hope everything adds up. Like the rest of this life, making your budget is about being willing to take on greater responsibility in exchange for greater control. The rest of this chapter is here to help you do just that.

**How to Create a Budget**

*Step 1: Gather information.*

This is the first step, but it is also one you'll need to be doing constantly, possibly forever. The more experience you gain, the more you'll know about what things will cost, how much money you can make from certain activities, and many other variables that will affect your budget. Smart money managers constantly take in new information and adjust their budgets accordingly. Every year, every season, even sometimes every day, you'll be updating your knowledge base. You can use that knowledge to make your household more financially efficient. This may sound like a lot of work, but once you've become practiced at it, it will become almost automatic.

But in the beginning, before you've got a lot of experience, gathering information will involve less personal observation and more research. You'll be doing most of this research already as you look into all the options that have been presented to you in this book so far. When you are deciding where to live, collect data about how much it costs to live there. When you're choosing your utilities, make note of the prices of each system. When you're planning what plants and livestock you'll have, estimate how much each will cost you. As you anticipate what you'll need for maintenance and emergencies, record what the upfront expenses of your supplies will be, and how much repairs and replacements will be. Taking this small extra step for all of your planning will leave you with a great foundation of information with which to build your budget.

*Step 2: List your expenses.*

Start with the basics: regularly occurring expenses like food, clothes, phone service, and medicines. Next, account for monthly, quarterly, yearly, etc. bills; this includes any debt you're paying off, such as car loans, student loans, and credit cards. You probably have a pretty good idea of all of these already. From here, start adding in all the other information you've gathered, like upfront expenses, including equipment and livestock; seasonal expenses, such as new plants or animal feed; housing and living expenses, including your estimated mortgage or lease payments; maintenance and medical expenses; the upfront cost of your utilities, as well as any ongoing expenses for them; taxes you'll be responsible for; and anything else that you came across in your research.

This list is not exhaustive but is meant to help jumpstart things for you. Everyone's list of expenses will be slightly different because different households have different needs. The idea is to write down absolutely everything you can think of so that you are never surprised by an expense. Don't forget to include a cushion for unexpected costs—you might not know exactly how much this should be, but use your best estimating skills. You can fine-tune this number later. While you're making this list, also write down when you will need to pay each expense. It can be helpful to make a rough list with all your information to ensure you don't forget anything, and then redo the list more neatly, organizing things by date and category.

*Step 3: Determine your monthly expenses.*

It's not very useful to have one big list of all your expenses, especially when some are monthly, some are yearly, some are one-time, and some might not have a set date. So, the next step is to determine how much money you'll need each month. You want to spread out big expenses over the year—basically, you'll plan to save a certain amount each month, so that when those expenses need to be paid, you've accumulated enough money to pay them. To get the amount you should save each month, divide each yearly expense by 12. If an expense is set at a different interval, determine the yearly cost and divide by 12 (i.e., if you pay a bill four times a year, multiply by four and then divide by 12). If you're not sure exactly when you'll need to pay an expense, use your best judgment.

Note that you might have big expenses in the first year or so that you will not have time to save for if you start saving after you start your homestead. You can plan to pay for these with savings you already have, or you can start incorporating those expenses into your monthly budget now with the intention of building up your savings before you make the transition. (You could also take out a loan for those expenses, but be very careful with this option, given that you may not have the ability to start paying it back for a few years.)

*Step 4: List your income streams.*

Just as you need to know how much you will spend and save each month, you need to know how much income you can count on. If you have a regular income that you know will continue, start with that. Then, add in any income from one-time sources, irregular sources, or any savings that you're comfortable including. You can include projected income—meaning income that you *think* you will make, but don't know for sure—but be careful not to rely too much on this. Homesteading can be very unpredictable, especially in the first few years, and you don't want to be left in the red because you anticipated getting paid for something and it fell through. As with your expenses, write down when you expect to get each stream of income.

*Step 5: Put it all together.*

There are a few different ways that you can do this. Some people prefer to calculate their total yearly expected income, and then divide that by 12 to get an estimated monthly income. After the division, you have a simple subtraction problem, money in minus money out. Some people do a similar method with quarters (three months at a time). The guiding factor here is what makes sense to *you*. However you divide things, the goal is to be able to predict the money you'll be spending for a certain period, and distribute the money you'll be making so that it covers that spending. For example, let's say that you know you'll make $6,000 in June, and your budget says you have $3,000 per month in expenses. This means that the money you make in June will cover your expenses for July and August, but you will need to make more income for your September expenses.

If creating your own system seems intimidating, don't stress; you can always gather all your expenses and income, and then input them into a premade budget. Apps like Excel often come preloaded with budget templates. You can also find templates online for both Excel and other programs like Google Sheets. If you're really feeling out of your depth, you could also consult with a professional accountant. However you do it, the important thing is that you create a budget that works and you stick to it.

**Homesteading on a Limited Budget**

The last part of this chapter will focus on tips for getting started when you don't have much money to work with. Yes, there are some parts of homesteading that can be very expensive. But even if you don't have the funds for big upfront expenses or a lot of land, you can still do this. In fact, switching to a homesteading mindset can actually help you save money in a lot of ways! Making food and clothing for yourself, being focused on reducing and reusing, and just generally being self-sufficient can cut down on your expenses and help you get more in control of your finances. Read on for advice on how to get started.

*Tip 1: Downsize your life.*

Many people's mindset, especially in the United States, is that more is always better. We like to do more and own more and be "more," but constantly accumulating things has a point of diminishing returns after which more stuff just means more to take care of, more to pay for, and for whoever's doing the housekeeping, more to clean. Take a hard look at what you're spending money on and ask yourself if those things *truly* make you happy. If that sounds daunting, try thinking of it in terms of the direction you want your life to go. If you focus on your goals and the purpose you want your life to have, then you have an inherent guideline for what's important in your life. Examine how you're spending your money, and ask yourself, "Is this taking me in the direction I want to go?"

I'm not advocating for you to eliminate anything you truly love, but so often we're spending money on things that we're only guessing will make us happy. Stop guessing, and start intentionally choosing your priorities based on where you want to go next. A good way to practice intentional purchasing is to ask yourself if something is a need or a want, and then only buy it if you need it. Classifying purchases into needs and wants will help you streamline your expenses, and this kind of focused buying will have the added benefit of helping you clarify and solidify your goals and plans.

*Tip 2: Be patient.*

The best way to change your life is to take small steps consistently. You've decided you want to change your life—great! That doesn't mean you should overhaul everything at once. If you're at the beginning of this journey, you'll likely have a lot of things you want to change. You can use those things as a guide, but remember the SMART goals we discussed in chapter one, especially the "A" for attainable. Take your big, long-term vision and break it down into very small parts that you can achieve a bit at a time. Make a list of all the things that you want to achieve, and then separate your list into things you can do now and things that you can't do yet. For the things that you can do now, make a plan on how you'll slowly integrate them into your life. For the things that you can't do yet, pick one or two that are top priorities for you and make another list of what needs to happen for those things to be possible. You can also separate that list into "now" and "not yet." Keep working like this until you have a clear plan of small steps that you can take now which can build into long-term change.

*Tip 3: Start with what you have.*

This covers a lot of the same ground as the last tip, but from a slightly different perspective. It's great for when you're feeling frustrated and far away from your goals, and it involves starting up your imagination and getting innovative. Take stock of your life and consider what parts of it can be adapted right now. Can you grow plants on your balcony? Can you start learning to sew? Do you have room for one or two small animals in your backyard? A few other ways to ask the same question: What skills can you acquire now that will serve you well in the future? If you're hoping to move eventually, what things can you build now that you can transplant to a new home when you're ready? This also dovetails into the first tip: while you're simplifying your life, look for things that you can save and repurpose. Containers, clothing, even old furniture all have possibilities of being reused as a part of your new lifestyle.

Expand this thinking beyond just your home. I've mentioned community gardens—find out if there's one near you. If you know someone with plenty of land, ask if you could use a small portion of it for a garden. Inquire at your local home and garden stores or nurseries about what happens to their leftover seeds at the end of planting season. Often, they will let you take them because they would otherwise be thrown away. If you learn to grow your own plants from parent plants, you can ask friends and family for clippings and start a garden that way.

Along with plants, there's another food resource that is surprisingly easy to get for free or cheap—chickens. We've discussed how chickens can be kept in a variety of situations. This sort of arrangement is becoming more commonplace and can be very easy to manage with just a small backyard. You can feed your chickens leftovers and water them with collected rainwater. When sourcing chickens, check the internet. Websites like Craigslist and Facebook can lead you to people giving away chickens or selling them for a low price so long as you are willing to come get them.

*Tip 4: Reconsider your job.*

For many people, a full-time 9–5 job is the pinnacle of financial stability. However, there are many times when a job like this can hold you back. The rigid hours can leave you locked into a daily schedule that leaves you no time to work toward the life you want. Some jobs can also be physically and mentally draining, leaving you with little energy or motivation. It's hard to focus on growing your own food when every day leaves you so tired that all you want to do is order fast food and be a couch potato.

Of course, it can be very difficult to leave a job, and I'm not advocating you just quit on a whim. Start by prioritizing your time; when you're on the clock, you're at work, and once you're punched out, that time belongs to *you*. Schedule time for your homesteading pursuits as if they were any other organized activity, and consider how you might start moving to a more flexible schedule. Could you go down to part-time for a while so you can build up a side business that you enjoy pursuing? Are there jobs available that you could do from home? Can you save for a year and have enough to support yourself while you transition to a more flexible job? Only you know the answers to those questions, and they will be slightly different for everyone. The point is, don't assume that a regular full-time job is your best option for a fulfilling and financially stable life.

*Tip 5: If you can't own, rent.*

It may seem as if you could only build on land that you own, but it is more common than you think for farming land to be rented. Usually, these rentals are on annual leases. You could potentially do a hybrid of renting and owning. If, for instance, you own a small amount of land with your house on it, but you're hoping to grow your operation, you could rent land from a neighbor for growing crops or grazing animals. If you're planning to do this, make sure your agreement is clear on who is responsible for what in regards to the maintenance of the property.

Another thing to consider is renting with the intention of buying. This is a specific kind of lease that you sign with a landlord, in which you agree to rent the property for a set amount of time, and when that time is up, you have the option to buy it. Not all landlords will agree to this, but if there's land that you're interested in, it is worth asking! Look for land that has been on the market for a while, as the owner might be more willing to consider a rent-to-own agreement. This is another time when imagination is a good resource, as properties that haven't sold aren't usually the most conventionally desirable ones. However, they often have a lot of promise if you're willing to put in some work.

There are a few things to be aware of in rent-to-own situations, and you will usually be required to pay a fee at the start of the lease. You should look over the terms carefully (as with all legal agreements) and make sure that the lease specifies things like who will be responsible for maintaining the property and how the eventual purchase price will be determined. Sometimes, the monthly rent you pay will go toward the price of the property, but sometimes it will not—this should also be clear in the lease. Be aware of the terms "lease-option" and "lease-purchase." Lease-option means you have the option to buy at the end of your lease; lease-purchase can mean that you are definitely agreeing to purchase. Again, read carefully, and if you're not sure about the meaning of anything, consult a lawyer!

*Tip 6: Get a loan.*

As with any loan, proceed with caution and only if you have a plan in place to be able to repay it. There are three specific kinds of loans for buying land without property on it. Raw land loans are for land with absolutely no development, improved land loans are for land with standard developmental markers such as road access and utilities, and unimproved land loans are for land that sits between those two, with some incomplete development. It can be very difficult to get any of these kinds of loans, and your best bet is probably small, local banks or credit unions that you have an existing relationship with. You'll also likely need great credit and proof of savings or other collateral.

**Next!**

One of the biggest expenses in your budget is usually housing, and this is especially true when you're looking at buying a new house or property. While you can homestead from anywhere and in any type of housing, if you're planning to buy a new place, you might have some questions and concerns. The next chapter will help answer and alleviate those by giving you an overview of homesteading properties.

# 8

# DIFFERENT TYPES OF HOMESTEAD PROPERTIES

B uying a new home can be very exciting, but it can also be incredibly stressful and frustrating. One of the best ways to alleviate the stress of this process is to be very prepared before you even start looking at properties. If you've made yourself a budget using the tips in the last chapter, then you hopefully have a good idea of what you can afford. The next step is to get a clear idea of what your ideal property looks like. While it's unlikely that you'll be able to find somewhere that exactly matches your ideal, knowing what you want helps you eliminate what you don't want. I recommend making two lists, one of the qualities that are absolutely necessary—things you cannot live without—and one of the things you would like to have if you could. Start with the first list, and use it to narrow down your options. Then, if you're deciding between proper-ties, you can use the second to help you pick the best one for you.

Timing is also important when buying a new property. The optimal time to shop for a home is when you're financially able to buy, but not in a rush. You don't want to feel that you *have* to buy, as that might lead you to buy somewhere that doesn't really fit your needs. Remember, this will be your home, so it will affect all other parts of your life. At the same time, don't get hung up looking for the "perfect" property. It doesn't exist! At least not yet—that's where you come in. If you can find somewhere that meets all your basic needs, then you can put your skills to work turning it into the perfect place for you. This chapter will help you know what to look for in a property, what types of properties are popular among homesteaders, and give you tips for where to find them and how to go about buying them.

**Types of Housing**

I want to introduce you to some housing options that you might not be familiar with, but remember that many homesteaders do live in traditional houses. If that's what will work best for you, that's what you should do. But if you're interested in what other options exist, this list will give you an overview of some of those possibilities.

*Cabins*

Many people are familiar with cabins as recreational areas or second homes, but they can also be used as primary residences. Cabins are a good option if you're hoping to build with local materials, especially if the land you're building on is wooded. Some cabins are very basic, while others are designed to offer all your modern conveniences in a smaller and more rustic unit. If you're interested in full-time cabin living, one tip is to look for a cabin rental that has a comparable level of off-grid living to what you desire. By renting the cabin for a few weeks, you can determine if that lifestyle works for you. You can even do this a few times, trying out different lengths of stay or in different seasons, to really get a feel for the way of life before fully committing to it.

*Tiny Houses*

Tiny houses have been an increasing trend for a few years now. You might have seen them on Instagram or HGTV. A tiny house compresses all the basic needs of a house down into a much smaller package—usually between 100 and 400 square feet. While this might seem impossibly small (especially to Americans, who are used to square footage about six times as large), downsizing to a tiny house helps many people discover that they really didn't need as much space as they thought. If you have a large family, a tiny house might not be the best idea, but if you're living alone or as a couple, they can be a great option—especially if you don't have a lot of land, or if you're planning to share the land with other residents. The small size also means less money for building materials, and in some places, the size can mean a tiny house is not restricted by normal building codes. Some tiny houses are designed to be easily mobile, meaning that you could travel with them, or they could go with you to a new property. This can be a great option if you don't need much space now but might like to scale up in the future; your tiny house could be moved to a larger property and used as a living space while your next home is built.

*Ecocapsules*

Ecocapsules are a specific brand of tiny house or "micro-home" designed by Nice Architects, an architectural company in Slovakia. Ecocapsules come with all the benefits of a tiny house, but with additional considerations for environmentally friendly living. Ecocapsules are around 100 square feet and have built-in systems for wind power, solar power, and rainwater collection with filtration. They are very portable and can be placed on a trailer to be towed easily behind a vehicle. One of the biggest positives of buying an Ecocapsule is that you will not have to build it yourself. However, the unit costs around €80,000 (about $97,000 USD), with additional costs for shipping and transportation to your property. If you like the idea of an eco-friendly tiny house and don't want the hassle of building it yourself, this could be a great option. However, if you'd rather have a house that is customized to your specific needs and aesthetics, you might prefer to just design and build your own tiny house.

*Earthships*

Earthships are another eco-friendly type of housing. The concept of Earthships started with the vision of architect Michael Reynolds and the company that he helped found, Earthship Biotecture. However, many people use the term to refer to any type of housing built in that same style. This includes being made of natural and/or recycled material and operating at least partially off-grid. There tends to be more variety among Earthships than many of the other types of housing discussed on this list because Earthships are not about a specific structure or style, but about using local materials to create a home that is sustainably built and maintained. Earthships range from the modest and practical to the large and luxurious. If you're feeling particularly adventurous, you can design and build an Earthship on your own, but you can also get plans from or have a consultation with Earthship Biotecture if you'd prefer to have the more complicated parts of the process done for you.

*Shipping Containers*

If you'd love to build your own home but you want to cut down on the new materials you use, you might consider converting a shipping container. You can use one retired shipping container to create a small house for yourself, or you can join or stack several together to make a bigger living space. In addition to your basic structure already being made, shipping containers offer good shelter and can be transported easily. Their rectangular space mimics the layout of most houses, and you can design the space inside as an open floor plan or add room separators for a bit more of a traditional feel. One thing to be aware of with shipping container homes is that being made of metal makes it hard to regulate the temperature inside. In particular, if you live somewhere that has extreme cold or heat, you might want to try a different type of housing or put some research into ways to securely insulate the space. You'll be much more comfortable, and your heating system will thank you!

*Underground Houses*

On the flip side, a type of housing known for its incredible insulation is underground housing. The idea of underground homes might bring to mind images of Hobbit holes, but in reality, a lot of people find underground housing to be an efficient and practical way of life.

Because your living space is surrounded by earth, it is naturally insulated. Another benefit of underground living is the automatic level of privacy that you'll get—but don't worry, you can still have windows and plenty of natural light if you design your home properly. The level of design and planning for these homes is probably the biggest drawback, as they need to be able to bear the weight of the earth without collapsing inward. They also need to be built in a way that doesn't negatively impact the surrounding environment. This can be intimidating, but it also often leads to some innovative designs that fit beautifully with the natural world around them.

*Yurts*

This tent-like home appeals to people who want to have as little impact on the land as possible, given that it sits on a platform and is built from a wooden frame and lattice walls covered with fabric. This also makes it one of the more affordable options on this list. However, yurts are definitely not for everyone; they are more durable and luxurious than regular tents, but residents still contend with much of the same drawbacks as tent campers. This includes less insulation (from both weather and noise), less privacy, not much storage, and a lack of security against bugs and animals. Just like some people enjoy camping and some do not, for some people this sort of living is fun and interesting, and for others, it is completely unappealing. I trust you'll know which of these you are!

**Where to Find Properties**

No matter what type of housing you choose, you'll need somewhere for it to go. Whether you're looking for a fully developed farm or an undeveloped plot of land, you need to start your search somewhere. It can be good to seek the help of a real estate professional, especially if you're not familiar with the process or you're feeling overwhelmed. However, even if you are working with a realtor, I recommend also doing some searching on your own. You never know when you might find something your realtor missed, or come across an option that you hadn't considered previously. And of course, if you're not working with a realtor, knowing where to look for listings is even more important.

*Mainstream Real Estate Sites*

These sites, such as Zillow, Realtor.com, and Trulia, will have a wide range of properties, so the challenge with them is to narrow down your options. Most of these sites have a similar collection of filters that you can use for this. Use the home type filter to eliminate any unsuitable options such as apartments, condominiums, duplexes, and townhomes, and use the lot size filter to look for properties in your preferred size. Checking at least an acre will remove most urban and many suburban properties, and leave you with more rural options. The higher the minimum acreage you set, the more of your search results will be rural. Another thing you can do is look for an off-grid option among the filters—try looking for an option that says "more filters" or similar if you don't see it right away.

*Sites That Specialize in Off-Grid, Sustainable, or Homesteading Properties*

These sites have done the work of narrowing the field for you, and only offer properties in their specific niche. Some will cover many different aspects of homesteading and off-grid living, such as eco-friendly, sustainable, alternative energy, and survival properties, while some may narrow their focus to just one or two of these. Two sites you can start with are Sustainable Properties Real Estate Listings and Survival Realty. Sustainable Properties has property listings throughout the United States, and Survival Realty has listings in the U.S. and a small amount of overseas properties as well.

*Social Media*

I wouldn't recommend this as a first or only choice for finding real estate, but it can work to expand your options or if you've had no luck and you're running out of options. You can always follow local real estate offices and brokers on social media, as they will often post about new listings. If you're in a particularly competitive market, you can alter your settings to send you notifications whenever these accounts post, which can help you get the jump on any new properties. Additionally, sites that have groups or communities, such as Facebook or Reddit, can work. Search for off-grid or homestead real estate and see what groups come up. You can then bookmark or follow these groups so that you can check them regularly to see what postings have been added.

**Questions to Ask When Buying Property**

I encourage you to make your own tailored list of questions in addition to these, and of course, you'll also have the list of necessities that you've made. Be sure to review all of those whenever you look at a property. But the following list of questions will make sure you remember the basics and can help jump-start your thought process as you contemplate what you need from a property.

*How much land do you need?*

This is really a question you ask yourself, and the answer will be entirely dependent upon your household needs. You might have a firm minimum or maximum amount of land, or you might be flexible to a certain degree. The important thing is to know what size of lot is acceptable to you. To help you estimate how much you'll need based on what you plan to do, here is a quick rundown:

- 5 acres is enough for a garden whose crops will feed an average-sized family, plus space to raise small and medium livestock.
- 10 acres is enough for a garden to feed a family and possibly sell the excess, as well as small and medium livestock plus a small herd of cattle or a few horses.
- 15 to 20 acres is enough for all of these above, plus growing hay and at least some of the food your livestock will need; if it is wooded, it might also supply most of your fuel needs.

- 25 to 50 acres is enough for a garden, whatever livestock you'd like, hayfields, wood for fuel (if in a wooded area), a barn, and possibly other structures (such as a greenhouse or a butcher shop), and growing crops. It will also likely have a much higher amount of natural resources.

*Where is it located?*

We've discussed the general location of homesteads in some depth already, and the importance of location in regards to laws and climate. Now that we've gone over all the different possibilities for your housing, your utilities, and many other choices you'll be making, you can see how choosing the right location affects all other areas of your life. Once you know the area where you're hoping to buy, make sure you look into the planning and zoning laws for that area. We've also discussed the benefit of a location with a lot of natural resources and the pros and cons of living in more remote locations versus more populated areas. Considering the location of a property also includes noting how far away you are from services that you might need, such as medical care. If the land is not developed, you'll want to inquire about the possibility of adding things such as a phone line or internet. You should also ask questions about the history of the area in terms of extreme weather and natural disasters.

*How will you get there?*

I don't mean just how you will get to the plot of land itself, but also to the place where the house sits or where you'd hope to build. If you're looking at relatively populous areas, the distance from the main road to your house might be short. But if you're looking at large amounts of land and/or in rural areas, the actual location of the house might be far away from publicly maintained roads. If there is a private road through the property, is it in good shape? What will it cost to maintain? Are you required to give anyone else access to it? Don't forget that in addition to getting yourself to and from the main road, you'll also need to transport supplies. This principle also applies to anywhere else that you'll need to get to on the property. If there is no legal, safe way to access the places on the property you need to go, there is no point in owning the property.

*What's nearby?*

This includes both residential and commercial properties. You should try to find out what is happening on adjacent plots of land and whether any of those activities will affect *your* land. Pay particular attention to any farms that are uphill or upwind from the property, as anything that enters their air or water can make its way to your air and water—especially if there is a water source that runs through both properties. Keep in mind that undeveloped land near yours might be developed in the future. You can check to see what zoning and restrictions exist for the area as a whole in order to get an idea of what it could or couldn't be used for in the future.

You can also ask "Who is nearby?" If possible, it is always good to see if you can meet the neighbors and get to know them a little. If you're lucky, you can find a place that you like where you also like the neighbors.

*What restrictions are there on usage or rights?*

As I briefly mentioned when discussing water systems, sometimes you can own land but not have the rights to the water on that land. There can be similar issues around mineral rights, and some deeds can also include restrictions on how the land can be used. Whether or not these things are deal-breakers is up to you, but it's important that you ask the question so you're making an informed decision. One thing to specifically look out for is land with covenants. Covenants are sets of rules that are designed to keep the usage of an area very uniform, and will often prohibit common homesteading practices such as gardens or livestock. Some might also dictate what types of structures you can build. As you consider all these restrictions, also consider what you might want to do with your property in the future. As you become more adept, you might want to expand your operation. Just because you don't want to raise livestock now doesn't mean you won't in the future. Think about long-term possibilities, and don't lock yourself into a limited range of activities just because you don't want to do any of those things immediately.

*How well is the house insulated?*

We covered the importance of insulation when discussing energy efficiency. The better the insulation, the easier it will be to heat and cool your house. If the house you're considering doesn't have proper insulation, you'll need to consider if improving it is something you'd be willing to do. You should be sure that what you end up paying for a property reflects the extra cost you'll incur for those improvements.

*What is the land itself like?*

Look at the way the land is laid out, especially in the context of how you plan to use it. For example, if wind power plays a major role in your plans, is there somewhere suitable to put your turbine? If you're planning to have fields for crops or for grazing, how difficult will it be to establish those? If there's a water resource you want to use, how far is it from the house (or where you expect to build)? If you're planning to hunt or forage for food, are those resources available on the land? Customize these types of questions to your personal plans for the property. Remember that you can change many things about a property once you purchase it, but those changes will take plenty of time and money.

*What is the soil like?*

Because almost all forms of homesteading involve growing food, it's a given that the quality of the soil will affect you directly. Avoid areas with a lot of clay or sand in the soil. As we discussed in chapter four, the ideal type of soil is rich and not too hard or compact, with good drainage and a balanced pH. You can use the tips from that chapter to examine the soil and determine how good it will be for growing. You can also check the USDA.gov website for more information about the area. Their site has soil maps and data for much of the United States.

*Where does the water come from?*

Whether you're buying undeveloped land or a full compound, there is a version of this question you need to ask. If there is already a water system in place on the property, you need to know what it is and how it works. If there is not, what water resources exist? Are they suitable for the lifestyle you're planning? You need to know if all this a) fits your needs, and b) needs any alterations or repairs for it to work as you'd want. Also remember to have the water tested by a state-certified lab before you buy, as we covered in the well water section of chapter three.

*Have you done a title search?*

If you've found a property you really like and you're strongly considering buying it, make sure that you look into the public records for the property. You can pay to have this done, or you can do it yourself. You want to be sure there are no encumbrances or liens on the property because those will become your problem once you are the owner. (An encumbrance is anything that dictates how a property can be used, including whether or not it can be sold; a lien is a specific type of encumbrance where a creditor lays claim to part or all of your property because of money owed to them.) It is also a good idea to just be sure that all the details of the property, including the owner's identity, are correct as they've been given to you. You might think that this is overkill, and it's true that most of the time these searches will turn up nothing. However, there are people who will be dishonest and try to hide these things, and you don't want to find out that's the case after you've bought the land. This is a simple step you can take that can save you a lot of time and hardship.

**Next!**

I've given you a lot of information to process, but I've also tried to contextualize that information, giving you the why and how in addition to the what. We have one last thing to talk about, and it's perhaps the most important context of all—the real-life context of a homesteading community. None of the decisions you make will happen in a vacuum, and the next chapter will discuss not only the importance of your community but how to get the most from it.

# 9

# BEING PART OF A
# HOMESTEADING COMMUNITY

I f you're particularly observant, you might have noticed that the idea of community has already come up many times in this book. We talked about it when we debunked the common myth that homesteading is about living in the middle of nowhere, surrounded by wilderness and with no company but your own thoughts. There are, of course, those people who will seek out extreme isolation—but for most, neighbors are a reality. And hopefully, they are not just a reality, but a welcome benefit.

This is why the idea of neighbors came up when we discussed plants and livestock, again when we talked about emergency preparation, and again when we went over what to look for in a property. The principle of returning to a more connected way of life that is central to most people's homesteading journey is not just about connecting to nature but also connecting to people. More conventional life is often about depending upon systems to help you in times of need—systems that can and do fail people. This life is about depending on yourself, yes, but it is also about developing a network of like-minded people that you know and respect. It is rebuilding society to its ideal of working together to make sure everyone can survive and thrive. Here are some reasons that you may want to find a local homesteading community.

### The Benefits of Having a Homesteading Community

*Safety*

The old adage that there's strength in numbers exists for a reason. Safety is a big part of why societies evolved in the first place. Our ancestors all got together and decided that it was easier to fight off predators and survive catastrophes if they were pooling their resources. The same is true of modern communities, and especially true in homesteading. Having a good relationship with the neighborhood will mean that you can all look out for each other. You can report suspicious behavior, and watch each other's homes when they're empty. Even something as simple as a neighbor noticing a light on when you said you'd be gone and calling to check that everything is okay can avert crime and keep everyone safer.

*Cups of Sugar (and Other Supplies)*

This is another well-known phrase associated with neighbors: "Can I borrow a cup of sugar?" Even if you do your best to prepare and plan, there will be moments when you discover you need something that you don't have. It might be what you need to make that cake you were planning, or it might be a tool that breaks when you have an important task to do. If you have the kind of rapport where you can walk or call over to the person who lives next to you and ask them for help, they might be able to save the day. And then, of course, you can return the favor next time they need something. This can extend beyond supplies to include actions, as well. Maybe you have a package to mail but you can't make it to town, but you know your neighbor goes in every week for a standing appointment and would be willing to mail your package when they go. In return, you might pick up or drop off something for them the next time you run errands.

*Advice*

We've already discussed how when you first move to a new location, your neighbors will be some of the most useful sources of information for you. They will be familiar with the area and have tons of accumulated knowledge that they will likely share if you just ask. Even after you have been homesteading for years, you will find that some neighbors have areas of expertise that you can draw on. You yourself will probably develop specialized skills that will be useful to others. It is impossible for one person or household to be good at everything or know all there is to know, but with every household sharing its own particular niche, a community can fill in gaps and ensure that everyone has what they need.

*Barn Raising (and Other Communal Efforts)*

It was common among communities in the past to hold a barn raising whenever someone needed a new barn. A barn raising was an event where everyone in the community came together to build a barn (or some other structure) for someone, with the understanding that the community would do the same for them when it was their turn. This idea doesn't just apply to barns! There are so many aspects of homesteading that will go much faster if done with others. Combining forces to make bigger and better things happen is a time-honored tradition, and it doesn't even have to be task-based. Perhaps there's an expensive piece of machinery that you'll only need for a small period each year? Ask your neighbors if they want to purchase it together—sharing the machine means sharing the cost, which is a win for everyone.

*Entertainment and Socialization*

Community is not just a practical consideration. It also fulfills the very human part of us that wants companionship and enjoyment. Having get-togethers with your neighbors is a great way to get to know one another, and also a great way to have some fun. Particularly if you are raising a family, the chance to meet up with other families and let the kids play while the adults chat can be a great way to blow off steam and relieve stress, whether it's a large, organized event or just a small gathering.

*Social Networking*

In the era of the earliest homesteaders, families often lived very close to one another, and this extended network was often utilized to help out with everything from childcare to getting your mail while you were out of town. Nowadays, it is much more common for people to live very far from their families, in different neighborhoods, towns, states, or even countries.

However, that doesn't mean that you can't find a network of people willing to look out for one another in those same ways. Many people find that after years of building relationships with their neighbors, those people have become a kind of family to them. Perhaps even more beneficial than the favors themselves, this sense of found family can be a boon to our mental and emotional well-being.

*Commercial Networking*

However you plan to make money on your homestead, it's a given that you will need contacts to do it. One of the best ways to make those contacts is to reach out to the people around you. Everyone in your circle will also have their own circle of people who might want the products or services you're offering. If people know you and like you, they are more likely to support your business. Neighbors who have been in the area for a long time might know just the right person to put you in touch with, while even neighbors who have nothing to do with your business can help you by promoting what you do to others. Again, this sort of thing is dependent upon establishing and maintaining relationships. You can't get just anyone to do these things for you—it will be the people who feel a positive connection with you that will go the extra mile to help you out.

*Help in Times of Need*

This is a thread that runs through most of the other items on this list. At its best, a community is a system that you can rely on to help you when you need it. This is because by building this community, you have essentially enacted a social contract or an unspoken agreement that you will all work together to make life easier and better for one another. At no point is this more crucial than when something goes wrong. If you get an unexpected illness or injury, it could seriously hamper your ability to work for days, weeks, or even months. However, while you're recovering, work still needs to get done. Having a good neighbor or several who are willing to drop by and pick up even small tasks, such as feeding livestock or watering your garden, can make all the difference in times like this. Just as I've pointed out several times throughout this book, small changes in your life can accumulate into big differences; this rings true here, as small acts of kindness and aid can add up to make the difference between success and failure. This is the biggest benefit that you can get from your community.

**Principles for Peaceful Living**

Now that we've established how valuable your community can be, let me give you a few tips for making that community as strong as possible. There are four principles that I always do my best to live by when interacting with others, particularly those in my own community. Putting these into practice will help you create the kind of harmonious coexistence that you and your neighbors will appreciate.

*Communication*

If you only pay attention to one of these principles, make it this one. A huge amount of conflict boils down to miscommunication—don't let that happen to you! The two pillars of communication are clarity and frequency. Clarity means making sure that you are expressing yourself clearly and that your neighbors always know what to expect from you and what you expect from them. Explaining why you did something or want to do something can mean the difference between your neighbor resenting you or them helping you out. Frequency means maintaining the lines of communication through consistent contact. Don't just talk to your neighbor when there's a problem or when you need something; try to build a valuable relationship with them, as well.

*Respect*

This goes hand in hand with communication since one of the best ways to convey that you respect someone is to give them the courtesy of a warning about any decisions you are making that might affect them. This might be as small as a heads up that you will be making noise at a certain time during the day, or as big as informing them that you will be putting up a wind turbine that they will be able to see from their property. (Bonus points if you give them the consideration of asking if they will be okay with big changes that affect them. It's your property, you don't have to—but doing so can go a long way toward making the relationship work.) And always respect the boundaries of your properties! Even if they've allowed you to cross or use their land in some way in the past, *always* be sure to ask before doing it so they know you respect their ownership of the land.

*Compromise*

This also goes hand in hand with communication. (Are you sensing a pattern? Communication is key!) Sometimes in a tense situation, you can figure out a solution where everyone gets exactly what they want. But much more frequently, conflict arises because there is no one solution that is perfect for everyone. In these cases, acknowledge that there is no bad guy, but rather that everyone involved is trying to do what they feel is best for them. To find the best compromise, carefully consider your own priorities. Draw the line between what you need to happen and what you would like to happen, and then clearly communicate those: "X is what I absolutely need to happen, but I'm flexible about Y." You'd be surprised how often offering to give something up will prompt the other person to do the same.

*Generosity*

Just as offering to compromise can engender goodwill in a conflict, offering something of value to your neighbors can foster a sense of community. There are many different ways you can put this into practice. It might be goods such as eggs, vegetables, textiles, or meat; it might be time and energy, such as helping them to put up a fence or with shearing their sheep; or it might even be space, such as sharing some of your garden space or a field you aren't using. Offering something of value without expecting anything in return illustrates that you are interested in the good of the community as a whole, not just your own self-interests. And the truth is, the wellbeing of the community *is* in your self-interest. The stronger the community, the better it will be able to take care of its own.

# CONCLUSION

At this point, I've covered all the basics you'll need to get you started on your homesteading plans. Let's take a moment to think back through everything you've learned.

First, we debunked some common myths and discussed all the different ways you could incorporate homesteading into your life. After this, we went over common legal issues and I walked you through the best states in the United States for homesteading. Next, we got into some of the nitty-gritty details of different aspects of homesteading: the options you have for water, power, waste, and heating; how to start gardening and raising livestock; how to be prepared for medical emergencies; how to keep your homestead in good working order; and how to create and stick to a budget. And finally, I introduced you to different types of housing, gave you tips on how to find property of your own, and gave you some perspective on how fostering community is a crucial part of homesteading.

**Things to Remember**

Now that you've made it to the end of the book, I hope you'll take some time to digest everything you've learned. There's a lot of information here, and it will take some time to absorb all of it. While I hope everything I've included will be of use to you at some point, I want to remind you of the most crucial things to remember:

*Planning and preparing can save you time, money, and frustration.*

Any endeavor you're undertaking, from growing herbs in a pot on your balcony to running a 100-acre farm, can benefit from a clear plan. Do your research and make informed decisions. Not only are informed decisions easier to make, but they can save you from expensive and time-consuming mistakes.

*Design your life for you, not anyone else.*

Informed decisions aren't just about knowledge of home-steading; they're also about knowledge of yourself. Don't forget to start with your vision of your ideal life, and let that vision dictate what you prioritize. The most perfectly planned and executed life is meaningless if it's not the life that *you* want to be living.

*Anyone can incorporate homesteading into their life.*

A lot of the more granular information in this book, such as buying property and installing self-sufficient utilities, may seem like it is only applicable to large-scale homesteading. However, the principles of these things can be applied at any level. If you're not currently able to become as self-sufficient as you'd like, practicing the tenets of homesteading on a small scale will help you develop the skills and mindset for when you *are* able to make the change.

*The best way to make lasting change is to take small steps over time.*

You don't need to jump headfirst into a new lifestyle. In fact, you shouldn't! It is *much* more sustainable to change your life a little bit at a time. Use your SMART goals (look back at chapter one for a refresher) to slowly achieve what you want to achieve; it will be much less stressful and *far* more permanent.

*Nothing will happen until you make it happen.*

This is the most important thing to remember! Your life is in your hands, and the only one that can change it is you. I've given you the information, but it's up to you to act on it.

And that's it! Now go forth and start homesteading. I hope that this book has been of help to you. If it has, consider leaving us a review on Amazon—it'll help even more people find this book and start planning their own homesteading dreams!

# A SPECIAL GIFT TO MY READERS

Included with your purchase of this book is your free copy of
Your Homestead Planner

Follow the link below to receive your free copy:
www.kellyreedauthor.com
Or by accessing the QR code:

You can also join our Facebook community
**Homestead Living & Self Sufficiency,**
or contact me directly via kelly@kellyreedauthor.com

# REFERENCES

15 Acre Homestead. 2018. "Getting Started Homesteading: Budgeting." Accessed June 6, 2021. https://15acrehomestead.com/getting-started-homesteading-budgeting/.

Advanced Water Solutions. 2017. "How Does Water Distillation Work?" Accessed June 22nd, 2021. https://advancedwaterinc.com/water-distillation-work/.

American Dairy Goat Association. 2020. "ADGA Breed Standards." Accessed June 10, 2021. https://adga.org/breed-standards/.

The American Goat Federation. n.d. "Meat Goats." Accessed June 10, 2021. https://americangoatfederation.org/breeds-of-goats-2/meat-goats/.

American Red Cross. n.d. "Make a First Aid Kit." Accessed June 5, 2021. https://www.redcross.org/get-help/how-to-prepare-for-emergencies/anatomy-of-a-first-aid-kit.html.

Ali, Shahraz. 2020. "Top 7 Survival Foods to Stock – When You Are Living Off-Grid." Off Grid Living. Accessed June 5, 2021. https://offgridliving.net/top-7-survival-foods-to-stock-when-you-are-living-off-grid/.

Atkins, Gordon. n.d. "Living off the Grid: Legal or Illegal?" The Homesteading Hippy. Accessed June 4, 2021. https://thehomesteadinghippy.com/living-off-the-grid-legality/.

Barnes, Steve. n.d. "6 Seldom Followed Tips for How to Buy Off Grid Land." The Off Grid Cabin. Accessed June 6, 2021. https://theoffgridcabin.com/the-6-must-know-tips-for-how-to-buy-off-grid-land/.

Bernard, Murrye. 2020. "Earth-Sheltered and Underground Homes Basics." The Spruce. Accessed June 15th, 2021. https://www.thespruce.com/what-are-underground-homes-1821786.

Brendza, Will. 2019. "How To Build A Root Cellar From The Ground Up For Survival." Skilled Survival. Accessed June 5, 2021. https://www.skilledsurvival.com/underground-food-storage-root-cellars/.

Brooke, Nick. n.d. "The Best Plants for Aquaponics." How to Aquaponic. Accessed June 22nd, 2021. https://www.howtoaquaponic.com/plants/best-plants-for-aquaponics/.

Brownlee, John. n.d. "Test Well Water Before Buying A Homestead – A

Helpful Guide." Country Homestead Living. Accessed June 22nd, 2021. https://www.countryhomesteadliving.com/should-well-water-be-tested/.

Burgess, Ross. n.d. "7 Common Misconceptions of Living Off the Grid." A Modern Homestead. Accessed June 2, 2021. https://www.amodernhomestead.com/misconceptions-living-off-the-grid/.

Cabin Life. n.d. "Composting vs. Incinerating Toilets." Accessed June 22nd, 2021. https://www.cabinlife.com/articles/composting-vs-incinerating-toilets.

Canadian Valley Electric Cooperative. n.d. "How Does Geothermal Energy Work?" Accessed June 22nd, 2021. https://www.mycvec.coop/how-does-geothermal-work.

Carlson, Riley E. n.d. "Beginner's Guide To Keeping Bees." Homesteading.com. Accessed June 5, 2021. https://homesteading.com/beginners-guide-keeping-bees/.

Carpenter, Dan. n.d. "Alternative Energy Solutions." Homestead Launch. Accessed June 5, 2021. https://homesteadlaunch.com/alternative-energy/.

College of Agriculture & Natural Resources. n.d. "Nucleus Colonies." University of Delaware. https://canr.udel.edu/maarec/nucleus-colonies/.

Copeland, Jayden. 2019. "What Is Homesteading And Is It For You?" Backroad Bloom. Accessed June 2, 2021. https://backroadbloom.com/what-is-homesteading-and-is-it-for-you/.

Copeland, Jayden. 2019. "11 Feasible First Year Homesteading Goals." Backroad Bloom. Accessed June 2, 2021. https://backroadbloom.com/2019-1-7-11-feasible-first-year-homesteading-goals/.

Counter, Angela. n.d. "Completely, 100 Percent Off-Grid: 9 Essential Foods You Should Grow." Off the Grid News Accessed June 5, 2021. https://www.offthegridnews.com/off-grid-foods/completely-100-percent-off-grid-9-essential-foods-you-should-grow/.

Crisis Times. n.d. "Raising Animals Off the Grid." Accessed June 5, 2021. http://crisistimes.com/offgrid_animals.php.

Culver, Blake. 2021. "How to Plan a Garden For 2021." An Off-Grid Life. Accessed June 5, 2021. https://www.anoffgridlife.com/how-to-plan-a-garden-for-2020/.

Davidson, Josh. 2021. "Off Grid Water Systems: 4 Proven Ways To Bring Water To Your Homestead." Tiny Living Life. Accessed June 5, 2021. https://tinylivinglife.com/2021/01/learn-how-to-build-off-grid-water-system/.

DeJohn, Suzanne. 2021. "Soak, Drip, or Spray: Which Is Right for You?" Gardener's Supply Company. Accessed June 22nd, 2021. https://www. gardeners.com/how-to/how-to-choose-a-watering-system/8747.html.

Department of Energy. n.d. "Solar Water Heaters." Energy Saver. Accessed June 5, 2021. https://www.energy.gov/energysaver/water-heating/solar-water-heaters.

Digital Public Library of America. n.d. "Primary Source Sets: The Homestead Acts." Accessed June 2, 2021. https://dp.la/primary-source-sets/the-homestead-acts.

Dodrill, Tara. n.d. "5 Off-Grid Water Sources and Systems." Homestead Survival Site. Accessed June 5, 2021. https://homesteadsurvivalsite.com/off-grid-water-sources.

Dodrill, Tara. n.d. "6 Features To Look For In Off-Grid Property." Homestead Survival Site. Accessed June 6, 2021. https://homesteadsurvivalsite.com/features-off-grid-property/.

Dodrill, Tara. n.d. "10 Best States for Homesteaders." Homestead Survival Site. Accessed June 4, 2021. https://homesteadsurvivalsite.com/top-10-states-living-off-grid/.

Drevets, Tricia. n.d. "8 Ways To Generate Power Off Grid." Homestead Survival Site. Accessed June 5, 2021. https://homesteadsurvivalsite.com/generate-power-off-grid/.

Earthship Biotecture. 2020. "Super Sustainable Buildings via Thermal Dynamics & Passive Solar." Accessed June 6, 2021. https://earthshipbiotecture.com/.

Ecocapsule. n.d. "Ecocapsule Home Page." Accessed June 15th, 2021. https://www.ecocapsule.sk/.

Ed., Old Farmer's Almanac. 2020. "Raising Chickens 101: When Chickens Stop Laying Eggs." The Old Farmer's Almanac. Accessed June 22nd, 2021. https://www.almanac.com/raising-chickens-101-when-chickens-stop-laying-eggs.

Federal Emergency Management Agency. 2021. "Build a Kit." Ready.gov. Accessed June 11th, 2021. https://www.ready.gov/kit.

Ferguson, Donna. 2014. "Greywater Systems: Can They Really Reduce Your Bills?" The Guardian. Accessed June 22nd, 2021. https://www.theguardian.com/lifeandstyle/2014/jul/21/greywater-systems-can-they-really-reduce-your-bills.

Folger, Jean. 2021. "Rent-to-Own Homes: How the Process Works."

Investopedia. Accessed June 14th, 2021.https://www.investopedia.com/updates/rent-to-own-homes/.

Gently Sustainable. n.d. "How to Homestead With No Money." Accessed June 6, 2021. https://www.gentlysustainable.com/how-to-homestead-with-no-money/.

Greene, Liz. n.d. "Trash on the Homestead: Everything You Need To Know." Homesteading.com. Accessed June 22nd, 2021. https://homesteading.com/trash-homestead/.

Happy Prepper. 2021. "Waste Disposal." Accessed June 5, 2021. https://www.happypreppers.com/waste-management.html.

Harbour, Sarita. 2021. "Off Grid Toilets: Which One Do You Want for Your Home?" An Off-Grid Life. Accessed June 5, 2021. https://www.anoffgridlife.com/off-grid-toilets/.

Harrington, Justine. 2018. "Regional Climates in the United States." USA Today. Accessed June 4, 2021. https://traveltips.usatoday.com/regional-climates-united-states-21675.html.

Harrington, Justine. 2018. "Climate Regions of the United States." USA Today. Accessed June 4, 2021. https://traveltips.usatoday.com/climate-regions-united-states-21570.html.

Haughey, Duncan. 2014. "A Brief History of SMART Goals." Project Smart. Accessed June 2, 2021. https://www.projectsmart.co.uk/brief-history-of-smart-goals.php.

Haynes, Sherry. 2021. "15 Best Goat Breeds for Meat." Pet Helpful. Accessed June 10, 2021. https://pethelpful.com/farm-pets/best-meat-goat-breeds.

Home, Garden and Homestead. 2021. "Soil Testing for Beginners." Accessed June 22nd, 2021. https://homegardenandhomestead.com/soil-testing/.

Hosfeld, Daniel. 2019. "Off Grid Electricity: What You Need to Know." An Off-Grid Life. Accessed June 5, 2021. https://www.anoffgridlife.com/off-grid-electricity-what-you-need-to-know/.

Howell, Elizabeth. n.d. "Five Kinds Of Off-Grid Living." HeroX. Accessed June 6, 2021.

Hunter, Jacob. 2021. "The Oh Crap! Guide to Off Grid Sewage and Septic Systems." Primal Survivor. Accessed June 5, 2021. https://www.primalsurvivor.net/off-grid-sewage/.

Incinolet.com. n.d. "Frequently Asked Questions." Accessed June 22nd, 2021. https://incinolet.com/frequently-asked-questions/.

Intrepid Outdoors. n.d. "How to Make a Bio-Filter." Accessed June 21st, 2021. https://intrepidoutdoors.com/make-bio-filter/.

Johnson, Jamie. 2020. "What's An Encumbrance In Real Estate?" Rocket Homes. Accessed June 22nd, 2021. https://www.rockethomes.com/blog/home-buying/encumbrance.

Johnson, Julie. n.d. "Everything You Need in Your Homestead First Aid Kit." Down to Earth Homesteaders. Accessed June 5, 2021. https://downtoearth homesteaders.com/everything-you-need-in-your-homestead-first-aid-kit/.

Jones, Anna Newell. n.d. "12 Good (Financial) Reasons to Get to Know Your Neighbors." And Then We Saved. Accessed June 6, 2021. https://andthen wesaved.com/know-your-neighbors/.

Josephine, Val. 2017. "7 Ways to Power Your Homestead." Medium. Accessed June 5, 2021. https://medium.com/@Valsephine/7-ways-to-power-your-homestead-homestead-power-series-intro-a050bb0453be.

Just Dabbling Along. 2017. "10 Myths and Misconceptions about Homesteading." Accessed June 2, 2021. https://www.justdabblingalong.com/10-myths-misconceptions-homesteading/.

Kanuckel, Amber. 2021. "Companion Planting Guide." Farmers' Almanac. Accessed June 22nd, 2021. https://www.farmersalmanac.com/compan ion-planting-guide.

Lamp'l, Joe. 2018. "Raised Bed Gardening, Pt. 1: Getting Started." Joe Gardener. Accessed June 10, 2021. https://joegardener.com/podcast/raised-bed-gardening-pt-1/.

Lee, Shannon and Bob Vila. n.d. "5 Things Homebuyers Need to Know About Septic Systems." Bob Vila. Accessed June 22nd, 2021. https://www.bobvila.com/articles/septic-systems/.

Lewis, Patrice. 2013. "Homestead Water." Backwoods Home Magazine. Accessed June 5, 2021. https://www.backwoodshome.com/homestead-water/.

Loftsgordon, Amy. n.d. "What Is a Property Lien?" Nolo Legal Dictionary. Accessed June 22nd, 2021. https://www.nolo.com/legal-encyclopedia/what-property-lien.html.

Love Property. 2020. "Incredible Earthships: Off-grid Homes You've Got to See." Accessed June 15th, 2021. https://www.loveproperty.com/gallerylist/76795/incredible-earthships-offgrid-homes-youve-got-to-see.

Magyar, Cheryl. 2019. "45 Self-Reliant Skills Every Homesteader Needs To

Know." Rural Sprout. Accessed June 2, 2021. https://www.ruralsprout.com/self-reliant-skills-for-homesteaders/.

Maxwell, Steve. 2012. "Homestead Water Sources and Options." Mother Earth News. Accessed June 5, 2021. https://www.motherearthnews.com/homesteading-and-livestock/self-reliance/homestead-water-sources-zm0z12aszkon.

McCafferty, Emily. 2017. "All About Off Grid Wastewater: Options, Septic, Code, and Advice." Accidental Hippies. Accessed June 5, 2021. https://accidentalhippies.com/2017/07/25/off-grid-waste-septic/.

McCafferty, Emily. 2020. "What Does It Actually Mean to be "Off The Grid"?" Accidental Hippies. Accessed June 2, 2021. https://accidentalhippies.com/2020/02/17/what-is-living-off-the-grid/.

MelissaKNorris.com. n.d. "12 Tips on How to Raise Pigs for Meat." Accessed June 5, 2021. https://melissaknorris.com/howtoraisepigsformeat/.

Meyer, Sarah-Jane. 2019. "Your Home Maintenance Checklist." PrivateProperty.co.za. Accessed June 6, 2021. https://www.privateproperty.co.za/advice/lifestyle/articles/your-home-maintenance-checklist/6977.

Mitchell, Ryan. 2018. "How To Start Homesteading On A Budget." The Tiny Life. Accessed June 6, 2021. https://thetinylife.com/how-to-start-homesteading-on-a-budget/.

Morning Chores. n.d. "12 Things You Need to Know Before Getting Your First Ducks." Accessed June 5, 2021. https://morningchores.com/about-raising-ducks/.

Morning Chores. n.d. "Homestead Maintenance: Taking Care of Your Tools and Equipment." Accessed June 6, 2021. https://morningchores.com/homestead-maintenance/.

Morning Chores. n.d. "Homesteading with Neighbors: 6 Tips to Avoid Disastrous Conflicts." Accessed June 6, 2021. https://morningchores.com/homesteading-neighbors/.

Morning Chores. n.d. " Housing Your Chickens." Accessed June 22nd, 2021. https://morningchores.com/chicken-housing/.

MSPCA–Angell. n.d. "Farm Animal Health and Veterinary Care." Accessed June 21st, 2021. https://www.mspca.org/pet_resources/farm-animal-health-and-veterinary-care/.

National Geographic. 2012. "United States Regions." Accessed June 4, 2021. https://www.nationalgeographic.org/maps/united-states-regions/.

Nicholas, Nick. 2020. "Common Types Of UV Lamps For Chemical-Free

Water Disinfection." Water Online. Accessed June 21st, 2021. https://www.wateronline.com/doc/common-types-of-uv-lamps-for-chemical-free-water-disinfection-0001.

Off Grid World. 2021. "Off Grid Living is Illegal! Sort of..." Accessed June 4, 2021. https://offgridworld.com/off-grid-living-is-illegal-sort-of/.

Off Grid World. 2021. "The Best Off Grid Heating Systems." Accessed June 5, 2021. https://offgridworld.com/the-best-off-grid-heating-systems/.

Off the Grid News. n.d. "The 3 Best Livestock For New Homesteaders." Accessed June 5, 2021. https://www.offthegridnews.com/how-to-2/the-3-best-livestock-for-new-homesteaders/.

Off the Grid News. n.d. "6 Quick Steps To A Debt-Free Homesteading Budget." Accessed June 6, 2021. https://www.offthegridnews.com/financial/6-quick-steps-to-a-debt-free-homestead-budget/.

Poindexter, Jennifer. n.d. 30 Best Cow Breeds for Meat and Milk You'll Want to Know About." Morning Chores. Accessed June 5, 2021. https://morningchores.com/cow-breeds/.

Poindexter, Jennifer. n.d. "Homesteading 101: What Is It and the Essential Steps to Get Started." Morning Chores. Accessed June 2, 2021. https://morningchores.com/homesteading/.

Rejba, Alex. n.d. "Living Off The Grid in the USA – Is It Illegal?" The Smart Survivalist. Accessed June 4, 2021. https://www.thesmartsurvivalist.com/living-off-the-grid-in-the-usa-is-it-illegal/.

Rhoades, Heather. 2021. "Plant Spacing Guide." Gardening Know How. Accessed on June 21st, 2021. https://www.gardeningknowhow.com/edible/vegetables/vgen/plant-spacing-chart.htm.

Robinson, Ed. n.d. "Raising Pigs for Meat." Mother Earth News. Accessed June 5, 2021. https://www.motherearthnews.com/homesteading-and-livestock/raising-pigs-meat-zmaz70mazglo.

Rural Living Today. n.d. "Best States for Homesteading: Know Your Options." Accessed June 4, 2021. https://rurallivingtoday.com/homesteading-today/best-states-for-homesteading/.

Schipani, Sam. 2019. "How to Prepare for Emergencies When You Live Off the Grid." Hello Homestead. Accessed June 5, 2021. https://hellohomestead.com/how-to-prepare-for-emergencies-when-you-live-off-the-grid/.

Schwartz, Daniel Mark. n.d. "Off Grid Water Purification: Safe and Low Cost." Off Grid Permaculture. Accessed June 5, 2021. https://offgridpermaculture.com/Water_Systems/Off_Grid_Water_Purifica

tion__Safe_and_Low_Cost.html.

Seaman, Greg. n.d. "Choosing Land for Homestead Living." Earth Easy. Accessed June 6, 2021. https://learn.eartheasy.com/articles/choosing-land-for-homestead-living/.

Sher, Savannah. n.d. "The Best Places in America for Off-Grid Living." Bob Vila. Accessed June 4, 2021. https://www.bobvila.com/slideshow/the-best-places-in-america-for-off-grid-living-578748.

Silbajoris, Alex. 2018. "What Are the Differences Between Bleach and Chlorine?" Sciencing. Accessed June 8th, 2021. https://sciencing.com/difference-between-bleach-chlorine-6516255.html.

Skilled Survival. 2019. "Best Non Perishable Food To Thrive During Times Of Turmoil." Accessed June 5, 2021. https://www.skilledsurvival.com/non-perishable-foods/.

Skilled Survival. 2019. "How To Build A DIY Aquaponics System For Food Self Sufficiency." Accessed June 5, 2021. https://www.skilledsurvival.com/diy-aquaponics/.

Tactical.com. 2020. "Homing In on Off-Grid Homes." Accessed June 6, 2021. https://www.tactical.com/offgrid-homes/.

Tamara, Nadia. n.d. "The Top 12 U.S. States for Homesteading." Crisis Equipped. Accessed June 4, 2021. https://crisisequipped.com/best-states-for-homesteading/.

Tomisch, Emma. 2021. "Land Loans: Everything You Need To Know." Rocket Mortgage. Access June 14th, 2021. https://www.rocketmortgage.com/learn/land-loans.

Unbound Solar. 2020. "What States Allow You to Live Off the Grid." Accessed June 4, 2021. https://unboundsolar.com/blog/off-grid-legal-states.

Vuković, Diane. 2021. "Best States for Homesteading". Primal Survivor. Accessed June 4, 2021. https://www.primalsurvivor.net/best-states-homesteading/.

Weather Atlas. n.d. "Monthly Weather Forecast and Climate Alaska, USA." Accessed June 4, 2021. https://www.weather-us.com/en/alaska-usa-climate.

Weather Atlas. n.d. "Monthly Weather Forecast and Climate Hawaii, USA." Accessed June 4, 2021. https://www.weather-us.com/en/hawaii-usa-climate.

Whittington, Amanda. n.d. "How To Keep Your Home Warm When Living

Off Grid." Homestead Survival Site. Accessed June 5, 2021. https://home
steadsurvivalsite.com/keep-home-warm-living-off-grid/.

Winger, Jill. 2019. "Become a Beekeeper: 8 Steps to Getting Started with
Honeybees." The Prairie Homestead. Accessed June 5, 2021. https://www.
theprairiehomestead.com/2014/05/get-started-honeybees.html.

World Population Review. 2021. "Best States To Homestead 2021." Accessed
June 4, 2021. https://worldpopulationreview.com/state-rankings/best-
states-to-homestead.

Ygrene. 2020. "What Are Solar Water Heating Systems?" Accessed June 5,
2021. https://ygrene.com/blog/renewable-energy/what-are-solar-water-
heating-systems.

Young, Olivia. 2018. "See inside the 104-square-foot tiny house that helped a
Canadian photographer 'house-hack' his way into living for free." Business
Insider. Accessed June 15th, 2021. https://www.businessinsider.com/tiny-
house-minimalism-zero-waste-saving-money-2018-12.

Zaheer, Kinza. 2020. "Growing Your Survival Garden for Off Grid Living."
Off-Grid Living. Accessed June 5, 2021. https://offgridliving.net/grow
ing-your-survival-garden-for-off-grid-living/.

# INSPIRING CHANGE

*"Happiness belongs to the self sufficient."*

— ARISTOTLE

When you boil it all down, the reason you came to be here, reading this book right now, is that you wanted to change your life.

You're here to absorb everything you can to make the changes you've dreamed of making for years, and I hope that by now, you're realizing that it really is possible.

There are many people out there who want to make similar changes, but the pace of modern life sometimes makes it seem impossible. I admit that Robert and I were daunted when we first began our journey, but piece by piece, it all came together. Our journey started with growing food, and little by little, we were able to build an entire homestead.

The fast-paced modern world is a distraction; there's no arguing with that, but as I hope you can see by now, it doesn't stand in your way. I want to help more people realize that and begin the journey toward self-sufficiency that they've been longing to make.

And this is where I'd like to ask for your help. To have the most impact possible, I need to reach more readers who are looking for this guidance, and a short review from you will go a long way toward making that happen.

**By leaving a review of this book on Amazon, you'll not only show new readers that this is possible; you'll show them exactly where they can find the guidance they need to make it happen.**

Simply by giving your honest opinion of this book and a little about how it's helped you, you'll show other readers that this is possible for them, too.

Thank you so much for your support. Sometimes, all it takes is a little inspiration, and your words have the power to provide just that.

## Customer Reviews

★★★★★ 2
5.0 out of 5 stars ▾

| | | |
|---|---|---|
| 5 star | | 100% |
| 4 star | | 0% |
| 3 star | | 0% |
| 2 star | | 0% |
| 1 star | | 0% |

See all verified purchase reviews ›

Share your thoughts with other customers

Write a customer review

# THE REGROWER'S HANDBOOK

A BEGINNER'S GUIDE TO SELF-SUFFICIENCY. USE YOUR GROCERIES TO REGROW FRUIT, VEGETABLES, HERBS, AND MUSHROOMS FROM ROOTS, SHOOTS, CUTTINGS, SCRAPS, AND SEEDS

# A SPECIAL GIFT TO MY READERS

Included with your purchase of this book is your free copy of
Your Homestead Planner

Follow the link below to receive your free copy:
www.kellyreedauthor.com
Or by accessing the QR code:

You can also join our Facebook community
**Homestead Living & Self Sufficiency,**
or contact me directly via kelly@kellyreedauthor.com

# INTRODUCTION

"In our society, growing food ourselves has become the most radical of acts. It is truly the only effective protest, one that can—and will—overturn the corporate powers that be. By the process of directly working in harmony with nature, we do the one thing most essential to change the world—we change ourselves."

— *JULES DERVAES*

Sometimes, the things you discover along the road become the highlights of your journey. Before we begin ours, let me tell you how growing fruit and vegetables changed my life.

My husband, Robert, and I are very resourceful people. We built our home together, learning and absorbing from the environment around us as we moved ahead with life. Our careers gave us enough—but the growing expenses surrounding a growing urban family became overwhelming at one point.

The time came when Robert and I spent nights awake, raking our hands through our hair with worry. Our children's school lives were around the corner, bringing academic and tuition fees along.

The house needed repairs. Day-to-day living was not getting any easier. Our financial stability was swinging back and forth like a renegade yo-yo, threatening our very peace of mind.

Ever the level-headed accountant, I scoured through our receipts, records, and spending habits to locate points where we could save more. I noticed that we were spending small sums on a regular basis—and though they did not seem like "too much" at the time, they had unfortunately added up to become the monster under our beds. We did what any other reasonable couple would do and focused on some cost-cutting solutions.

We thought and thought. What was more important, and what could we do without? Compromise was a given. It was coming to an agreement that had become a slippery slope. Robert cherished things that didn't mean as much to me, and vice versa. Plus, we had to consider our children's happiness. Indeed, that was the most important point.

## THE IN-BETWEEN

We tried a million odd things. We became persnickety about our power usage and turned off lights and fans like our lives depended on it. Regular date nights and restaurant outings stopped—but that was okay since we're both homebodies.

We chose to save some extra money by not using the air conditioner, switching to a different service provider and ditching some luxuries like dehumidifiers. I put together an allowance and decided to not spend above that but it became very difficult.

Do you know what felt worse? When we sat down with our receipts a month after we became this fastidious, we found that we were still spending far more than ideal. This forced us to turn to the one area we'd been religiously avoiding simply because working on cost-cutting there would be very tricky.

Groceries.

That sneaky little fiend! How she exhausted our earnings, dollar by dollar!

Cutting the grocery budget wouldn't be hard if we only wanted to save. Boxed and canned goods sold for much lower prices than their fresh counterparts and were also available in larger quantities. The problem here was that we didn't want to play around with our family's health and nutrition.

My family loves fresh produce. Our meals are like a religion to us, because we cherish each fruit and vegetable that goes on our plates. There's something so beautiful about the simple glory of freshly grown produce. Plump, ripe, and healthy—there can be nothing better than seeing something so wonderfully nourishing grace your repast.

How could we keep this love alive while saving money?

Well, sometimes inspiration jumps in on us from the unlikeliest of places. At this time, the call changed everything for us.

## THE GREAT POTATO EPIPHANY

I doubled as a real estate executive. At the time, I was receiving multiple client requests for large yards or homes with enough land to make homesteads. As my husband woefully declared that we'd have to supplement our meals with tinned goods (much to my horror), a client called me and began discussing her plans to buy land to grow her own produce.

I thought then—is this the way? Can we be creative and self-sufficient enough to grow our produce and stop depending on corporate giants for our food once and for all?

The more I researched, the more intrigued I became. I found that we could grow food all year-round, so long as we factored in the climate and seasons typical of our locality. Even if we wanted to raise animals—think backyard chickens or ducks—it was feasible. The land would save us, giving us the sustenance we needed.

I had dabbled in gardening before, but that was simply a hobby. It was a start, however—having a green thumb gave me a natural instinct and love for tending to greenery. To me, the earth and all of its soil—red or black, wet or dry—was gold.

My grandparents had a beautiful kitchen garden which always had enough to make a hearty soup or a summer salad. When I went on holiday to their house, I took on small tasks like watering tomatoes or picking green beans.

My father had imbibed my grandmother's love for produce—he had his own tomato garden where he'd grow six healthy tomato plants of different, robust varieties each year. The mere remembrance of this makes my mind happy and leaves my tongue salivating.

The humdrum business of my professional life had kept me from seriously considering having a little garden. I didn't think I had the time or resources to get down to it while I was working and tending to my family. It always figured in my "someday, when I retire" list.

I wouldn't say that I came to an immediate decision the very night I began my research. This happened about two weeks later when I had what my family now loves to call "the great potato epiphany."

While cleaning our kitchen, I came across a sack of old, forgotten potatoes neatly tucked behind a storage space. The potatoes had sprouted shoots: long, green, thin tendrils reaching out in every direction, clamoring for air and life. I stood there, looking at this miracle in my kitchen, a tingling in my fingers.

The plants we ate still had a semblance of life in them for a very long time from when they were uprooted. I thought this again and again—a sharp realization thudding in my heart.

This wasn't all. That night, while going through what we had in our refrigerator, I wondered what else could be regrown. What if I could grow root vegetables from other cuttings and offshoots—and fruit too? The old, withered lettuce sitting in the corner—could I grow fresh lettuce from that?

The issue of food wastage had been bothering me for a while, perhaps there was a way for me to counter that now. Until then, I'd always seen lettuce as a relatively cheap product.

I'd buy two to three heads at a time, and some would inevitably end up in the trash. While throwing away one lettuce didn't seem like much at the time, the thought of how many I'd wasted along the way was troublesome, to say the least.

I turned to books and forums yet again. It wasn't long until I discovered the answer I instinctively knew: Yes, I could do it. I could use different parts of fruit and vegetables to grow my produce, saving not just on groceries but on the resources I'd otherwise invest in buying seeds, cuttings, and saplings.

There she was. My family's insurance, love, and safety married into one composite whole, staring at me from a sack of over-ripe potatoes.

## A Note to You

It has been more than a decade since we made this discovery. Today, my husband and I have the homestead of our dreams. Almost all that we grow—fruit, vegetables, mushrooms, and herbs—come from our own hands. We compost most of the waste we generate, so we give back to the earth as much as it nurtures us.

The whole experience is mostly about frugality, in the comprehensive understanding of the term. There is so much less waste in my family's life than there was before. This applies not just to our resources, but to the very manner of our existence. Anxiety no longer plagues my household, for we are as close to Mother Earth as it gets. She teaches and heals us every day.

There is nothing like the vision of your own plants growing in the fertile soil that you parent. Nothing gives the peace and regeneration of walking through your garden full of life and growth after a long day, feeling the wind in your hair, the smell of wet soil wafting into your nostrils as you water and feed all the life sprouting around you. It is a universe in itself—the most beautiful one there can be.

It has been a journey from the grocery aisles to the rows of plants now welcoming me every day when I wake up. And today, I sit in my study, overlooking my life's work, with one thought in my mind.

The learning that I have gained belongs out there in the world. It should become a part of households like yours and mine, where people thrive on the concepts of growth and sustenance.

The magicking of your grocery scraps into plants in full bloom in your own homes is one of the most beautiful things you will experience. Today, I hope to be the guide who will show you the way.

I must confess—the onset of anything new is equal parts exhilarating and terrifying. You never quite know what you're getting into. Much like everyone else, I was immensely worried about the copious amounts of research I'd need to do on gardening and regrowing methodology. When regrowing became a way of life for me, I made up my mind to share what I learned to make life easier for every future gardener.

It isn't as hard as it seems. Most things, once you truly get knee-and-elbow deep, get easier not because of their inherent "doability," but because you're willing to do what it takes to get there. And that is what makes something worthwhile.

Most of us want to live a simple, wholesome life. Today, if this book has found its way into your hands, I can take a guess at who you are. Much like me, you may be a being with a deeply immersive love for nature and the soil. Gardening calls out to you but you're unsure of where to begin. What you firmly believe is that access to good health shouldn't be a privilege, but a priority.

When I started out on my regrowing journey, my emphasis was on developing a self-reliant family. Thriftiness was our friend, the trick up our sleeves, the tool in our pockets. We never imagined that scraps could become a way of living—until they did. Like me, you too may be in a place in your life where cost-cutting would be optimal.

We're thrifty people at heart. We believe that food shouldn't have to be expensive to be sustainable. And many of us know that if we could just learn how to make regrowing a lifestyle choice, we could help others in the community.

Well, this is just what I will be showing you.

This labor of love is a collection of everything I have picked up along the way. It's all you need to maintain your produce from grocery scraps that you'd never think to cast a second glance at.

One of our goals will be an exercise in frugality—to study how you can cut back gardening costs with regard to soil, tools, fertilizers, offshoots, and so much else. Through six meticulously crafted chapters, we will take different aspects of regrowing and unfolding its roots and shoots.

We will begin by foraging into the world of regrowing. Our first chapter together will be a deep dig into the benefits of regrowing and what it takes to do it successfully. In the next few chapters, we will tackle one product at a time, discussing growth, care, and harvesting options. From veggies and mush-rooms to herbs, spices, and fruit—you will discover a new world waiting for you at each step.

I hope that what you pick up along the way ends up making this a well-beloved friend on your bookshelf. One that you keep coming back to whenever the green in your thumbs begins to itch. Yes, this is about financial stability, but it is also an adventure.

Your own secret garden awaits you at the turn of the page.

# 1

# FROM SCRAPS TO BOUNTY - UNLEASHING THE POTENTIAL OF REGROWING FRUITS AND VEGGIES

R egrowing your produce is a lot like recycling materials. Your garden will be a living, breathing, and beautiful creation because it is entirely recycled. You are giving back to the earth a part of what you are taking from her.

The returns are two-fold. You get a self-sufficient lifestyle where you run things based on your wants and desires. Additionally, you contribute to a greener, more sustainable environment.

## BENEFITS OF REGROWING FRUIT AND VEGGIES FROM SCRAPS

Life itself is an act of transience. There's not much that's given. This is truer in the context of our contemporary lifestyle.

These days, how much you have is relegated to "how much you can buy." Our philosophy is to move a hundred steps back from this kind of living.

Instead, we take a more holistic route, which ensures that (at least some) things in life are yours for the taking, whenever you want them. That's the beauty of growing your own fruit and veggies.

The most obvious benefit will be evident when you sit down to do your financial planning a few months after beginning your regrowing projects. Taking the time and effort to grow your food—even if it's just the essential things in your freezer or on your plate (think tomatoes, potatoes, beans, apples, or chilies)— allows your finances room to breathe.

As it happens, the hardier kinds of produce can grow in cups and bowls that you have lying around in the kitchen. Waste not, want not! You don't even need anything extravagant to begin with so long as you have some space.

Next, you are intimately aware of what's going on your plates. When you grow your own food, you know that the fruit and vegetables your loved ones and you are consuming are organic, bereft of harmful pesticides, and as fresh as possible.

The lingering worry of needing to wash your veggies in water that often drains essential nutrients (especially water-soluble ones like vitamins B-complex and C) is no longer valid. You gain the assurance that what's going inside you is as wholesome and close to nature as it gets. Nutritious, healthy, and safe.

For many of us, regrowth is a passion brought to life. It's that hobby that you "keep putting aside for when the time is right." The beauty of finally beginning is that you get to see your vision, your dream, coming to life through little shoots and leaves every single day. I cannot tell you how uplifting that feels.

My kitchen walls are full of little polaroid compositions of vegetables growing into their own. Every time I look at the progress I've made, I know that this is the hobby that goes on giving. The plants that you grow in your garden can produce fruit and vegetables—which can then sustain your family.

And then, of course, there's the aesthetic value. The sheer simplistic beauty of rustic table decor is inexplicably magical. You won't ever return to glaring plastic decor to spruce up your kitchen.

Think wicker baskets full of plump, fresh veggies; window displays of potted plants bursting with fat, red and green chilies; little herb gardens that welcome you with an impossibly seductive smell the moment you step foot in the kitchen—it's a paradise. One that you'll wake up to every single day of your life from here on.

### *So How Can Growing Food Make You Financially Stable?*

How many of you have heard the song "Banana Pancakes?" It's one of my favorites, and the man behind it is someone who continues to inspire me every day. Jack Johnson is lesser known for his home gardening pursuits—but he is a gardening enthusiast like you and me. From Swiss chards to eggplants and sugar snap peas, his home in Hawaii is all about self-sustenance.

He's not alone. The secrets of growing your produce have begun reaching American households as folklore whispers into eager ears through the generations. Today, more than a third of US homes practice cultivating part of their consumption.

There's a very legible financial benefit that constitutes the core of the home gardening philosophy. The National

Gardening Association estimates that a well-kept garden has the propensity to yield a half-pound's worth of produce per square foot area every growing season. If you even allocate a 600-square-foot yard for your gardening needs, you will likely generate about 300 pounds of fresh produce. That could amount to a food cost savings of $600 US annually.

Yes, there is an initial investment. In your case, it doesn't include expenses involving seeds or plants. A start-up garden (that has pretty much everything aside from what you don't need) will initially cost you between $200 and $300, though this will vary depending on whether you already have land to work with, or are starting from scratch.

**Gardening: The Essential Costs**

The total cost to begin a 10-foot by 10-foot garden adds up to $300. This includes tools, soil, and seeds. The tools cost $100, the soil is about $35 per cubic yard, and the seeds you won't need.

The bare minimum tools that you'll need include a hoe ($30), a spade ($30), and a trowel ($30). As time goes by and you become more familiar with your hobby, you can choose to invest in other tools. Additional tools include what you need to water your plants: a watering can ($10) or a sprinkler ($8) and a hose ($15).

Some plants may be easier to handle if you have a pair of gardening gloves. They'll cost you about $10. Then there are the rake ($15), aerators ($30), and pruning shears ($15). My advice is to begin with a list and narrow down the essentials before you begin.

When it comes to soil, you may need to check for fertility. If your soil is depleted of the nutrients essential for growing plants, it'll give you a hard time. A fertility testing kit will cost $15 and give you the necessary information.

In all likelihood, you will need to top up your soil with a nutrient-rich substitute from a garden center. The amount you need will depend on your garden's size. You can get a 3/4-cubic-foot bag of topsoil for $5 or less. The soil for a 10-by-10-foot garden will be about $200. You can invest in bags of potting mix—each costs about $9. You don't need to buy compost—it can easily be made at home.

If you want to invest in a raised bed kit, the average cost will be an additional $145. Kits for raised garden beds may be made from a variety of materials, with prices ranging widely. Wood, PVC, vinyl, alloy steel, and composite wood are all common kit components (Purnell, 2022).

The most expensive kinds are made from composite wood, while galvanized steel ones are usually the more affordable. Composite wood will set you back by $210. In contrast, galvanized steel comes in at $104.

Beginner DIYers and gardeners on a budget might benefit from a raised garden bed kit. You'll need a larger budget if you want a personalized garden bed or additional material alternatives. In a raised bed, a mound of dirt and plants is held in place by its sidewalls. The average cost per square foot of construction materials is $18.39.

There will be a maintenance cost (including the water bill) that will depend on how many items you grow and how big your garden is (Regly, 2022). The returns you'll experience, even if you don't sell your produce (in terms of merely saving grocery costs) will be high.

Your best bet is to get together with a gardening enthusiast— ask around or join a forum online. This will get you on the best footing.

And here's another eye-opening statistic. According to the 2019 data collected by the Bureau of Labor Statistics, people in the United States spend an average of $386 a month on groceries. That's $4,643 spent annually. The savings created by investing in a garden allow you to cut back on this kind of spending.

**Something for Everyone**

You may think that it's easier to do this if you're in a greener and larger locality than if you live in a crowded urban space— but wait. In 2016, Reuters shared the experiences of some home gardeners, including those residing in urban regions.

Divya Sangam features in this article as a 32-year-old public relations specialist residing in Edison, New Jersey. Ms. Sangam lives in a two-bedroom apartment with no yard space, and yet every day she nurses her dream of growing some of her food at home.

She grows some beloved tropical herbs like lime leaves, blue ginger, curry leaves, and lemongrass in a planter on her porch. After the expenses of planters and soil, she still saves $100 each year (*How Gardening Could Save You $600 on Groceries*, 2016). Additionally, she gets flavorful and healthy herbs that are much more delicious than what you'd find in most supermarkets.

The financial benefits for you will be more significant because you won't be incurring the costs of purchasing seeds. If you grow your food from the scraps you've collected from what you already have in your kitchen, you bypass the need to buy a plant or a pack of seeds. For you, it's a cycle that doesn't end because, once you consume the produce that grows from the scraps, you can reuse the scraps from the new lot of produce to grow subsequent plants.

Additionally, if you get a large yield that is in surplus of what you and your family need, you can preserve and sell the excess produce in local markets. There is considerable demand for organic and homegrown produce. For instance, a pound of organic tomatoes from Whole Foods is $3.40 as of 2023, but a package of heirloom tomatoes that you grow organically from scraps can sell for $3.50 to $5.00 a pound.

If it's legally permissible within your community, you can also sell from your own garden by setting up a makeshift stall one day a week. You may even sell to a local restaurant. Contact a manager to gauge their interest in purchasing local, organic produce once you've reached a comfortable and consistent production level.

If you don't want to go down the selling route, you can also trade produce with your neighbors. You can barter what you grow for what you don't—even for fresh eggs, milk, or other products.

Be abreast of current developments, for you never know when you'll strike gold. There was a mounting lime crisis recently, which led to many bars and restaurants offering complimentary refreshments in exchange for homegrown limes.

### That's the Financial Bit—Now, How Does Growing Food Make You Healthier?

In very rudimentary terms, the most apparent health benefit is that what you see is what you get. Since you survey and control your produce, you can ensure the quality, which isn't possible when it comes to mass-produced items.

You have the ultimate say on what nutrients, chemicals (if any), and compost you add to your soil. By controlling what goes into your fruit and vegetables, you control what ultimately goes into the bodies of those you love, including yourself.

The food you grow and then put on your plate is in its rawest and most pure form. It hasn't been shipped, distributed, or subjected to questionable hygiene standards before coming to you. Produce always retains the most nutrients when consumed just after harvesting

With commercial items, you never know whether what you're buying was harvested yesterday, last week, or sometime in the previous month. The older it is, the less nutrient value it has.

Additionally, having a home garden gives you the keys to picking your produce when it is ripe and ready, unlike supermarket or store-bought produce which is often harvested before reaching the fully mature stage. The quality and flavor you get from freshly picked fruit and vegetables will always surpass the chemical-laden ones you have to buy and wash.

And the fun thing is that you get in some handy exercise! Gardening is a brilliant way to spend time outdoors engaging in physical activity.

It's been proven time and again that being involved in growing your garden can improve your heart and gut health, enhance your immune responses, decrease stress, and promote overall flexibility and body strength. You gain a sense of balance, fine and gross motor skills, and actively work to reduce depression.

You can burn as many calories as you would at a fitness center by gardening, which improves agility and stamina. Digging, raking, and mowing are some of the most calorie-consuming activities.

You also get a healthy dose of vitamin D in your system in the process! Vitamin D helps your bones and gives you that serotonin rush when you wake up, walk into your garden, and witness the fruits of your labor. It's hard to be sad when life is growing all around you. It is indeed a win-win situation.

### Are You Giving Back to the Environment, Too?

Yes, you are—and in myriad ways. To begin with, most supermarket fruit and vegetables travel an average distance of 1,500 miles to the supermarket shelves. We call this prolonged journey "food miles" which covers the distance from the farmer's field to your home.

Pause for one second here, and think of the fossil fuel consumption that happens during this extended journey. Each day, whether the produce travels by air, road, or water, it causes enormous energy expenditure—of the non-renewable and wasteful kind.

An added issue with supermarket produce is that many exotic variants are not locally sourced, but rather imported from regions where both energy and labor expenditures are intensive and questionable.

The imported produce is generally brought via airplanes which emit ten times more carbon emissions than what you'd have with road transport. The more carbon emissions, the more $CO_2$ concentrations in the global environment, bringing us closer and closer to a mammoth global warming crisis. Many of us might think, "What difference will one small homegrown garden make?"

Well, it'll make an enormous difference.

Even if it were just one garden, and it's not. Locally grown fruit and vegetables do away with food miles altogether. So, every one of you who reads this book and decides to go the more sustainable route is contributing to a marginally less polluted environment. Small contributions can move big mountains.

Furthermore, you contribute to reducing plastic consumption and waste. With store produce, the packaging is an essential component of keeping fruit and vegetables in optimum condition.

Those plastic shopping bags which seem so insignificant can add up to a significant amount of waste. The United States alone generates 42 million metric tons, or 92 billion pounds of plastic waste each year. Most of the waste ends up polluting oceans and landfills, destroying native and sensitive ecosystems. They are ingested by turtles, whales, and even seabirds, harming and killing them.

A Greenpeace report found that seven of the top UK supermarkets generated 59 billion pieces of plastic packaging—about 2,000 pieces for every household—in the environment on an annual basis (*Checking out on plastics: A survey of UK supermarkets' plastic habits*, 2019).

Data collected in the United States suggests that food containers and packaging produce over 82 million tons of waste every year (Helmer, 2021). The largest plastic waste contributor is the single-use plastic packaging that protects store-bought products, including fruit, vegetables, and herbs.

This is just an account of two nations. Imagine how much global waste is piling up, one country at a time.

And, I cannot begin to emphasize how much you'll be helping the world by reducing pesticide production and use. Chemical fertilizers are a common component in commercial farming. They're known to increase plant growth and overall productivity. Since farmers rely on volume sales, chemical fertilizers become the dreaded means to an end.

The issues happen when these harmful chemicals seep into the soil and work their way inside the crops. They can be ingested when we consume the produce, and indeed, they are. In the United Kingdom, a report analyzed by the Pesticide Action Network (PAN) found that commercially grown fruit and vegetables were covered in a "cocktail" of poisonous pesticides (Javed, 2021).

A 2019 article published in *The Nation* (in the United States) discovered the very real dangers of consuming commercially grown and marketed products. What is a cause for great concern is that over 90 percent of Americans have pesticides or pesticide byproducts in their systems—generally from consuming conventionally grown produce (Gross, 2019).

The chemicals in commercial produce also harm the environment around us. They contaminate the water, impact insects like bees, and decrease biodiversity. When we consciously reduce the demand for commercially produced goods, we diminish the utilization of chemical pesticides and fertilizers in addition to ensuring they're not going inside our own stomachs.

These chemicals can cause dangerous hormonal imbalances which can impact the sensitive workings of your system over time (including causing life-threatening cancers). There's also the issue of not knowing what's happening inside your body if you continue to consume commercial produce.

So, when you grow your fruit and vegetables at home, you become an organic part of the ecosystem that is larger than you, and intimately connected to your well-being. The soil itself reaches out and embraces those who learn to treat it like the precious resource it is—nurturing, preserving, and compassionate.

## Summing Up

With so many plausible benefits, growing your produce from scraps will be one of the best decisions you make. You'll also meet new people in the process, and get to know minds that are creative, tender, and generous.

The gardening community is a collection of people who understand the value of the Earth as our one home. The returns are not just financial, they are beneficial for your whole system—internal and external.

In the next chapter, we will begin our journey into regrowing vegetables. Get excited, because a whole new and green world is about to open its welcoming arms and embrace you!

# 2

# CULTIVATING SUSTAINABILITY - REGROWING YOUR STORE-BOUGHT VEGGIES

One of the most beautiful things about knowledge is that there's no end to it. You can keep sharing it with the world—and who knows who'll be blessing you for helping them! This was something I learned when I shared my love for regrowing with a dear friend, Jane.

Jane and I had grown up with a deep love for fresh produce and coloring our plates with vegetables. But, much like me, a time came when she was seriously considering cutting back on her grocery spending so that she could save on bills that were piling up.

One day, we were sitting down to a hearty lunch. I roasted sunchokes and bell peppers and served them with a garlic sauce. After the first bite, she sighed and sat back in her chair. "This is so good, Kelly. You've no idea how much I miss eating fresh veggies."

This was when she told me she'd been avoiding spending on commercial produce because of mounting grocery bills. As we talked about our savings, I asked her if she was throwing her vegetable scraps out.

She'd never done anything differently, so she naturally presumed that the only thing you could do with them (after eating the vegetable) was throw them out. I told her how I was growing my artichokes from scraps and at first, she thought this was impossible—it had to be a practical joke. But I came with ten years of experience in regrowing my produce from roots, shoots, scraps, and cuttings.

So, over the next hour, I told her what she had to do. When she left, I made her promise to at least try. After that, life got in the way—as it often does. We got busy with our homes and jobs, and I didn't hear from her until almost two years later. She'd called me, bubbling with joy and anticipation.

"Kelly! It worked! I finally got down to it and tried to regrow my vegetables, and I've got the most beautiful little vegetables! I can't stop looking at them, and you wouldn't believe how much I've saved so far this year on grocery bills!"

Ah, but I did believe it. You can do that too. This brings me to a very important question.


WHY ARE VEGETABLES GOOD FOR YOU?

A diet that includes vegetables is a wholesome one. Vegetables can lower blood pressure, reduce the risk of chronic cardiovascular and lifestyle diseases, and even act as a shield against some forms of cancer. They protect your bone, heart, gut, and eye health and also have a positive effect on blood sugar.

Non-starchy vegetables like cruciferous and leafy greens can even aid in healthy and sustained weight loss. Their low glycemic index acts as a shield against blood sugar spikes that cause hunger pangs. When it comes to growing your own vegetables, there's no limit to the varieties you can cultivate.

At least nine different families of veggies and fruit exist in the world, and each has hundreds of different plant compounds that benefit your health. By growing your vegetables at home, you can also ensure that they don't get sprayed by toxic chemicals which have to then be washed off.

Your goal should be to grow what you can manage. Think of the kind of veggies you'd like to see on your plate. A variety of colors will give you a mix of nutrients and essential vitamins.

You may find this hard to believe but some of our favorite foods are in categories you wouldn't believe. So, when you look for or come across something that seems out of place, it meets the criteria. The most common example is that the humble little tomato is actually a fruit!

With this in mind, let's look at some vegetables that you can start your regrowing journey with.

## REGROWING ARTICHOKES (JERUSALEM)

Juicy, with a slight hint of mellow bitterness, artichokes are a wonderful vegetable that can spruce up any meal. Here's how you can grow it from scraps.

### General Notes About Growing

To plant Jerusalem artichokes, all you need are tubers from the original vegetables that you bought to eat. It helps if the original sunchokes don't have cuts or nicks, and are clean and firm to the touch.

Jerusalem artichokes are beginner-friendly. They thrive in the temperature range of 65°F–90°F (18°C–32°C).

### Preparation and Planting

- You can get tubers for sunchokes or Jerusalem artichokes from your local grocery store.
- You can grow sunchokes from whole or partial tubers. Each section or each tuber should have 2 to 3 eyes (bulging nodes).
- The ideal planting temperature is 50°F (10°C). Planting during late winter or early spring is optimum.
- Make 4"–6" (10–15 cm) deep trenches in the soil. Add compost or kelp meals to increase fertility.
- Plant your tubers 12"–18" (30–45 cm) apart.
- Fill the trenches with soil and keep them evenly moist. Mulch 2"–3" (5–7.5 cm), and add a good root barrier since they spread very fast and can overtake other plants.

- You should see tubers sprouting between 7–14 days.
- If you are planting the tubers in a pot (this makes harvesting easier), supplement the existing soil with compost or potting soil.
- Plant one tuber or one piece in each pot, going 4"–6" (10–15 cm) deep.
- Keep the pot in the sun, and if possible, ensure that one-third of its depth is in the soil to allow for more stability and heat insulation.
- Water deeply once 7 days have passed. Fertilizer isn't essential.

### Care Instructions

Jerusalem artichokes can withstand most kinds of soil—clay, sand, or loamy. They prefer light soil that is porous and has good fertility.

- Mulch the soil surface so that no unwanted weeds show up.
- When the flowers have pollinated, they will begin to grow seeds. You need to cut off the flower stalks before this happens to encourage tuber growth.
- Row coverings, mulch, or a greenhouse are all options if the weather forecast calls for excessively frigid temperatures.

### Harvesting

Jerusalem artichokes are harvested from late fall to winter. They usually taste richer after 2 frosts (harvests).

- After 150 days, add some potting mix and let your plants grow for two weeks more.
- Begin harvesting 162 days after planting.
- Locate and gently dislodge the roots using a fork or a hand rake. You should feel the tubers growing around the plants—they'll feel like plump ginger to the touch. Work without damaging them.
- These tubers can either be consumed or used for subsequent harvests.
- For the best taste, consume immediately after harvesting. Otherwise, you can store them for up to a week in your refrigerator.

## REGROWING BEAN SPROUTS

Tender, crisp, and the ideal component of summer salads, bean sprouts have a home in every kitchen.

### General Notes About Growing

- When we talk about "bean sprouts" most of us usually mean the mung bean (small, green, and round dried bean) sprouts.
- Mung bean plants prefer warm climate conditions and can take 3–4 months to reach a mature stage. Ideal temperatures for growing are between 82°F and 86°F (28°C–30°C).
- The beans themselves can sprout 2–3 days after the plants have reached maturity.
- They're versatile and can be grown both indoors and outdoors.
- Sandy, loamy, and fertile soils that are well-draining are the best for growing mung beans.

### Preparation and Planting

- Gather up some of the mung beans you have lying around your house. If they have already germinated (the sprouts are out), go ahead and plant them in the soil.
- If they haven't started showing sprouts yet, follow these steps.

- Wash your mung beans in water. Once clean, soak them in clean water for 8–10 hours.
- Strain the beans to remove any excess water.
- Place a colander in a large bowl, and ensure that there's 3"–4" (7.5–10 cm) of space between the base of the colander and the bowl.
- Transfer the soaked beans into the colander.
- Dip a cotton towel in room-temperature water and squeeze all the water out.
- Cover the mung beans with the towel.
- Keep the bowl in a cool, shaded place for 24 hours.
- The next day, repeat the process of wetting the cotton towel, squeezing out the excess water, and covering the beans again so they don't dry up.
- In 4 days, you should see the beans beginning to sprout. You can either consume them or transplant them into your garden.

- Prepare the soil by removing weeds, clods, large rocks, or any debris. Work compost 2" (5 cm) deep into the soil.
- Sow the beans 1" (2.5 cm) deep into the soil and at a distance of 2" (5 cm) from each other. If you are planting them in rows, plant them 3"–5" (7.5–12.5 cm) from one another.

### Care Instructions

- The planting area has to be weed-free.
- Fertilize your mung bean plants with a nitrogen-phosphorus-potassium ratio of 5-10-10. The nitrogen content should be low.

### Harvesting

- Mung beans will begin to form when the plant is at a height of 18″ (45 cm) and the pods will grow darker as they mature.
- The best time to harvest is when at least 60 percent of the pods have reached maturity.
- Once the pods have fully matured, the plant has to be pulled up and hung overhead. You can do this in a shed or the garage.
- Place a clean paper towel or soft fabric below the plant so that all the pods that dry and fall are collected on it.
- Dry the seeds completely by spreading them out on a newspaper in the open air.
- Mung beans, once completely dry, can be stored in an air-tight glass canister for several years.

REGROWING BELL PEPPERS

The best items to color your plate with splashes of red, sunshine yellow, or deep green, bell-peppers are easy on the eyes and lift up the palate.

### General Notes About Growing

- Peppers grow well in sunny and warm areas where the soil has enough air, is sandy, well-draining, loamy, and rich in nutrients.
- The best temperature range for growing bell peppers is 70°F–80°F (21°C–27°C).
- Bell peppers grow best in containers and raised beds.

### Preparation and Planting

- Always choose mature or ripe peppers when singling out scraps.
- Remove all seeds (the little white things inside the pepper that you usually scrape and throw away) and spread them on a clean paper towel or a tray.
- Place the paper towel or tray out in the sun. Leave the seeds to dry—this should take about an hour.
- Don't leave them out for too long because this can reduce their growing power. You can also dry them under a ceiling fan or in a dry, shaded area.
- Fill a planting tray with soil and then plant the seeds a 1/4" (6 mm) into the soil.

- Keep the soil moist by sprinkling water, and keep the seeds near a heating pad if you have to.
- After 1–3 weeks, the seedlings should have sprouted, which means they can be transplanted outdoors.
- 10 days before planting the seedlings outdoors, slowly introduce them to the outside environment by taking them outdoors for small periods of time each day.
- Gradually increase the time, beginning from 10 minutes to an hour.
- The slow introduction will help them acclimatize to the outside climate and prevent stunted growth.

### Care Instructions

- Always mulch the soil well. Grass clippings are great for bell peppers.
- Bell peppers require 1"–2" (2.5–5 cm) of water each week.
- Ensure that your plant gets enough sunlight.
- Low-nitrogen compound fertilizers are ideal for your bell pepper plants and will allow them to grow without hampering fruit production or yield.
- Stake your plants from time to time. This can keep the plants positioned off the ground and away from harmful pests.
- Use organic insecticides to keep pests like aphids and fleas in check.

## *Harvesting*

- Bell peppers need between 60–90 days to ripen—this depends on the kind you are dealing with.
- Green peppers are the most bitter of the lot, and also the least mature. If you leave the green pepper on the vine, it will eventually turn yellow, and then orange, before transforming into a fully ripened red pepper.
- To harvest a bell pepper, take a sharp knife or garden scissors and separate the fruit by cutting it from the plant. Make sure to leave 1" (2.5 cm) of the stem intact on the plant.
- Don't tear the fruit off the plant with your hands because you could cause unnoticed damage to it.
- Use a refrigerator crisper drawer to store peppers. Raw peppers will last between 1–2 weeks in this drawer, while the cooked variants will last for 3–5 days.

## REGROWING BOK CHOY

Most of us cut off the base of the bok choy and either dispose of it (it's hard and doesn't taste as good) or use it as a compost component. However, it can be the secret to growing a whole new bok choy!

### *General Notes About Growing*

- Bok choy needs well-draining soil that is rich in nitrogen, phosphorus, and potassium (NPK). It also requires an adequate amount of sunlight.
- To regrow bok choy, you will need one shallow container, the base of the vegetable (just use the base that you cut from the veggie before cooking it), and water.

### *Preparation and Planting*

- Cut off 2"–3" (5–7.5 cm) of the base from the bok choy leaves once you buy the vegetable from your grocery store.
- Fill a container with 1" (2.5 cm) water and stand the base of the bok choy inside the container.
- Set the container on the windowsill or in another sunny location.
- If the water grows cloudy after a few days, replace it.
- Spray the plant's center occasionally to keep it well-hydrated.

- Watch it for a week. Gradual changes should follow within a couple of days.
- The outside of the bok choy will slowly turn yellow. Work compost or fertilizer into your soil at this time.
- Loosen the soil by tilling it. Make ridges for easy planting.
- Plant the bok choy with potting mix when the center begins to show leafy growth.
- When planting, just the tips of the new green leaves should be pointing out of the soil.
- Bok choy grows well in fall and spring.

### Care Instructions

- Weed your garden regularly.
- Bok choy thrives on 1" (2.5 cm) of water every week.
- Thin down the weaker plants so that the healthy ones grow and sprout full heads.
- A healthy dose of NPK fertilizer will help with the fast growth of the veggie. You can also use your homemade compost as a fertilizer.
- Monitor spring harvests in case there are early signs of flowering.
- If you see a plant bolting (producing a flowering stem) harvest it immediately so you don't lose the whole crop.

*Harvesting*

- If there is no bolting, wait for the bok choy to reach a mature size. The standard varieties reach 12"–24" (30–60 cm) tall. Baby varieties grow to 10" (25 cm) tall.
- You can begin harvesting the plant once you see consumable leaves popping up.
- To harvest, use a knife (not your hands—don't tear the plant) and cut the plant at ground level.
- Always try to harvest bok choy in usable quantities because it has a short shelf life.
- If you must store it, it can keep in a container in your fridge for 3–4 days after being harvested.

## REGROWING BROCCOLI

You can regrow your broccoli from the stalks of veggies that you'd usually cut and throw away.

### *General Notes About Growing*

- A cool-weather plant, broccoli is easy to grow and thrives in conditions where many other plants wouldn't.
- Broccoli can be harvested when the main head stops growing in size and the buds are tight and dark green. If the buds start to open or if any yellow starts to show through, harvest as soon as you can.

### *Preparation and Planting*

- Don't use the stems (stalks) of spoiled broccoli heads. The fresher your veggie, the better.
- Cut about 8" (20 cm) of the broccoli stalk from the vegetable. Remove the leaves and florets, only keep the stalks.
- Take a clean glass cup or jar.
- Add enough water to the glass cup to cover up to 2" (5 cm) of the broccoli stalks.
- Don't add more than 3–4 stalks to one jar or cup.
- When the water in the container turns dark brown, replace it.
- After a couple of days, the broccoli stems will start to show new roots. You can leave them in the container

until the new roots and leaves grow a bit more—2 to 3 more days maximum.

- Get your potting mix ready. Fill a good container with potting soil.
- If you plant it in garden soil, top it off with coarse sand, shredded or chopped wood, and compost.
- Transplant the shooting broccoli stalks from the water to the soil.
- If you plant in a pot, only plant 1–2 stalks in each.
- Insert each stalk into a hole that can accommodate the entire root.
- There should be a 3"–5" (7.5–12.5 cm) space between stalks.
- Feed your plants with low-nitrogen fertilizer after transplanting. You can also use chicken droppings or compost tea as natural fertilizers.

## Care Instructions

- Broccoli plants thrive in partial shade and good ventilation. Choose a spot with 2–6 hours of sunlight for your containers.
- Broccoli does best with 1"–2" (2.5–5 cm) of water every week.
- Watch for weeds and remove any that arise so that there is no competition.
- Hot soil can make broccoli bolt (this will yield broccoli that tastes bitter). To prevent this, cover your soil with a layer of mulch—especially during warmer seasons.

*Harvesting*

- Keep a close eye on the color of the florets. If they begin to turn yellow, it means they are likely to bloom (bolt). Harvest immediately if you see this.
- Use a sharp knife to cut the broccoli's head off of the plant.
- Cut the broccoli head stem by 5" (12.5 cm). Then, remove the head with a swift cut.
- Do not cut the stem because this can damage the plant and ruin your chances at a side harvesting option later on.
- After harvesting the main head, you can also harvest the side shoots from the plant. They will grow like tiny heads at the side of the main head. When they sprout into florets, you can cut them off.
- Broccoli can be enjoyed fresh after a harvest, or you can keep them in the crisper drawer of your refrigerator for 3–5 days.

## REGROWING BRUSSELS SPROUTS

These veggies taste delicious when blanched and oven-baked with a dash of balsamic vinegar, hot honey, and salt. And you need nothing but the old Brussels sprouts lying around in your fridge to grow new ones.

### *General Notes About Growing*

- You can regrow Brussels sprouts from your grocery scraps. For best results, use Brussels sprouts that aren't too old.
- Ideal temperatures for Brussels sprouts are 45°F–75°F (7°C–24°C).
- They are best harvested in the fall, so you should plant them at the onset of summer.

### *Preparation and Planting*

- Wash the Brussels sprouts over the sink to remove dirt or grime. Check the bottom of each of them and peel away any yellowing or dead leaves.
- Using a clean, sharp knife, slice the flat, bottom portion of each sprout.
- Fill a container with 1/2" (13 mm) water.
- Place the Brussels sprouts with the bottom part down in the water. Don't cram too many of them into one container.
- If the water gets cloudy, change it. Remove any dead leaves that may float on the surface.

- Measure the Brussels sprouts with a ruler every week until they seem at least 3" (7.5 cm) tall.
- Once they reach this height (preferably in late summer), transplant them to your garden in an open, sunny area. Keep a gap of 18"–24" (45–60 cm) between each of the sprouts.
- Cover the roots completely with soil. Sprinkle with water.
- Keep measuring the growth. Once the Brussels sprouts reach 12" (30 cm) in height, apply a nitrogen-rich fertilizer. Apply again in 4 weeks.

### Care Instructions

- Brussels sprouts thrive with 6 hours of sunlight each day.
- The soil has to be well-draining and fertile.
- Mulch the soil regularly to retain moisture and keep the plants cool.
- Use a row cover (fabric sheet to shield plants) from pests.
- If you see yellow leaves forming at the base of the plants, gently remove them to retain plant health.

### Harvesting

- Fall is the best time for harvesting Brussels sprouts.
- The sprouts will mature upward from the stalk's bottom. Harvest when these sprouts measure 1" (2.5 cm) in diameter.

- To harvest, simply twist the sprout until it breaks off from the stalk.
- Consume fresh or store in a crisper for 10–14 days (preferably in a bag).

## REGROWING CABBAGE

A versatile and healthy vegetable, you can easily regrow cabbage from the original vegetable you bought during a grocery haul.

### *General Notes About Growing*

- To regrow cabbage from scraps, you need the core of the original vegetable. You can also use the leaves, but they need to be attached to the core.
- The core is the hard, stem-like structure at the bottom of the vegetable.
- Separate the whole core from the rest of the vegetable with a knife. You will use this to grow a new cabbage.

### *Preparation and Planting*

- Fill shallow containers with water and place the cores on top of the water. Do not submerge them.
- Use one container for each core.
- Change the water every 2 days.
- The core should sprout leaves and roots in 4–7 days.
- Prepare the soil by adding a potting mix.
- When roots and leaves mature, remove them from the water and transfer them to your garden or pots.

*Care Instructions*

- The best soil temperature for growth is between 60°F–65°F (16°–18°C).
- Mulch the soil to retain moisture and regulate temperature.
- Water 2″ (5 cm) per square foot every week.
- Fertilize with a balanced (10-10-10) NPK fertilizer 2 weeks after your transplant.
- After 3 weeks, add nitrogen-heavy fertilizer.
- Crop rotation will help counter soil-borne diseases. Crop rotation is growing different kinds of crops in the same area over a number of growing seasons.

*Harvesting*

- Harvest when cabbage heads reach the desired size and feel firm. Green cabbage varieties should take 70 days to mature from when they are transplanted.
- To harvest, cut the cabbage head at the base using sharp gardening shears or a knife.
- Bring the cabbage head indoors or keep it in a shaded region.
- Cabbage can be kept in the refrigerator for two weeks. It should be dry before storing.

## REGROWING CARROT GREENS

If you are looking to utilize everything that comes into your kitchen and minimize waste, you can also regrow carrot greens from the carrot tops of the vegetables you buy at the grocery store! We usually throw these tops away, or use them as compost—but they can be used to yield leafy greens which are delicious.

### General Notes About Growing

- To grow carrot greens, choose carrots that still have some of the green leaves attached to the tops of the vegetables (the veggie heads).
- Carrot greens like nutrient-rich, moist soil and bright sunlight.
- Ideal growing temperatures are between 60°F–70°F (16°C–21°C).

### Preparation and Planting

- Using a clean knife, make a precise cut at the top, so that you have about a quarter inch of the head of the carrot with the greens attached to the head.
- Place them with the cut side of the head facing down in a flat, shallow jar or container with a little bit of water. The container should be transparent.
- The tops of the carrot tops should not be submerged in water—only the base. You can use a toothpick to

position the carrot top so that only the bottom part touches the water in the container.

- Keep the container in a warm spot with shade.
- Monitor your plant. Carrot scraps will start producing new green shoots.
- After a few days, the roots of the carrot will begin to sprout from the bottom.
- Once you see the roots, you can transfer the tops to soil. The soil should have enough compost and nutrients mixed into it.
- Dig 10" (25 cm) holes in the soil and insert the tops. Cover them gently, exposing only the greens to the open air.
- Immediately after planting, water the carrots.

### Care Instructions

- Mulch to allow the soil to retain its moisture, enhance the germination process, and keep the sun from hitting the tender carrot roots too intensely.
- Ensure that the carrots get 1" (2.5 cm) of water every week.
- Weed while taking care not to disturb the roots of the plant.
- Fertilize 5–6 weeks from the date of planting. Low-nitrogen fertilizer is ideal for carrots.
- If you grow the plants in indoor pots, expose them to 3 to 4 hours of sunlight every day after a week from transplanting. This will help harden the veggies and give you a robust yield.

*Harvesting*

- Once the carrot greens start shooting up comfortably, you can pinch small leaves and use them for garnishes.
- You can also let the greens grow and become tall, and then cut them to make pesto.
- If you leave some of the stems attached to the plants, they'll keep yielding new edible shoots, giving you a perennial supply of delicious carrot greens.

## REGROWING CAULIFLOWER

Versatile and nourishing, cauliflowers are among the easiest veggies you can grow from leftovers.

### General Notes About Growing

- To regrow cauliflowers, you will need scraps or a head —you can simply use the scraps from your kitchen leftovers.
- Cauliflowers thrive in soil that retains moisture.
- The ideal temperature range for growing cauliflower is 60°F–65°F (16°C–18°C).

### Preparation and Planting

- Fill shallow containers a quarter of the way with water. The rule of thumb is for the water not to swallow the entire stalk.
- Place the stalk scraps of your cauliflower in the water.
- You can also use the base of the cauliflower heads (scraps) but it helps to cut off some parts of the cauliflower with the bases.
- Allow the scraps/stalks to receive 2–6 hours of sunshine.
- Change the water every 2 days.
- Give the scraps a week to sprout roots and leaves.
- Once you detect fresh roots and leaves emerging from the cauliflower leftovers, you may transplant them to the garden or into pots.

## *Care Instructions*

- Mulch the soil as needed.
- Cauliflower plants require 2″ (5 cm) of water per square foot each week.
- After 3–4 weeks, apply high-nitrogen fertilizer.
- If you see brown heads, it's possible the soil has low amounts of boron. You can supplement the soil with liquid seaweed or drench it with a solution of 1 gal (approximately 4 L) of water and 1 Tbs (15 ml) of Borax.
- Be sure to compost regularly.

## *Harvesting*

- Plants will be ready to harvest 50–100 days from when you transplanted them.
- When the heads appear white, firm, and compact and are about 6″–8″ (15–20 cm) in diameter, cut them off with a large knife.
- Leave a few of the leaves around the head when cutting.
- Store the heads in a sealable bag in your crisper drawer for up to a week.

REGROWING CELERY

You can easily regrow and enjoy your next celery dish from your vegetable scraps. Let's find out how.

**General Notes About Growing**

- The ideal daytime temperature range for celery is between 60°F–70°F (16°C–21°C).
- Celery thrives in nutrient-rich and compost-added soil.
- For optimum yields, plant at a time that allows you to harvest before it grows too hot.

**Preparation and Planting**

- Slice 2" (5 cm) from the root end of your celery bunch.
- Fill a shallow glass bowl or jar with enough water to submerge 1" (2.5 cm) of the root end. Set the celery in this bowl or jar.
- Keep the container somewhere it can get natural light.
- Change the water every 2 days, ensuring the root end remains submerged.
- In a few days, small leaves will emerge from the top. You will also notice tiny roots forming around the base.
- Add a pesticide-free potting mix to your soil.
- When these new roots are 1" (2.5 cm) long, make a hole that is deep and wide enough to hold the plant from the root to the cut end, and plant your celery.
- Ensure that the emerging stalks and leaves are above the soil.

- Keep the soil moist.

### Care Instructions

- Immediately after transplanting, mulch the soil with peat, sawdust, or mown grass.
- About 10 days after planting, nourish the soil with a complex fertilizer. Feed again after another 14 days.
- To get the finest quality root, you have to pull the top part out of the ground in the middle of the summer and break off the side roots.

### Harvesting

- 85–120 days from the date of planting, you can consider harvesting your celery.
- Measure the lower stalks to see if they have reached a height of 6" (15 cm) from the ground to the first node (the area from where the first leaf grows).
- For harvesting whole plants, wait until they are 3" (7.5 cm) or more in diameter. They should be compact, tight, and not have any open spaces around the stalk's center.
- Cut off the individual stalks or simply slice the whole plant at the soil line.
- Either consume fresh or keep the heads whole and wrap them in aluminum foil before placing them in the refrigerator crisper. Done this way, they should keep for 2–4 weeks.

REGROWING CUCUMBERS

Consume it fresh, pickle it, juice it, make kimchi with it—the uses of cucumber are many. It really helps to regrow such a refreshing fruit from what you have lying around the house!

*General Notes About Growing*

- Don't use diseased cucumbers. You'll know a cucumber is rotting if it feels soft and squidgy to the touch and has a thin, white layer of film (resembling powder) on its skin.
- The best temperature for growing cucumbers is 75°F–85°F (24°C–29°C).
- Cucumbers do best when planted during spring and summer.
- Try growing cucumbers from different varieties to ensure proper pollination.

*Preparation and Planting*

- Take a ripe cucumber. Make sure your cucumber is of a natural variety and not a hybrid or artificial fruit.
- Keep the cucumber in a shaded region for 4–5 days to allow the seeds to mature.
- Remove the fruit's top and bottom halves. Because they lack seeds, they will not develop plants.
- You can scoop out the seeds and consume the remaining flesh. Alternatively, follow the steps below.

- The remainder of the fruit should be sliced into 1/2" (13 mm) pieces.
- You may either plant the cuttings directly into the soil, or you can remove the matured seeds from the individual pieces and cultivate them as independent cucumber plants.
- Always look for the hard seeds if you're removing them from the cuttings.
- Prepare a potting mix using half garden sand that has been altered with compost and the other half regular sand for your plants.
- Choose a basket with sufficient drainage and an 8" (20 cm) diameter for the cuttings.
- Place cucumber scraps in three-quarters of the potting mix.
- Cover the cuttings with 1" (2.5 cm) potting mix.
- After planting cucumber leftovers, you must hydrate the soil and keep it in moderate shade.
- 5 to 7 days later, you'll notice tiny seedlings.
- Cucumber seeds usually germinate in 10–12 days.
- If you want to transplant outside, now is the time.
- To begin, till the ground by hand using a shovel or other suitable implement. Make sure each hole is at least 6" (15 cm) deep before proceeding.
- Cover the bottom of the hole with a 3" (7 cm) covering of compost. Fill up the remainder of the hole with regular garden soil and then plant the cucumber plant.
- It is recommended that just a few inches of the plant's stem remain above ground level.
- After that, be sure to thoroughly moisten the seedlings.

- Make sure that the cucumber plants are protected from direct sunlight throughout the day.

### Caring Instructions

- Water the soil 1" (2.5 cm) deep every week.
- Mulch regularly and fertilize every 10 days.
- Cucumbers are self-pollinating. However, trellising may help as it will allow the blooms to be pollinated to the fullest extent possible.
- Plant flowers that attract pollinators, such as daisies, dahlias, and coneflowers.
- You may use a nylon trellis, a tomato cage, or a chain-link fence to support cucumber vines.
- Using a trellis to train cucumbers requires that the plant be at least 1' (30 cm) long.
- Once it has reached the recommended size, carefully wrap the vine around the trellis 2 or 3 times.

### Harvesting

- Cucumbers typically ripen their fruit after 60–70 days on average.
- Cucumbers should be picked when they are at least 5"–8" (12.5–20 cm) long and have a hue between medium green and dark green.
- Harvest during the morning.
- Cut the stem of the cucumber off with a sharp knife, holding it in one hand.

- Don't grind or pull at the cucumber. It might harm the remainder of the plant's development.
- If you want to produce cucumbers again next season, you may leave one cucumber on the vine after you've picked all the others.
- Consume fresh or store in your crisper drawer for 1–2 weeks.

## REGROWING EGGPLANT

It's not too hard to grow eggplant. If you have a kitchen garden, eggplant is a must-have.

### *General Notes About Growing*

- You need an eggplant that is a good size, is not infected, has tiny seeds in it, and is not a hybrid.
- The tiny seeds that are inside the eggplant will be used to grow new plants.
- Plan the deseeding of the vegetable so that you can plant it during the onset or middle of summer.

### *Preparation and Planting*

- Slice the eggplant in half.
- Scoop out the pulp with the tiny seeds from inside the eggplant and place the scooped-out flesh on a plate.
- Next, separate the seeds from the flesh.
- Place the seeds in a fine-mesh strainer and rinse them off to remove any stubborn flesh that may be sticking to them.
- Dry the seeds completely and store them in an airtight container or plastic bag once dry.
- When the seeds are ready to plant, speed up the germination process by keeping a damp cloth around them and storing them in a shaded area for 7 days.
- Next, moisten your soil and plant the seeds.

### Care Instructions

- Water well after planting.
- Mulch the soil to prevent weeds.
- Add a balanced fertilizer every 14 days.
- Stake the taller plants so that they don't fall over due to the weight of the fruit once they begin to produce.

### Harvesting

- The ideal time to harvest is 65–80 days from planting, when the fruit is ripe.
- The fruit's skin should be glossy and without any wrinkles. The color should be uniform.
- Don't pull at the plant when harvesting. Take a sharp knife and cut close to the plant's stem, right above the green cap at the top. The green cap can be prickly, so use gloves if necessary.
- Eggplants taste best when fresh, or can be stored in a crisper drawer for 7–10 days. You can save the seeds for a future harvest.

## REGROWING GARLIC

Given that garlic is a common ingredient in most of our savory dishes, the news that you can regrow it from scraps should come as a blessing!

### *General Notes About Growing*

- You can regrow garlic from the cloves of the original vegetable. The cloves are the separate white portions that you peel and consume.
- During the first 2 months of growing, it thrives in temperatures between 32°F–50°F (0°C–10°C). It does well in most temperatures after maturing.
- Moist, well-draining soil is good for growing garlic.

### *Preparation and Planting*

- Separate your garlic cloves using a sterilized paring knife.
- Remove the outer skin from the surface of the cloves.
- Prepare your soil by digging 10" (25 cm) into it and adding a layer of organic compost.
- Position the cloves 6" (15 cm) apart and in rows. Every row should have a distance of 12" (30 cm) between them.
- Place the cloves 2" (5 cm) into the ground with the tips (the pointy ends) facing up and the flat ends into the soil.

- Add the soil around the cloves and water generously for the first time.

## Care Instructions

- When the first leaves begin sprouting, supplement the soil with slow-feeding nitrogen plant food.
- Water 2"–3" (5–7.5 cm) each week.
- Mulch the soil to contain weeds and retain moisture.
- During the summer months, the garlic will stop yielding new foliage and bulbs will start developing. When this happens, remove all mulch.
- Stop watering during the summer. Allow the soil to dry out—even if it feels hard and brittle.

## Harvesting

- Garlic will be ready to harvest once the leaves turn dry and yellow and begin to fall off the plants. This usually happens during late summer to early fall.
- Dig up the bulbs carefully after loosening the soil around the plants with a garden shovel. You can also use a garden fork.
- Garlic bulbs are very susceptible to bruising, so be gentle.
- Spread out the bulbs in a well-ventilated area and let them dry.
- If you slice through a bulb by mistake, consume it immediately.

- To store your garlic, bundle 8 to 10 stems containing the bulbs together and hang. The bulb's side must face down in a cool, dark space.
- Allow the bulbs to stay this way for a month.
- Once the roots and tops dry, cut them off and clean your matured garlic by removing the thin layer of papery skin forming on the outside.

REGROWING LETTUCE

Lettuce is a kitchen staple. It adds volume and nourishment to your salads, sandwiches, soups—you name it. Now you can learn to regrow it from your kitchen scraps!

***General Notes About Growing***

- Most kinds of lettuce that you buy at the supermarkets as an intact bunch or a whole "head" with the stem can be used for regrowing.
- The stem of the lettuce is also edible, but we usually throw it away and only consume the leaves.
- Ideal temperatures for growing lettuce are 60°F–65°F (16°C–18°C).

### Preparation and Planting

- Start by slicing the leaves from the stems, leaving about 2" (5 cm) of the base intact. If you have a smaller length available, try your luck with it anyway.
- Position the base in a shallow container with enough water to cover half of the stem.

### Caring Instructions

- Keep the container somewhere sunny and change the water if it gets too dirty or evaporates.
- As an optional step, you can add hydroponic fertilizer to the water.
- In a few days, you'll see green leafy shoots growing.

### Harvesting

- Regrown lettuce can't be planted in the soil since it doesn't have a root structure.
- All you need to do is to keep observing the shoots as they form in your shallow container.
- After around 10 to 12 days, the regrown lettuce is ready to harvest from the container. Don't wait longer than 15 days because the leaves will become bitter.
- Just snip off the new leaves with a pair of scissors, and enjoy!

REGROWING OKRA

Stir-fried, roasted, or baked into crisps, there's a variety of uses for okra. And all you need to grow your own is the tiny, gelatinous seeds that exist inside each vegetable (and pop in your mouth when you chew on them!)

*General Notes About Growing*

- Okra grows well in stable, warm weather between temperatures of 65°F–70°F (18°C–21°C).
- Since transplanting okra from containers to soil can be complicated, it is best to germinate the seeds directly in the soil.

*Preparation and Planting*

- Split open the vegetables and scoop out all the seeds. You will notice that there is a thin, slimy film over them. Wash the seeds, then let them dry in a sunny spot until they darken.
- Store the dried seeds in the refrigerator overnight.
- Germinate the seeds by adding them to ready-made peat pellets. These are compressed soil discs that are made from peat moss and are ideal for beginners.
- Simply push the seeds 1/2" (13 mm) into the peat pellets and water until the soil is moist.
- Once seedlings sprout, dig holes large enough to hold each peat pellet. While digging, remember to keep 9"–12" (22.5–30 cm) distance between each hole.

- If you are growing multiple okra plants, plant them in rows. Keep a distance of 3'–6' (90–180 cm) between the rows.
- Once the holes are ready, place the pellets with the seedlings in them.
- Cover them with soil, taking care to keep any leafy growth above the soil.

### Caring Instructions

- Get rid of weeds when your plants are young.
- Mulch 4"–8" (10–20 cm) of the soil.
- Apply a balanced liquid fertilizer once a month.
- 1" (2.5 cm) of water every week is ideal.
- Prune the tops of the plants when they reach 5'–6' (152–182 cm) in height.

### Harvesting

- 2 months after planting, the plants will be ready to harvest. Wait for the seed pods (the sprouting vegetables) to be 1–2 days old or 2"–4" (5–10 cm) long.
- Cut above the sprouting vegetable with a knife.
- You can also dry the seeds from the fresh vegetables for growing new okra.

REGROWING ONIONS

Most of us lean on onions as a base for all our savory cooking. You can easily regrow your next batch of grocery scraps.

### General Notes About Growing

- You can easily grow your own onions from scraps of other onions. All you need is the base of the vegetable that often has those thin, wiry roots protruding from it —which you'd otherwise throw away.
- Onions grow well in temperatures of 53°F–77°F (12°C–25°C) in the initial phase of planting, and 60°F–77°F (16°C–25°C) for bulb development.

### Preparation and Planting

- Leaving the skin on, cut off the bottom third of the onion (the root end). For accurate measurement, aim for a 1/2"–1" (13 mm–2.5 cm) thick slice at the widest part of your vegetable. The more of the bottom you have, the better!
- To generate numerous full-size young onions from a single onion bottom, split it with a sharp knife.
- Dry the bottom (or bottom halves) for a few hours to 2 days in an area that has plenty of shade and ventilation. You will notice callouses beginning to form.
- If you have starter pots, fill them two-thirds with potting mix and push the mix down until it feels tight and compact.

- Make indentations in the center of the pots to hold the onion bottom, or halves, bottom facing down.
- Once you have placed the bottoms into the indentations, cover each with a very thin layer of soil.
- Water enough for the soil to be moist without going soggy, and keep the pot somewhere sunny.
- Once the onion has grown a few leaves, take it out of the pot.
- Take off the old onion skins.
- Replant it in a garden bed that has been prepared with potting soil.
- Cut the leaves down to a third of their size so the bulb can grow. The onion will grow those leaves back faster and with less stress.
- If you want to plant the onion bottoms directly in your garden, ensure you have soil that has good drainage abilities. Your onion bottoms will also need 6 hours of sunlight daily.
- Give the onion bottoms 1" (2.5 cm) water each week.

### Caring Instructions

- Weed the garden regularly if you are growing the onions outdoors.
- From time to time, fertilize your garden with a nitrogen-rich fertilizer.

### Harvesting

- Onions are ready to harvest when they start producing flowers. This will be about 90–120 days from the date of planting.
- Loosen the soil with your garden shovel and gently pull the green foliage on top of the onion to get it out of the soil.
- The green shoots can also be cooked and consumed, and have a sweet, nutty taste. Consume your harvested onions now, or store them somewhere dry for future use.

## REGROWING POTATOES

Bake it, boil it, mash it, or roast it—there's no end to the number of ways a simple potato can spruce up an entire meal. And, with the instructions below, you will regrow your potatoes from scraps of old potatoes!

### *General Notes About Growing*

- Potato scraps are leftover peels (skin) from potatoes that are not used. You can even use whole potatoes which have been lying around for too long.
- Sometimes, store-bought potatoes are treated with chemicals that stop them from maturing. But that is just what we want for regrowing them. When the potato matures, its skin begins to develop little black buds, also known as eyes because that's what they look like. You need skin with eyes to grow new potatoes. Your best bet is to have a bunch of seed potatoes.
- 45°F–50°F (7°C–10°C) is the best range for planting potatoes. The best soil temperature for potatoes to grow after planting is between 60°F–70°F (16°C–21°C).

### *Preparation and Planting*

- If the potato is small, you can plant it directly into the soil. If it is large, cut it in half, keeping the skin intact. Each half must contain at least one eye.

- If you want to grow new potatoes from potato peels, leave some flesh attached to each peel. Each peel should also have at least one eye.
- After cutting the potatoes into halves, let them dry for 2 days. If you use peels, place them on a tray with the skin side down, and let them dry for 24–48 hours.
- Potatoes do well when planted in rows.
- Dig trenches are at least 8" (20 cm) deep. Keep 3' (90 cm) of space between each row.
- Plant seed potato halves or peels with the cut side facing down. Then, cover with 3" (7.5 cm) of potting mix.

### Caring Instructions

- They need 1"–2" of water every week.
- When the potatoes/peels start sprouting leaves, gently fill the trenches with 2" (5 cm) of soil without covering the tops of the sprouting plants.
- Continue covering these trenches every 2 weeks. This process is called hilling and it keeps the plants shielded from the harsh effects of direct sunlight.

### Harvesting

- When potato plants begin to wilt and become yellow—usually 13–17 weeks from planting—it means they are ready for harvesting.
- Gently loosen the soil around each plant. Avoid shovels so you don't accidentally hit the outside of the potato.

Using your hands (wear gloves if you wish to), dig up the potatoes.

- Brush excess dirt from the potatoes with your hands and keep them in a dry, shady area for a few days. After 2–3 days, transfer them to a dark and cool spot in your kitchen.
- Avoid keeping onions and potatoes together. Onions release a gas that can spoil the potatoes pretty quickly!

## REGROWING PUMPKINS

Sweet pumpkins are best enjoyed roasted, in soups, or baked into pies. They are a complete delicacy, and very easy to regrow!

### General Notes About Growing

- If you have an excess of pumpkins lying around after Halloween, it's time to end your worries! You can plant the seeds inside the store-bought pumpkins and grow your own!
- The best temperatures for growing pumpkins are 65°F–95°F (18°C–35°C). The best time to begin growing them is early summer. This ensures you will have a harvest by fall.
- Pumpkins thrive in sandy soils, but will pretty much accommodate any soil so long as it has good drainage properties.

### Preparation and Planting

- Begin by slicing the pumpkin open.
- Take a big, flat spoon and scoop out the core portion that has seeds attached.

- Separate the seeds from the pulp by rinsing them in a colander.
- Once you have the seeds separated, spread them on a paper towel and let them dry for 24 hours. This will speed up the germination process.
- After 24 hours, transfer the seeds to a re-sealable bag and store them in a cool, shaded place for 5 days.
- Prepare your garden soil by adding potting mix.
- Plant each seed 1" (2.5 cm) deep. Space the seeds 8"–12" (20–30 cm) apart in rows that are 6"–18" (15–45 cm) apart.
- Ensure that the soil receives 6–8 hours of sunlight every day.

### Caring Instructions

- Provide nitrogen-rich fertilizer at the onset. This will encourage growth and protect the health of the vine. Avoid pesticides and herbicides because this will reduce helpful pollination.
- Pumpkin plants need about 1" (2.5 cm) of water each week. When you water, aim for late afternoon or early morning and only water the soil, not the sprouting foliage.
- Inspect the top 2"–3" (5–7.5 cm) of soil to get a feel of the dryness each week. If it feels too wet, reduce the watering frequency.
- After the fruit develops, prune the fuzzy ends of the plant's vines.
- Consider growing multiple pumpkin plants to increase the likelihood of their flowers cross-pollinating.

### Harvesting

- Pumpkins take about 3 to 4 months to grow from the date of planting.
- You will know your pumpkins are ripe when the stems begin to shrivel and dry. The color will also become bright and they will feel hard to the touch.
- When the pumpkins are ready, cut each stem about 2"–4" (5–10 cm) above the fruit. Don't tear the stem with your hands, use gardening shears.

- Ripe pumpkins can last for up to 3 months provided you have a cool, dry space for storing them. The optimal storing temperature is 55°F (13°C).

## REGROWING RADISHES

If you like the sharp taste of radishes, and how they can uplift any salads or curries, you can now regrow them from store-bought radishes!

### General Notes About Growing

- All you need to regrow radishes are the tips with the roots attached to the original vegetable. We generally throw these away, but now, you don't need to.
- The ideal temperature for growing radishes is between 60°F–70°F (16°C–21°C). Spring and fall are ideal planting seasons.

### Preparation and Planting

- Slice off the root end of the radish using a clean knife.
- Cover the entire root end that you've just cut with germination gel. You can make your own gel at home by adding 1 Tbs (15 ml) of cornstarch to 1 cup (250 ml) of lukewarm water, and heating this on low heat until it reduces to a gel-like consistency.
- Select a sunny spot in your garden. Dig holes 2" (5 cm) deep for each root end.
- Place the root ends (with the cut side facing down) into the holes and cover with soil.
- Keep 2" (5 cm) distance between each radish cutting and 10" (25 cm) between each row.

### *Caring Instructions*

- Radishes thrive in fertile soil. Add a balanced fertilizer from time to time to ensure optimum growth.
- Water 1″ (2.5 cm) deep every week. Drip irrigation is ideal for these plants.
- The plants will need about 8 hours of sunlight each day.
- Once the seedlings are 2″ (5 cm) tall or a week old, thin the radish plants. To do this, snip the greens at the soil line.
- Weed frequently to allow the radishes room to grow.
- Mulch the soil from time to time.

### *Harvesting*

- Radishes can be harvested within a month from the day you planted them. If you live in an area where the temperature is less than 50°F (10°C), the plants may take 50 days to reach maturity.
- You should feel or see the top part of the radish pushing up from the soil.
- Gently dislodge the vegetables and cut off the tops and the thin root.
- Wash the radishes and dry them.
- You can either consume the vegetables fresh or store them in re-sealable bags in the refrigerator's crisper drawer.
- The radish greens are edible and can also be stored for up to 3 days.

## REGROWING SPINACH

Versatile and healthy, spinach can work in most savory dishes and also add volume (and nourishment) to your smoothies. You can easily regrow these healthy greens from your grocery scraps!

### General Notes About Growing

- The key to regrowing spinach is to have the cuttings from a fresh bunch. Don't buy spinach that looks old and wilted. The tastiest ones are dark green and look vibrant. As a bonus, when shopping for vegetables at your grocery market, try to find ones that have their roots intact.
- Optimum temperatures for growing spinach are 50°F–60°F (10°C–16°C).

### Preparation and Planting

- Slice off the leaves and consume them as you normally would. You'll be left with the main stem, the branches, and the roots (if they are still intact).
- If any branches look weak or wilted, remove them.
- Prepare containers with potting mix. If you plant outdoors, prepare your soil by adding a layer of potting mix to it.
- Create holes that can accommodate the cuttings.
- Plant one cutting in each hole.

- Keep the containers in a well-ventilated area that receives 2–6 hours of sunlight every day.
- If you plant outdoors, ensure there's 3"–5" (7.5–12.5 cm) space between each cutting.
- Water gently, just enough to moisten the soil.
- After a week to 10 days, your cuttings will show new growth. Mix in a nitrogen-rich fertilizer.

### Caring Instructions

- Use row covers to keep the soil cool and keep bugs away.
- When the seedlings are about 2" (5 cm) tall, thin them out so that they are 3" (7.5 cm) apart. You can consume them. Thinning means removing some of the plants growing too close together, ensuring the survival of the fittest.
- Water 1" (2.5 cm) deep each week.
- Mulch regularly.

### Harvesting

- When the spinach leaves reach the desired size, you can harvest the outer leaves or the entire plant by cutting the stem at soil level.
- Don't wait too long, because overmature spinach can taste bitter.
- Increasing daylight (over 14 hours) and warmer temperatures can cause spinach to develop large stalks

with narrow leaves, also making them taste bitter. If the weather becomes too warm, harvest as soon as you can.

- Fresh spinach leaves can last for up to a week. Wash the leaves, pat them dry with a paper towel, and store in a freezer bag along with the paper towel to prevent excess moisture.

## REGROWING SWEET POTATOES

If you have a sweet potato that's already sprouting, it may be difficult to consume it. Rather than throwing it away, you can easily plant the sprouting section (called a slip) and grow your own sweet potatoes. Store-bought sweet potatoes work just fine and regrowing them is a simple process.

### General Notes About Growing

- You should start with good-quality sweet potatoes.
- The best temperatures for growing sweet potatoes are 65°F–95°F (18°C–35°C).
- Always aim to plant sweet potatoes during a time when the soil is warm and there is no chance of frost.

### Preparation and Planting

- Begin by washing your sweet potatoes. Either cut them in half or in large sections.
- Place the sections in a jar of water with the cut side facing down. You can use toothpicks to hold the sections in place. Half of the sweet potato should be below the water and half should be above it.
- Position the jar on a window ledge with plenty of sunlight. Keep an eye on the water and replace it if you need to.
- In a few weeks, your sweet potatoes will be covered with roots at the bottom and leafy sprouts at the top.

- After the sprouts begin to form, you need to separate them into slips. Carefully twist each individual sprout off the sweet potato.
- Place each sprout in a shallow bowl, with its bottom half submerged in water. The leaves of the sprout should hang out over the bowl's rim.
- In a few days, each individual sprout will begin to produce its own root system.
- When the roots are 1" (2.5 cm) long, it's time to transplant your sprouts to the soil.
- Add a layer of compost to your soil and ensure that it is loose and well-draining.
- Plant the sprouts about 12"–18" (30–45 cm) apart in rows. Each sprout should be planted about 4" (10 cm) deep.
- Water generously after planting, and continue watering every day for the first week. Reduce the watering to 3 times during the second week.

### Caring Instructions

- Choose a sunny spot that will receive a few hours of shade to grow your sweet potato sprouts/slips.
- Once established, water 1" (2.5 cm) deep every week.
- Sweet potatoes love well-draining soil rich in organic matter. You can top off your soil with a layer of compost, chicken droppings, or coffee grounds from time to time.

- 3 or 4 weeks before harvesting, stop watering your sweet potatoes. This will keep mature tubers from splitting.

### Harvesting

- 3–4 months from the date of planting, sweet potato tubers should be ready for harvesting.
- If you like to consume sweet potato leaves as greens, you can harvest them in moderation throughout the growing season. But leave enough on the plants to help them keep growing.
- You can dig up the tubers once the foliage becomes yellow.
- Be gentle when you dig. The tubers will grow close to the soil's surface and can be damaged if handled roughly.
- Don't store sweet potatoes in the refrigerator. Instead, store them in a well-ventilated, dry, and cool region like a root cellar or basement.

REGROWING TURNIP

Turnips are great for soups and meat dishes. The greens go into making salads. Regrowing turnips from kitchen scraps is easy and does not take much time.

*General Notes About Growing*

- Turnips need full sun.
- Grow them best in spring or fall.
- 40°F–75°F (4.4°C–24°C) temperature is suitable for turnips.
- Mix aged manure or compost into the ordinary garden soil to help turnips grow.

*Preparation and Planting*

- Cut the tops off your store-bought turnips.
- Put them in water.
- Within a few days, new green tips appear.
- Roots take about a week to develop.
- Prepare the soil as the roots get stronger.
- Add 3" (7.5 cm) of compost or aged manure to 7" (17.5 cm) of soil to enrich it.
- Transplant the turnip tops with the green leaves above the soil. The part with the roots should be covered with soil.
- Soil should be loose, moist, enriched, and well-draining.
- Plant them in rows 8" (20 cm) apart. Keep a gap of 3" (7.5 cm) between the plants.

### Caring Instructions

- Turnips need sunlight with partial shade during the heat of midday.
- Water regularly but adequately—about 1" (2.5 cm) per week.
- A layer of mulch in winter prevents freezing.

### Harvesting

- Harvest turnip greens when the plants are 4" (10 cm) tall.
- Turnip greens will regrow from the roots.
- Roots are best when small. They are ready after about 2 months.
- Tug the plant and pull it out of the soil along with the root.

REGROWING ZUCCHINI

Not only is it great because of its clean, refreshing taste, but zucchini is also a house favorite because of how easy it is to regrow it from grocery scraps!

*General Notes About Growing*

- Zucchini thrives in regions with lots of sunlight and rich soil.
- The best time to grow zucchini is when the soil has reached a minimum temperature of 65°F–70°F (18°C–21°C). It will grow well in temperatures between 65°F–84°F (18°C–29°C).

*Preparation and Planting*

- The first step is to prepare the scraps. Choose scraps from a vegetable that is mature. If you plant scraps from an unripe zucchini, they may not germinate.
- Scoop out the zucchini seeds from the scraps with a clean spoon.
- Place the seeds in a container and wash to remove any zucchini flesh from their exteriors. Once all the flesh has been removed, dry the seeds with a paper towel.
- Let the seeds dry for 2–3 days or more by spreading them over a newspaper or on a clean tray. Leave them in a well-ventilated place and turn them over each day.

- In the meantime, prepare your potting mix by adding a balanced amount of compost, coarse sand, dried leaves, and peat moss to your soil.
- Moisten the potting mix with water.
- After the seeds have dried, plant the seeds 1"–2" (2.5–5 cm) deep and 4" (10 cm) away from each other.

### Caring Instructions

- Zucchini thrives in soil that has a slow-release fertilizer like 10-10-10 fertilizer added to the potting mix. This is a balanced fertilizer with equal parts nitrogen, phosphorus, and potassium (NPK).
- The planted region should receive 6 hours or more of daily sunlight.
- Water the soil 1" (2.5 cm) deep each week.
- Get rid of weeds.

### Harvesting

- When the zucchini grow to a length of 6"–8" (15–20 cm) they are ready to be harvested.
- The vegetables should also look dark green, yellow, or white (depending on which variety you are regrowing) and feel firm. If it feels squishy and soft when you touch it, it's probably rotting and should be removed from the plant.
- When you harvest, don't pull the vegetable or tear it from the plant. Instead, use a pair of gardening shears and cut it from the plant at the stem level.

- Store zucchini that hasn't been washed in an open or perforated plastic bag for approximately a week, or freeze it to use later.
- You can also wash the fruit, cut it into 1" (2.5 cm) cubes, and freeze them in freezer bags. Either way, zucchini can be frozen and kept for up to 3 months.

With this, we have reached the end of the chapter on regrowing vegetables from what you buy at the supermarket. In the next chapter, we will look at regrowing fruit so that you can experiment with what you have at home, or what you've bought in your last grocery haul.

---

# 3

# HARVESTING FRESHNESS - REGROWING FRUIT FROM YOUR GROCERIES

My children always found creative uses for fruit peels that we wouldn't consume. While I couldn't help admiring their ingenious ways of annoying each other by tossing these peels, it was a huge hassle for me to clean up after them—every time!

When I began my journey into regrowing fruit, veggies, and herbs from what I could find in my kitchen, I discovered that almost all can be regrown. There are exceptions for example where the seeds or roots are absent. Not only did I find creative ways to utilize fruit scraps, but I also cut back on expensive bills.

One of my biggest grocery woes used to be the amount I needed to spend on fruit. Regrowing my own at home helped me cut back and save up for essentials. Plus, it has also been a great way for me to bond with my family.

In this chapter, we will discuss what fruit you can regrow from your grocery hauls and kitchen waste. For each fruit below, we will cover general instructions that'll give you an idea of optimum temperatures, and simple information pertaining to preparing, planting, growing, caring for, and harvesting your fruit.

Generally, fruit takes more time and care than vegetables because most grow on bushes or trees requiring prolonged maturing periods. However, regrowing your own fruit is well worth the time investment given that fresh produce is your reward.

## REGROWING APPLES

"An apple a day keeps the doctor away" may be a worn out and clichéd term. But regrowing your own apples from the seeds inside the mature fruit bought during your grocery haul will certainly keep your mounting grocery bills away!

### *General Notes About Growing*

- You can certainly regrow apples from fruit that you buy in the grocery stores. For seeds to grow, they need to be taken from fruit that is already ripe.
- Apple seeds need cold and damp conditions for 60–90 days to get ready for germination.
- Not all apple seeds will sprout. Some types, even after sprouting, may not always germinate. To increase your chances, start with a variety of apples so that you know which ones are the most likely to bear fruit.
- If your apple seeds grow and bear fruit, they will not be the same as the fruit you began with. Every apple seed contains a different combination of genes. Nonetheless, you will get tasty yields every time your trees bear fruit.
- Abundant sunshine is required since it considerably impacts the fruits' coloring. Most apple trees do well in places where the average temperature won't exceed 90°F (32°C).
- The best time for planting apple trees is in the spring.

### Preparation and Planting

- Select apples that have a bright color, appear strong, and smell fruity. They should be adequately ripe.
- Consume the apples and keep the seeds inside the core on a moist paper towel. Store in a food container bag for 2–3 days in a cool, dark room.
- After 2–3 days, move the container to the refrigerator. The best fridge temperature will be 40°F (4.4°C).
- Most apple seeds will need 60–90 days in cool, moist conditions to germinate. Don't let the paper towel become dry. Check every 4 days and moisten as needed.
- Within 60–90 days, the seeds should sprout. They are then ready for planting.
- Choose a sunny, well-draining, and fertile spot in your garden. The location should have good air circulation.
- Plant each apple seed 1/2" (13 mm) deep, 12" (30 cm) apart.
- Cover the seeds lightly with a potting mix. Add 1"–2" (2.5–5 cm) of sand to the mix.
- Water the apple seedlings every 10 days until they are well-established.

### Caring Instructions

- Bees are your friends. Apple trees need pollen from other apple trees to bear fruit. This process of cross-pollination is enhanced by insects like bees. Poor pollination reduces fruit numbers and quality.

- Refresh mulch from time to time, but always ensure you place it away from the trunks of the apple trees.
- You will need pesticides depending on the stages of fruit and flower development. Research your local climate and variety of apple trees so that you can apply organic pesticides at the right time.
- Prune the trees on a yearly basis. Remove any branches that look diseased or weak, interfere with the growth of healthy ones, and grow straight upward or inward into the trunks of the parent trees.

### Harvesting

- Be patient with the process. Apple trees are unlikely to sprout fruit in a year. Dwarf varieties begin producing fruit in about 2 years, while standard-sized trees may take 8 years to bear fruit.
- The apples can be plucked when the main color isn't green (except Granny Smith apples—these will have a pink or yellowish blush when adequately ripe).
- The stem should part readily from its branch. Don't yank the apple, just move it around and then up, to break it from the stem.
- If you get any overripe or soft apples, you can preserve the seeds for regrowing and cook the fruit into jams, sauces, or pickles.
- The harvest season can stretch from early to late fall. Only store mid- to late-season apples.
- The apples you store shouldn't have any imperfections or blemishes. Store by wrapping individual fruit in

newspapers or soft tissue rolls. The fruit should not touch each other.

- Store in well-ventilated, airy locations. You can wrap and store them individually in the crisper drawer of your fridge for 4 to 6 weeks.

## REGROWING AVOCADOS (HASS)

If you love guacamole or avocados on toast, don't throw away the avocado pit, use it to grow a new avocado instead! I prefer regrowing Hass avocados since cross-pollination isn't required for them. Cross-pollination will, however, yield a bigger harvest. Let's quickly look at how you can do it, should you wish to.

Avocado trees produce two types of flowers—A and B—which influence how they pollinate. Each tree has parts for male and female genders that are active at opposite times.

The flower of the avocado is "complete," but it acts in a strange way called "protogynous dichogamy." To increase the chance of cross-pollination even more, the flowers of some avocado trees open in the morning as operationally female, close, and then open again as operationally male the next afternoon (type A flowering sequence).

Other avocado tree flowers first open in the afternoon when they are operationally female, close, and then open again the next morning when they are operationally male (type B flowering sequence).

Hass avocado trees are type A. The female flowers on these trees are the ones that open in the morning and close in the afternoon. The next afternoon, they open again as male flowers that make pollen. You can add a B-type avocado plant, like Zutano, to enhance cross-pollination.

Cross-pollination works best when bees can thrive.

### General Notes About Growing

- The best temperature for growing avocados is 60°F–80°F (16°–27°C).
- Rich, fast-draining soil with a layer of potting mix is best for growing avocados.

## Preparation and Planting

- Carefully remove the pit from inside the avocado fruit. Don't cut or mark it.
- Wash the pit thoroughly and make sure there's no flesh sticking to it.
- Pierce the sides of the avocado pit evenly with 3 toothpicks.
- Rest the bottom half of the avocado in a jar of water. The upper half should be above the water's surface.
- Change the water once a week to stop any mold, fungus, or bacteria from growing.
- Keep an eye on the pit for 6–8 weeks. At this time:

  - The top of the pit will dry and form a crack.
  - The crack will go down to the bottom of the pit.
  - A tiny root will emerge.
  - A small sprout will show from the top of the pit.

- Prune the top 2 leaves every time the sprout grows to 6" (15 cm).

- When the sprout reaches 12″ (30 cm) transfer it to a pot or to the garden. The soil should be well-draining with potting mix added.
- Keep the top part of the pit exposed when transferring.
- If you use pots, keep them on a sunny windowsill.

## Caring Instructions

- Ensure that the trees get 6 hours of direct sunlight every day.
- In the beginning, water every 2–3 days. Once the trees are established, reduce watering to twice a week, keeping the top 2" (5 cm) of the soil moist.
- Along with a balanced fertilizer, spray Zincubor on your trees from time to time.
- Prune during late winter by removing the tallest protruding branch from the tree.

## Harvesting

- Avocados need to be harvested by hand. If you don't pick the fruit, they aren't likely to fall off the tree.
- The longer the fruit stays on the tree, the richer it will taste. Just don't let them go too brown or rot.
- The fruit will have a darker color, and be lightly soft without feeling squidgy or mushy.
- Firm and uncut avocados will keep in the fridge, individually stored, for up to two weeks.

## REGROWING BLACKBERRIES

Berries are among the richest sources of antioxidants. When you bite into a blackberry, have you noticed a little "pop" sound when the seed inside bursts in your mouth? These seeds can be dried and used to regrow the fruit!

### *General Notes About Growing*

- Blackberries grow best under full sun and in well-draining soil.
- It is possible to regrow blackberries from the seeds of the store-bought blackberries.
- Blackberries produce plenty of fruit in regions where the temperature is 45°F (7°C) or below for 300 or more hours every year.
- The best time for planting blackberries is in the spring.

### *Preparation and Planting*

- Choose berries that are deep purple or burgundy.
- Put the berries in a blender and, on low speed, blend until the seeds have separated from the pulp. You can also mash the fruit to separate the seeds.
- Pour the pulped fruit into a colander and separate the juice from the pulp. Pick out the seeds with your fingers or tweezers.
- It helps if the seeds have scratches or nicks. You can also gently nick the surface of the seeds using a knife.

- Fill a food container about halfway with peat moss. Put the seeds in the container, buried in the moss.
- Layer 1/2" (13 mm) of peat moss on top and put a piece of paper over your container.
- Keep the container in the refrigerator for 3 months. Check on the peat moss every 4 to 5 days, and mist it whenever it feels too dry.
- In the meantime, you'll need to prepare a makeshift nursery. You can just use a few pots and fill them with seed-starting soil mix.
- After 3 months, spread the seeds on the seed-starting soil mix. Just place one seed in each compartment.
- Sprinkle a thin layer of the same soil over the seeds.
- Mist with water and keep the pots in a flat region that is sunny and warm.
- Ensure the soil stays evenly moist and spray with water if it feels too dry.
- Prepare your final planting site by loosening the soil to a depth of 6" (15 cm). Spread 2 cu yds (1.5 cu m) of compost for every 100 sq ft (9 sq m) of your planting soil.
- Till the soil until compost is at a depth of 6" (15 cm). Smooth everything with a rake.
- 10 days before you transplant the seedlings from the nursery to the permanent site, harden them off by placing them outdoors in shaded regions for 3–4 hours every day. Increase the sunlight duration by 30 minutes daily.

- Place the plants in well-draining soil in a location with full or partial sun. Put a trellis behind the seedlings to help their canes stay upright.
- Before you plant each seedling, make sure the hole is large enough that the roots don't get bent.
- Plant the seeds 2' (60 cm) apart, and leave 7 ' (210 cm) between rows.

### Caring Instructions

- Spread 2"–3" (5 cm–7.5 cm) of organic mulch around the base of the seedlings. Keep a thick mulch layer around the plants at all times
- Irrigate consistently to ensure that the soil stays evenly moist. Ensure the plants get 1" (2.5 cm) of water each week.
- Blackberries thrive with an organic balanced fertilizer with equal parts nitrogen, phosphorus, and potassium (10-10-10 fertilizer).

### Harvesting

- Wait for blackberries that are fully black. Mature berries will be plump and firm, possess a deep black color, and pull free from the plant without you needing to yank on them.
- Every 2 days is the ideal frequency for picking blackberries when they are ripe.
- Harvest when the temperature is lower. Refrigerate the berries as quickly as possible after picking them.

- Blackberries are extremely perishable, even when refrigerated, and will last a maximum of 4–5 days.
- While nothing beats the freshness of newly-harvested fruit, it is possible to preserve blackberries by canning, freezing, or preserving.

## REGROWING BLUEBERRIES

Are there any overripe blueberries lying around your pantry? Now, you don't need to throw them away—just use them for growing new, delicious berries!

### General Notes About Growing

- Optimum temperatures for growing blueberries are 35°F–55°F (2°C–13°C).
- Late fall or early spring are the best seasons for planting blueberries.

### Preparation and Planting

- Put the berries in a re-sealable bag. Store this bag in the freezer for 3 months to cold stratify them. This is an essential step for successful germination.
- Next, retrieve the blueberries from the freezer. Keep the bag at room temperature for 2 hours to let the berries thaw.
- Pour fresh water into a blender until it's three-quarters full, then add 3/4 cup (190 ml) of blueberries. Put the lid on and blend on high for about 10 seconds.
- Pour the pulp into a mixing bowl and let it sit for 5 minutes. Some pulp will float to the surface. You have to discard that.
- After 5 minutes, strain and then add fresh water. Repeat the process of letting it stand for 5 minutes.

- Pour the mixture through a sieve or colander with wire mesh. Get the small, rust-colored seeds out of the sieve. Put them on a paper towel to dry.
- Fold the paper towel to cover all the seeds, and moisten it with water.
- Put the towel in a re-sealable bag and close it.
- Place the bag in a warm, dark location like a pantry.
- Keep an eye on the towel. If it becomes too dry, moisten it once again.
- The seedlings should sprout within a few weeks to a few months.
- Once the seedlings sprout, plant them in pots topped with a soilless potting mix. The best kind will have 40% peat moss, 20% vermiculite, 20% pine bark, and 20% sand.
- Keep the pots in a sunny area like a windowsill.
- Once the blueberry seedlings grow into bushes that can be transplanted, begin hardening them by leaving the pots out in the sun for increased durations each day for a week.
- Get your permanent planting site ready. Dig holes 20" (50 cm) deep and 18" (45 cm) wide.
- Space the bushes 4'–5' (120–150 cm) apart in rows. Keep a distance of 8' (240 cm) between the rows.
- Mulch the top of the soil using the same soilless potting mix referred to above.
- Set a bush into each hole, and pack it tight with soil.

## *Caring Instructions*

- Fertilize 1 month from the date of planting by using 1/2 fl oz (15 ml) of a 10-10-10 fertilizer. This is a balanced fertilizer with equal parts nitrogen, phosphorus, and potassium.
- Remove any branches that cross (rub) against one other, arch to the ground, or block off too much sunlight from the core of the bush.
- Mulch regularly.
- Water 1"–2" (2.5–5 cm) every week.
- Pinch back any flowers or blossoms growing on new plants so that the sole focus of the plants remains on fruit production.

## *Harvesting*

- Typically, blueberries growing from seeds will bear fruit in their second year. So, be patient.
- Once the fruit is a deep purple in color, lightly tickle the branches to see which berries fall off. You shouldn't have to pull the berries from the branch.
- You can either consume them fresh or dry them and store them in the freezer for 2 weeks. In the refrigerator, they should keep for 4–7 days.

## REGROWING CANTALOUPE

Fresh and full of water, cantaloupes are an ideal summer fruit. You can regrow them from store-bought cantaloupes. However, many store-bought varieties are hybrids and don't come with seeds inside—so look for fruit that are ripe and organic.

### General Notes About Growing

- Cantaloupe sold in grocery stores may be developed from hybrid plants, so the melon you grow won't be like the one you originally had. It will still be edible and delicious.
- The best temperature for growing cantaloupe is 65°F–75°F (18°C–24°C).
- Cantaloupe prefers warmer weather, so spring is the ideal planting time.

### Preparation and Planting

- Slice open a ripe cantaloupe and scrape out the seeds and membrane.
- Remove all strings and drop the seeds into a bowl.
- Fill the bowl halfway with water and add a pinch of dish soap. You need this to rinse away any sugar clinging to the seeds.
- Drain the water, rinse the seeds twice with clear water, and lay them on a paper towel.

- Allow the seeds to dry thoroughly. This will take 2 to 3 days. Once dry and brittle, pour into an envelope and mark the date.
- Place the envelope in a completely dry air-tight jar. Shut the lid and keep it in the refrigerator until the next spring.
- Close to that time, prepare your garden patch for planting.
- Remove rocks and weeds, and mix a 3" (7.5 cm) layer of compost into the soil.
- Raise the soil to form a flat-topped hill (do it for 6 seeds each). Each hill should be 1' (30 cm) tall and 2' (60 cm) across.
- Plant 6 seeds into each hill, and spread soil over the entire surface. Make sure to bury each seed 1" (2.5 cm) deep.

### Caring Instructions

- Once they sprout, cover the ground around the seedlings with an even layer of mulch.
- Water 1" (2.5 cm) deep every week. Aim for the soil and stems, not the leaves.
- Fertilize once the plants reach a height of 4" (10 cm).

### Harvesting

- 90 days after planting the seeds, cantaloupes are ready to be harvested.

- Ripeness is indicated by tan or yellow rinds. There should be a faint aroma of cantaloupe.
- When your melon is ready to be picked, the connecting stem will look cracked.
- Make sure that the fruit vines are dry and don't hurt them when you pick the fruit.
- Overripe cantaloupes that have fallen off the vine should be composted.
- You can consume cantaloupe fresh, or store the fruit uncut in the fridge for 7–10 days.

## REGROWING CHESTNUTS

Sweet and healthy, chestnuts are becoming more and more popular in different cuisines. It is absolutely possible to regrow your own chestnuts from store-bought ones.

### General Notes About Growing

- Always grow chestnuts from store-bought varieties that are fresh and organic. The more processed the nuts are, the less likely they will be able to produce new yields.
- Chestnuts need to spend a while in a cold environment to sprout properly.
- The chestnut tree can withstand temperatures as high as 81°F–88°F (27°C–31°C) and as low as 3°F (−16°C), and it can adapt to a climate with mean monthly temperatures exceeding 50°F (10°C) for at least 6 months without suffering any harm.
- Fall is a good time to plant chestnuts.

### Preparation and Planting

- Plant 1 to 2 chestnuts in a pot of compost and leave it outdoors over the winter. Chilly weather and frost help the chestnut rest, and when the weather gets warmer in the spring, the nut will start to grow.
- Another option is to put the chestnuts in a re-sealable bag and leave them in a cold place, like the fridge, for 4 to 6 weeks. Then, take them out and plant them in pots of compost.

- Most of the time, you will see signs of growth in the pots 3 to 6 weeks after sowing the seeds.
- Once the seedlings have grown tall enough, move them to their permanent spot, which should have a lot of sunlight and soil that drains well.
- Dig a hole that is at least 1.5 to 2 times wider and deeper than the root ball of the seedling you want to plant.
- It is very important that when you plant your trees, only the roots and none of the stems are in the ground.
- Fill the holes with soil and tamp them down to make sure the trees stand up straight.

### Caring Instructions

- Make sure to water your young trees well right after you plant them. After that, give each tree about a gallon of water every week.
- Every few weeks, weed and add mulch.
- You will need to prune to get rid of any low-growing branches on younger trees and any secondary limbs with narrow crotch angles.
- To make the soil more fertile, you can add compost several times a year, or you can add fertilizer just as the trees are coming out of dormancy in late winter or early spring.

### Harvesting

- Most types of chestnut trees don't start making nuts until they are 3 to 7 years old.
- Early- to mid-fall is when nuts will start to fall from the trees. They will still be in their large, prickly shells, which will start to dry out and split open.
- Now is the time to start gathering the crops. If the hulls are green or haven't split, they aren't ready yet.
- Wear gloves every time you pick chestnuts.
- If you don't plan to use the chestnuts right away, you can keep them in their shells in the fridge for up to a month or freeze them for up to a year in temperatures below 25°F (4°C).

## REGROWING COCONUT

Be it for the sweet flesh inside or the water inside a young fruit, coconuts are incredibly nourishing. Did you know you could regrow the tree from just one store-bought fruit?

### *General Notes About Growing*

- Use a whole coconut that has gone entirely brown at the husk level and has developed hair-like fibers all around it.
- Ideal temperatures for growing coconut are 68°F–89°F (20°C–32°C).
- When young, coconut palms grow slowly, but as they age, they grow faster. If you live in a colder region, keep your baby coconut tree inside and supplement sunshine with artificial light.

### *Preparation and Planting*

- Ensure the coconut is fully mature and has the 3 eye-like structures at the top intact. The shoots and roots will come out of one of these eyes.
- The coconut should have water inside it.
- You'll need a bucket and a rock.
- Fill the bucket with warm (not hot) water to speed up germination.
- Submerge the coconut completely in the water. Use the rock to weigh it down—or any other heavy object. Be careful not to damage the coconut in the process.

- Keep the bucket in a warm spot for 3–4 days.
- After that time, take a re-sealable bag and splash some of the bucket water into the bag. Just a tiny bit—you don't need to submerge the coconut any longer.
- Place the coconut inside the bag with all eyes facing upward. Place the bag in a bowl with the eyes of the coconut still facing up.
- Move the bowl to a warm, dark place.
- Put the bag next to the water heater if you have one. If you can't, just put it somewhere warm and dark.
- It could take anywhere between a few weeks to a few months for the seed to sprout, but it shouldn't take more than 3 months.
- When the roots start to grow, you can take the coconut out of its sealed bag. Wet a paper towel and wrap it around the roots.
- Put the coconut back into the bag and make sure to check on it regularly.
- When the roots are between 6" and 8" long (15–20 cm), your fruit is ready to be moved into soil.
- Dig a hole between 2'–5' (60 cm–1.5 m). Fill most of the hole with layers of peat, sand, and topsoil.
- Plant the coconut with the root facing downward and cover half of it with another layer of peat, sand, and soil. Allow the seedling and the top part of the coconut to remain on top of the soil.

### Caring Instructions

- Water the plant twice a week.
- Treat your coconut trees with a fungicide like Fosetyl-al to thwart fungus growth.
- Mulch regularly.
- Fertilize once every 4 months.
- Prune any dead leaves using a sharp knife.

### Harvesting

- Examine each coconut husk. Coconuts with brown husks are ready to be plucked off the tree.
- In some cases, ripe coconuts will also fall to the ground for you to collect easily.
- For a tree that's yielding plenty of fruit, harvest from the tree or get the fruit that falls off the tree every 40 days.
- For ones that don't yield as much, check back and harvest every 90 days.
- Consume the water fresh or use it to cook with. You can grate the coconut flesh and store it, or eat it as is.

## REGROWING DRAGON FRUIT

Densely juicy and sweet, dragon fruit can yield flesh that's blood-red, purple, or yellow. It's a great fruit to consume raw, and now, you can regrow it in the convenience of your home!

### *General Notes About Growing*

- To regrow dragon fruit from store-bought fruit, all you need is the seeds inside. I love to munch on these little seeds because of their delicious "popping" sounds, but now, you can grow new plants with them!
- The best temperatures for growing dragon fruit are 32°F–90°F (0°C–32°C).
- Summer is the best time for growing dragon fruit.

### *Preparation and Planting*

- To grow dragon fruit, choose a location with at least 6 hours of direct sunshine each day, whether that's in your yard or on a sunny windowsill.
- Pick a potting soil that drains effectively and has a high organic matter content. It should also have good moisture retention properties. I prefer the Miracle-Gro seed starting potting mix for its foolproof nature—and it is very reasonable on the pocket as a pack that is 1.8 gal (7 L) costs about $4.
- Scoop the black seeds from a ripe dragon fruit after slicing it in half.

- Lay out the seeds on a damp paper towel for a minimum of 12 hours to remove any remaining fruit flesh and pulp.
- Next, sprinkle the seeds across the surface of the soil. Cover them with a thin layer—you don't have to worry if the soil barely covers the seeds. They needn't be planted too deep.
- Water consistently to ensure the soil is evenly moist.

### Caring Instructions

- As the seedlings begin to grow, thin them periodically to give them room for growth.
- Once the plant reaches a height of 12″ (30 cm), it will demand a support system, much like cucumbers. Set up a trellis or stake to help the plant grow upward.
- Prune any dying, diseased, or dead branches.
- Fertilize once a month.
- Water the soil 1″ (2.5 cm) deep every week.

### Harvesting

- A plant grown from the seed may take up to 5 years to bear fruit, so be patient.
- Dragon fruit trees are simple to harvest once they've begun producing.
- Look for ripe fruit with wilting "wings" (the skin flaps on the exterior of the fruit).
- Gently twist to harvest. As soon as it's mature, the stem will disintegrate and the fruit will fall off. Do not let the

fruit fall from the plant on its own—this likely means the fruit is overripe.

- When stored in the refrigerator, unpeeled dragon fruit will last for up to 2 weeks.

## REGROWING DURIAN

Known for its size and smell, the durian fruit is very sweet on the palate. It is an acquired taste, but if you love it, then you can rejoice! It's absolutely possible to regrow the fruit from the seeds of the original fruit.

### General Notes About Growing

- The ideal temperature for growing durian is 75°F–86°F (24°C–30°C).
- Always plant during the hottest and rainiest part of the year in your region. Durian is a tropical fruit.

### Preparation and Planting

- Take out the durian core (the seed of the fruit), remove any flesh sticking to it, wash it and let it dry.
- Soak the core in water for 2 days to speed up the germination process.
- Dig a 1.5′ (45 cm) hole and mix organic compost into the soil.
- Place the seed on top and push it down a little bit with your finger. The majority of the seed should be visible.
- Water the seed well.
- You should notice sprouting within a week.
- If you live in cold climates, it is possible to grow the seed indoors.

○ Put your seeds and a wet paper towel in a plastic bag and seal it.

○ Put the bag in a spot that gets direct sunlight for 4–6 hours. Try a windowsill or use a grow light.

○ After 4–5 days, roots should start to grow from the durian seeds. Find small yellow or brown appendages coming out of the seeds, and plant them whenever the roots are lengthier than the seeds themselves.

○ Put the seeds on top of the compost and potting soil in a pot. Gently push the seeds into the soil, but don't let them go all the way in.

○ Make sure that your durian gets 1–2 gal (4–8 L) of water every day. Water should be spread out between morning and afternoon.

## Caring Instructions

- Fertilize once a month with a nitrogen-rich fertilizer.
- For the first year, water the seed with 1–2 gal (4–8 L) every day.
- Weed regularly.
- Prune after the first year.

## Harvesting

- Harvest durian fruit by cutting the stem 1"–1.5" (2.5–4 cm) from where the fruit is attached.
- Use a sharp knife or any other cutting device.
- In some countries, durian is also harvested by skilled tree climbers.

- Consume durian fresh. After opening, if you need to store it, always use air-tight containers because the smell will overpower other items in your fridge. It will keep in the fridge for 5 days.

REGROWING GRAPES

Sweet-tasting and so attractive to look at, you can regrow grapes as long as you have the stems from the original fruit. So, when getting the fruit from the stores, always choose the bunches that are on the stems and not stored individually in plastic containers.

***General Notes About Growing***

- Grapevines prefer moist, well-draining soil.
- The ideal temperature for growing grapes is 77°–90°F (25°C–32°C).
- Although grapevines may take some shade, if fruit development is the main aim, they must be placed in direct sunlight.
- You should also consider the structure you'll employ to hold the vine. When they reach their full maturity, they may become rather hefty as a climbing plant.
- Building a sturdy framework before planting the vine is highly recommended. Examples of such a framework include an existing trellis, fence, or house wall.
- Grapes prefer loose, well-draining soil.
- Ideal time for planting grapevines is spring after the first frost has passed.

### *Preparation and Planting*

- Begin by removing the grapes from the stems. Try to select a bunch with a central stem at least 4" (10 cm) long.
- Remove the side shoots from the main branch, saving 1 or 2 at the cutting's top using scissors. Try trimming the branch's bottom at a 45-degree angle.
- Dip the bottom into a rooting hormone. A 2 oz (55 g) bottle comes at about $5.
- Prepare your pot with a seed-raising mixture.
- Make a hole in the soil with a dibber. They are available for about $11–$14.
- Position the cutting within the pot gently and firmly, and cover the soil around it.
- Water well.
- Keep the pot in a warm, humid location. It will take a few weeks for the cuttings to show growth.
- Once a cutting shows leaves, you can transfer it to a larger pot.
- When ready to transplant outside, choose a spot that has a good amount of sunlight.
- Make a hole equal to the pot's depth so the vine can be placed at the same depth as it was in the pot.
- Once you plant the vine, mulch around the base of the plant to a depth of 2"–4" (5–10 cm) and ensure the ground retains as much moisture as possible.

*Caring Instructions*

- During the first year of growth, the grapevine shouldn't be pruned, but some of the branches may need to be tied to some form of support.
- When the plant goes dormant, trim the trunk to 3 buds. This requires cutting down a large amount of the vine, which may appear severe, but will foster a thick central stem.
- Green branches emerge along major stems. After a year, these new branches will yield grapes. In areas with high nitrogen levels, these may develop too many shoots. When this happens, too-closely-spaced shoots must be removed to regulate leaf and shoot development and keep the vine productive. Each bunch of grapes needs 15 sun-exposed leaves to mature properly.
- When bunches appear in early June, stems should be thinned and spaced 3"–4" (7.5–10 cm) apart. To maximize grape quality, thin bunches to 1 per stalk.

*Harvesting*

- Grapes are best judged on taste. Each variety has its own flavor, so knowing what yours "should" taste like will help. Grapes should be sweet, not sour.
- Check your grapes. They should be uniformly dark, and for green grapes, slightly yellowish. Grapes are the appropriate color before they're totally sweet, so don't go on appearances alone. After displaying the

appropriate color, grapes take 1 to 3 weeks to reach maximum sweetness.

- Grapes should be plump, thick, and juicy. If they're shriveling, you've waited too long.
- Grapes contain the most sugar on warm, bright days and preserve well without surface moisture.
- Support a bunch of grapes in one palm and clip the entire cluster off the vine. Breaking off the cluster can injure the plant, so use a sharp instrument.
- Put each cluster in a bucket or pail.
- Consume fresh, or store in a well-ventilated location in your fridge for 4–7 days.

REGROWING GUAVA

Prized for its juicy taste, guava can be enjoyed raw, made into jams, or juiced. Most guava trees will bear fruit in their third year. And yes, you can absolutely regrow them from the seeds in the fruit you buy from grocery stores!

### General Notes About Growing

- You need to take good care of your guava trees. Poor care can result in no fruit production.
- Guava can be regrown from the seeds of the fruit you buy from grocery stores.
- Ideal growing temperature is 73°–78°F (23°C–26°C).
- Spring or fall seasons are best for planting guava seeds.

### Preparation and Planting

- Guava is among the easiest fruits to germinate. The main concern is to start with seeds from a fresh, healthy fruit.
- Rinse the seeds in soft water (contains little or no dissolved calcium or magnesium) at room temperature.
- Wrap the seeds in a paper towel and let them dry for 2 hours.
- Next, pour them into a cup of warm water, and soak them for 3–4 hours.
- To give the plant the room it needs to establish roots, use a pot at least 3 gal (11 L) in capacity and 10" (25 cm)

in diameter. Choosing a clay container with enough drainage holes at the bottom is the best option.

- Prepare the pot with the seed mix and sprinkle the seeds into it.
- Keep the pot in a warm, well-lit spot, such as a windowsill.
- Water with a misting spray.
- The seeds should germinate within 2–8 weeks.
- Plant outdoors when the spot reaches 6–8 hours of sunlight.
- Dig 2' (60 cm) into the ground. When digging, be sure to clear the area of any rocks or other debris.
- Using the instrument you used to dig the hole, loosen the earth at the bottom a little bit.
- Place the seedlings within this hole, ensuring that all foliage stays above the soil.
- After you've filled the hole, avoid compacting the earth too tightly; instead, let it stay loose.

### Caring Instructions

- Water your seedlings 2 to 3 times a week.
- After a year, fertilize once every 3 months. Scatter the fertilizer around the tree without letting it come in contact with the trunk.
- Start pruning 3–4 months after the tree has sprouted. If the tree has multiple trunks, find the middle one and cut the others away at the base. Cut any branches sprouting from other branches, as well as any damaged or dead branches.

- If you live in a cold region, cover your tree with a tarp during times of frost.

### Harvesting

- Color change is an indicator of maturity. Red or pink guava can be picked when the peel is light green to yellow.
- White guava should be picked when it is full-sized and green to light green in color.
- Don't wait until the guava fruit start falling on their own. They can burst on the hard ground and cause a mess. Instead, when they look and feel ripe enough, twist them off the branches gently.
- Ripe guava can be kept in the fridge for 5–7 days.

## REGROWING HAZELNUTS

Hazelnuts are prized for their sweet flesh and innumerable health benefits. And guess what? You can completely regrow them at home!

### General Notes About Growing

- Hazelnuts don't do well in extremes of heat or long dry seasons.
- The best temperatures for growing hazelnuts are 55°F–60°F (13°C–16°C).
- Work with hazelnuts picked during late summer, which have shells of a solid, brownish-red color.
- Hazelnuts need to be cross-pollinated. Plant them in pairs with other hazelnuts, and always begin with a good variety. Research your local climate conditions to know which 2 or 3 hazelnut varieties will grow best.
- You will need a germination mat for regrowing hazelnuts. The simple ones cost as little as $10.

### Preparation and Planting

- Rub the side of each nut with a fine-grained rasp. This will weaken the outer hull.
- Continue rubbing until you see a pale patch forming on the surface.
- Place the nuts in cold water for a day. Scoop out and throw away any nuts that float to the surface. These won't germinate as they should.

- Retrieve the hazelnuts that have sunk to the bottom.
- Prepare 8" (20 cm) containers with half coarse sand and half seed compost mixture.
- Plant the hazelnuts to a depth of 1"–2" (2.5–5 cm).
- Keep each pot in a clear, large plastic bag. Leave the tops of the bags open.
- With the pots inside, keep the bags in your refrigerator or anywhere with an optimum temperature of 32°F–40°F (0°C–4.4°C).
- Let 2 to 4 months pass. Moisten the mixture in the containers from time to time if they get too dry.
- After this period, remove the bags and transfer the containers to a partly-shaded cold frame on a germination mat.
- Keep the temperatures set to 70°F (21°C) at night and 80°F (27°C) in the mornings.
- Add water to the sand mix whenever necessary.
- Look for sprouting in a month's time. Leave the germination mat in place after the initial sprouts show up.
- Acclimate the seedlings to full sun for 2 weeks in the early fall.
- Once they are 8"–10" (20–25 cm) in height, move the seedlings to a partly shaded area and grow them in your permanent soil.
- Transplant them to a bed which has acidic, moist soil. Keep a distance of 15'–20' (4.5–6 m) between the plants.

## Caring Instructions

- Water the soil 1" (2.5 cm) deep every 10 days.
- Hazelnuts will naturally develop into a shrub, but you may also trim them into a tree. To construct a tree shape, pick 6 sturdy branches toward the top section of the bush and cut anything below, including any low-hanging branches.
- Sprinkle composted organic matter or a balanced fertilizer with equal parts nitrogen, phosphorus, and potassium in spring. Fertilize 100 sq ft (9 sq m) with 2 lb (900 g) of the fertilizer.
- Check for any weeds, and mulch from time to time.

## Harvesting

- Hazelnuts planted from seeds need 7–8 years to bear fruit, so don't lose patience too soon!
- When the husks turn yellow in the fall, you can harvest the sweet nuts.
- You can pick them off the tree, and if they're ripe enough, they'll easily come off if you shake the branches.
- Keep the nuts in containers, nets, cloth bags, or slatted boxes in a dry, well-ventilated place.

## REGROWING KIWIFRUIT

The kiwifruit is the perfect blend of sweet and tart. Regrowing from store-bought ones is possible and an enjoyable process.

*General Notes About Growing*

- The black seeds inside the kiwifruit can be used to regrow new fruit.
- Kiwifruit will do well in most climates that experience a month of temperatures below 45°F (7°C).
- Early spring or late fall is the best time to plant.

*Preparation and Planting*

- Always choose an original fruit that is fresh, adequately ripe without being rotten, and organic.
- Take the seeds out of the kiwifruit. Start with a few varieties because once they grow, you need to make sure you have both male and female plants for producing subsequent fruit.
- Put water and kiwifruit seeds in a blender to detach the seeds from the sticky membrane. Use a colander to wash seeds in the sink.
- Put the seeds on a moist paper towel and put them in a re-sealable bag.
- Put it somewhere warm.
- Check the seeds regularly until you see them sprouting. Make sure that the paper towel is always damp.

- Plant a few of the sprouted seedlings in a pot. In case the seedlings are stuck to the paper towel, tear it into small chunks and plant them with the paper in the pots.
- Keep the pots on a sunny windowsill.
- When tiny leaves form, separate the plants and only keep 2 per pot.
- At this point, it will take the kiwifruit plants about 3 weeks to grow more leaves. After that, they will use energy from the sun to keep growing.

### Caring Instructions

- As the leaves grow further, transplant each plant to separate pots and fertilize using a starter fertilizer to boost growth.
- Pollen is made by the many stamens on male flowers. Female flowers have an ovary that is well-developed and long, gooey stigmas in the middle that hold the pollen.
- For pollination to work, you need at least 1 male plant for every 5 female plants. Keep them near to each other in their own pots, and nature will take care of the rest.
- Remember that kiwifruit grows on vines that can get as long as 30' (9 m) and weigh a lot. Like other climbing plants, they grow best on vertical structures that give them support and let in more light.
- Your plant will start to send out shoots as it grows. You will need to wire the vines to the trellis so that these shoots will grow up the support. Once a year, you should prune kiwifruit plants.

*Harvesting*

- Your plants should start making fruit after a few years, or even in the same year if they are hardy or super-hardy. Yields may start out small, but as the plant grows, they usually increase every year.
- Cut a sample fruit to see if the seeds inside are black. This is an indicator of your plant being ready to harvest.
- When the fruit's skin starts to change color, cut it off at the stem.
- Kiwifruit can be stored for up to 4 to 6 months at 31°F–32°F (0.5°C –0°C), as long as they are kept cold and distant from other ripe fruit.
- They will last longer if they are kept at a colder temperature.
- For kiwifruit to last up to 2 months, pick them while they are still hard and put them into the fridge right away in a plastic bag with holes.

## REGROWING LEMONS

Lemons are among the most useful fruits to have around the house. They are wonderfully citrusy and come with a good dose of vitamin C. It is possible to regrow new lemons from store-bought ones.

### *General Notes About Growing*

- Lemons prefer temperatures of about 70°F (21°C).
- The best season to grow lemons is spring.
- You can regrow lemons from store-bought ones using the seeds in the fruit.
- Seed-grown trees are not exact copies of their parents. It can take 5 years or more for them to bear fruit, and the fruit is usually not as exemplary as that of the parent tree. Even so, they will taste great and be very good for you.

### *Preparation and Planting*

- Populate a seed-raising tray up to 3/4" (2 cm) from the top with moist seed-raising mix. Press down on the soil in the tray to make it firm.
- Cut a lemon in half and remove the seeds with a knife. To get rid of the pulp and sugar, clean the seeds in a bowl of warm water.
- Put the clean seeds in a bowl of water and leave them there for 8 hours.

- Scatter the lemon seeds on the surface of the soil while they are still slightly damp. Spread a 1/2″ (13 mm) thin coating of seed-raising mix over the seeds and gently press the soil down.
- Mist the top of the soil with water to keep the soil moist while the seeds are growing. To help the soil keep its moisture, stretch plastic wrap over the tray.
- Keep the tray in a warm location.
- In 3 to 6 weeks, the lemon seeds should start to grow. After the seeds sprout, take off the plastic wrap and put the tray near a sunny window where it will get indirect sunlight.
- Fill 6-inch pots with moist potting soil that drains well. Place one lemon seedling in the middle of each pot at the same depth it was sown in the seed-raising tray.
- Put the pots in an area that is 60°–70°F (16°C–21°F) and gets direct sunlight for at least 4 hours a day.
- After the last frost date, put the seedlings in the garden when they are big enough to handle. Put them in the ground at the same depth they were in the pots.

### Caring Instructions

- Keep the soil moist while the plants grow and get their roots set. Water about twice a week, and change how often you water after it rains.
- Use a citrus plant food or a fertilizer with a nitrogen-phosphorus-potassium ratio of at least 2-1-1 to feed the lemon plants.

- As the lemon tree grows, you should trim it in early spring.

## Harvesting

- When the skin goes from green to yellow and shiny, lemons are ready to be picked.
- The width of the fruit should be between 2"–3" (5–7.5 cm), and it should be easy to squeeze.
- You can also pick lemons when they are still a bit green and let them ripen at room temperature.
- Don't pick lemons while they're still dark green, tough, or have a tough skin.
- Picking lemons by hand is the best way to do it.
- To get the fruit off the tree, hold it in your hand and lightly twist it.
- Lemons can also be kept for up to 3 weeks in the crisper drawer of the fridge.

## REGROWING MANGOES

Sweet and juicy, mangoes are the ideal summer fruit. You can regrow it from the seed of the original store-bought fruit. The fruit you grow won't be exactly like the one you originally bought, but will still taste delicious.

### *General Notes About Growing*

- The best time to plant mango trees is summer.
- For best growth, mango plants need a humidity level of at least 50 percent.
- Mangoes thrive in temperatures warmer than 50°F (10°C). They can live in temperatures as low as 40°F (4.4°C), but very cold weather or frost can hurt them.

### *Preparation and Planting*

- Start with a ripe mango.
- Next, gently rub the pulp and stringy parts of the mango fruit off of the husk.
- When most of the pulp is gone, dry the husk with a towel and put it somewhere to dry for another day or 2.
- The next step is to cut the husk open.
- Cut off the edges with good scissors. You could also hold the husk in a vice and cut off the edges with a fine wood saw.
- Gently pull the seed out of the husk and peel away any paper-like layers that are loose around it.

- Put warm water on a cloth until it is damp but not dripping.
- Wrap the wet cloth around your mango seed and put it in a plastic bag.
- Put the bag somewhere warm and make sure the towel doesn't dry out.
- Open the paper towel every few days and look for signs of growth.
- If you need to, wet the paper towel again.
- Once the seed starts to grow, move it to a pot that is 6" (15 cm) deep.
- Fill the pot with potting mix and put the sprouted seeds on top.
- Cover the seed with an inch of potting mix, water it, and add more potting mix on top.
- Put your plant somewhere sunny, but not directly in the hot sun, where it could dry out.

- Keep soil moist but not soggy.
- Once the mango plant is 1 or 2 years old, you can move it outside.

### Caring Instructions

- About 26 gal (100 L) of water are needed for each young tree every week. Once the plant is established, it only needs water when it is flowering or producing fruit.
- Mango trees don't need to be pruned often, except to get rid of diseased or broken branches and infrequent growth that doesn't belong.
- For first-year saplings, fish emulsion is a wise choice of fertilizer. Use a 6-6-6 fertilizer that also has magnesium 6 times a year for the tree's second and third years, and then only 4 times a year after that.

### Harvesting

- Mangoes are usually ready to be picked when they are still firm but ripe. This can happen anywhere from 3 to 5 months after they bloom, depending on the type and the weather.
- Most of the time, the color will change from green to yellow, maybe with a touch of pink. When the fruit is ready, the inside has gone from white to yellow.
- To harvest your mangoes, pull on the fruit. It's ready when the stem comes off easily. You can continue to

pick the fruit this way, or you can use pruning shears to remove them.

- Once mangoes are ripe, they should be put in the fridge. Whole, ripe mangoes can be kept in the fridge for up to 5 days.

## REGROWING ORANGES

The next time you eat an orange, keep the white pips aside. Did you know how useful these tiny life-givers are? You can grow new orange trees from them!

**General Notes About Growing**

- The ideal temperature for growing orange trees is 77°F (25°C).
- Early to mid-spring constitutes the best season for planting oranges.
- When growing the fruit, always try to ensure that the original fruit you take the pips from is organic and as fresh as possible. For best results, use pips from a ripe, juicy orange.

**Preparation and Planting**

- Wash the orange pips in warm water.
- Make 4 drainage holes in a plastic container and fill it halfway with disinfected potting soil.
- Plant the seeds about 1/2" (13 mm) deep in the potting soil. Add just enough water to hydrate the soil, but not so much that it becomes soggy.
- Wrap the container with plastic wrap or put it in a plastic bag.
- Place the pot in a warm location. At this point, sunlight is not required.
- Check regularly to ensure that it is still moist.

- Once the seed has sprouted, relocate it to a sunny location and discard the plastic.
- Ensure the soil remains moist at all times.
- When the seedling has grown enough, move it to a more permanent container or outside.

### Caring Instructions

- Growing orange trees often need 1"–1-1/2" (2.5–4 cm) of water each week.
- Each tree should have 1–2 lb (450–900 g) of nitrogen each year for a maximum yield of edible oranges. Fertilizer should include potassium, phosphorus, and a variety of micronutrients.
- Prune any branches that are less than 1' (30 cm) from the ground. Remove any damaged or dead branches as soon as they are discovered.

### Harvesting

- Choose oranges with a sweet, citrusy, and fresh smell (not moldy). Taste a single fruit before harvesting a whole tree.
- Grasp the ripe fruit in your hand and twist it gently until the stem detaches.
- Consume the fruit fresh, or store it in the crisper drawer for up to a month.

## REGROWING PAPAYA

Ripe papayas are delicious and nutritious. The stunning orange-yellow fruit is a rich source of vitamins A, C, and folates. Regrowing papaya from store-bought fruit is possible from the seeds.

### General Notes About Growing

- The black seeds of the papaya fruit are used to regrow papaya plants.
- Papayas grow well in tropical and subtropical climates with temperatures between 70°F–90°F (21°C–32°C).
- They can be sown in spring, during the summer months, or in early fall.

### Preparation and Planting

- To ensure growth choose a variety that is locally grown. Chances are, the more exotic or distance-sourced fruit may not be suited to your climatic zones.
- The fruit should be healthy, ripe but not rotten, and organic.
- Cut open the fruit and collect the black seeds from inside.
- Papaya seeds are sown directly into the soil. They do not like transplants.
- Prepare a bed in the sunny part of the garden to sow the seeds.

- Papaya grows best in well-draining, loamy soil. A raised bed around the plants will ensure adequate drainage of the soil.
- Sprinkle as many seeds as possible in the bed; if possible, sow them in multiple beds to increase the chances of productivity. Cover the seeds with compost soil.
- Cover the topsoil with mulch to retain moisture.
- Water regularly and adequately. Prevent waterlogging as excess water can kill the growing plants.
- Saplings appear after a month. Thinning them out will ensure a better supply of resources for each plant.
- Plants can be male, female, or bisexual. The male plants do not bear fruit. At this stage it is impossible to distinguish them; hence, allowing enough plants to grow will increase the chances of pollination.
- After 3 months, add a slow-release fertilizer to the soil to improve plant nutrition.

### Caring Instructions

- Let the plants grow to a height of 3' (90 cm). This is the time they flower. Bees and insects are the pollinating agents.
- The male plants bloom first; the flowers are thin-stalked with many small blossoms.
- The female flowers are bigger, closer to the tree, and single. One male plant per 10–15 plants is sufficient for pollination. Remove the rest of the males from the bed.
- Papayas need sunlight.

- Water the plants regularly with a sprinkler to avoid excess watering.
- Papayas are heavy feeders, so add compost from time to time. Use a fertilizer with good nitrogen content. Be sure to water after adding fertilizer.

### Harvesting

- The plants bear fruit after about 10 months. Young green fruit can be used in stews, curries, and salads.
- The best time to harvest ripe papayas is when the skin of the fruit starts to turn yellow. Papayas bear fruit throughout the year as long as they get proper sunlight. The other requirements are well-draining, fertile soil and adequate water.
- To ensure a year-round supply, plant papayas regularly.

REGROWING PEACHES

The warm-toned peaches are deliciously sweet with a hint of acidity. A medium-sized peach is surprisingly low in calories and rich in fiber and vitamins like A and C. Grow juicy peaches in your garden from store-bought fruit.

### General Notes About Growing

- Peach belongs to the *rose* family and is widely grown in warm temperate climatic zones.
- Peaches cannot grow where winter temperatures fall below 10°F to 15°F (23°C to 26°C). On the other hand, they also seem not to grow well where the winters are mild. Most varieties need specific chilling hours of winter temperature between 32°F–45°F (0°C–7°C) to break winter dormancy and get into normal growth and bloom.
- The plant grows well in well-draining gravely or loamy soil.
- Early spring is the best time to sow the seeds, a month before the last frost.

### Preparation and Planting

- Clean the peach pit with a soft-bristled brush, wash it, and pat dry.
- Put the pit in a plastic bag or a jar filled with moist potting soil containing peat moss, vermiculite, or sand. Mark the date on the bag with a pen. Store in the

refrigerator between 33°F–41°F (0.6°C–5°C) for 3 to 4 months.

- Thick white root sprouts will appear; considering that the best time to sow is a month before the last frost, the seed can be kept in the refrigerator until that time, taking care it does not mold.
- A container with drainage holes should be filled with organically enriched, well-draining soil. Half peat moss and half sand mixtures, perlite, or vermiculite, are suitable. Peaches can also be directly planted in the garden soil.
- Sow the seeds 2" (5 cm) deep in the soil in a pot or 12" (30 cm) deep in the garden soil. Press the soil gently.
- Keep the pot in bright but indirect sunlight.
- Water by spray misting immediately after planting. Water regularly and uniformly throughout the growing season. Peaches do not tolerate excess water. The optimal temperature for the plant's growth is 70°F (21°C).
- Once the shoots sprout, shift the pot to a sunny area with ambient temperatures between 55°F–70°F (13°C–21°C).
- Reduce watering, allowing the soil to dry out between waterings.
- When the plant shows 5 to 6 leaves, transplant it into a larger container with enriched, well-draining soil or into the garden.
- Plant the trees 15'–20' (4.5–6 m) apart.

### Caring Instructions

- Growing peach plants need nitrogen-rich fertilizer. The ideal NPK or nitrogen, phosphorus, and potassium fertilizer ratio should be 10-10-10. Add 1 lb (450 g) of fertilizer after 6 weeks of planting.
- The next spring, add 3/4 lb (340 g) of fertilizer and repeat in early summer to ensure good crop production.
- From the third year onward 1 lb (450 g) of nitrogen-based fertilizer in early spring when new growth appears is adequate.
- Stop fertilizing 2 months before the start of fall.
- After harvesting in late summer to early fall, peach trees should be pruned regularly to keep them healthy.
- Peaches grow from lateral spurs left from the previous season's growth. To ensure healthy fruit production, reduce weak spurs by two-thirds, remove the ones older than 2 years, and shorten those that are less than 2 years old by half.
- Clear grass and weed growth around the plant. Add mulch to this encircled zone to retain soil moisture and prevent weed growth.

### Harvesting

- Harvest ripe fruit from late summer to early fall.
- Pick fruit that feels plump and soft in your hands.
- Pluck them carefully, avoiding bruises.
- Slightly unripe fruit will mature at room temperature.

## REGROWING PEARS

Light green pears with a hint of pink blush are the favorite fruit of many people. Their seeds look tiny but growing trees from store-bought fruit is possible.

### General Notes About Growing

- You can grow your own pears in the yard or even in a container.
- Pear trees are not self-pollinating, and planting multiple trees will ensure fruit production.
- The trees can take a few years to bear fruit. Once they start, they will produce pears in abundance.

### Preparation and Planting

- Like peaches, ripe seeds can be germinated in the refrigerator during late winter. This allows the requisite chilling time for the plant.
- Cut the fruit lengthwise with a paring knife, and scoop out the seeds gently. Removing many seeds for planting ensures better chances of growing the trees.
- Soak seeds overnight in water. Reject seeds that float on the surface.
- Soak the viable seeds for 10 minutes in a solution of 10 parts of water to 1 part of bleach .
- Pat them dry.
- Take a plastic bag with moist peat moss or potting soil, and plant up to 4 seeds per bag.

- Seal the bag, tag it with the date, and keep it in the crisper compartment of the refrigerator.
- Check the soil occasionally. If it feels dry, moisten it with some water.
- The seeds take 3 months to germinate.
- Remove the seeds once the temperature outside is 40°F (4.4°C).
- Soak them in warm water for 2 days to soften. Reject those that float on the surface.
- Fill a small pot with a potting mix. Plant the seeds 1/2" (13 mm) deep along the edges of the pot. Space them out evenly.
- Water the soil to moisten it. Do not waterlog.
- Expose the pot to sunlight for 3 weeks.
- When the plants give out shoots with 4 true leaves, transplant them into the garden in well-draining, moist, fertile soil.
- Water the plants.

### Caring Instructions

- The growing trees will need support with wooden sticks or twigs.
- In the first year, water the plants once per week—more frequently in dry spells.
- Pears, during the growing season, need 1/8 lb (55 g) of ammonium nitrate per tree multiplied by the number of years the tree has been planted in fertile soil.
- Use less fertilizer once growth peaks at more than 1' (30 cm) per year.

- Prune the plants in early spring and whenever branches or leaves dry out.
- Shape the trees with the help of spreaders so that they grow more outward than upward.

*Harvesting*

- Pears should be harvested before ripening. They ripen unevenly when left in the trees to ripen.
- Take a fruit in your hand and tilt it horizontally. A mature fruit will disengage itself from the branch while an immature one will stick to it.
- Pears ripen at 70°F (21°C). Keeping the mature fruit in a plastic bag or inside food grain canisters will quicken ripening. Pears also ripen when kept with fruit like apples or bananas.

## REGROWING PINEAPPLES

Regrowing pineapples from store-bought fruit is possible. Grow them and enjoy their juicy sweetness. The taste of garden-grown pineapples is different from the store-bought ones.

### General Notes About Growing

- Pineapples are easily grown indoors from a fresh store-bought fruit.
- Select a large-sized fruit with a ripe smell and plenty of leaves on the top. Check for any rot or mushy appearance.

### Preparation and Planting

- Using a sharp knife, cut off the top 2" (5 cm) of the fruit along with the foliage.
- Wash off the dirt.
- Dry the cut section (scarring) for a few days until it is completely dry.
- Take a large-mouthed glass jar that fits the pineapple head and fill it with tap water to just below the rim.
- Place the pineapple head on the rim so the bottom is 1" (2.5 cm) into the water.
- Secure the head with toothpicks all around its perimeter.
- Roots appear after about 3 weeks as long thin filaments.

- To ensure rooting, select a warm environment like the top of the refrigerator or dishwasher.
- Ensure bright light but not direct sunlight.
- Change the water once per week or when it clouds up. If molds or spores are seen floating, the fruit has to be discarded to start anew.
- Within a month of the appearance of the roots, consider transplanting.
- Plant the whole thing in the soil with a high-grade potting mix. Sow them indoors in colder climates.
- Once new leaves appear, the plant has been successfully transplanted.

## *Caring Instructions*

- Pineapple plants are slow to bear fruit; it may take 2 to 3 years to appear.
- Pineapples grow best at 75°F (24°C). Temperatures below 60°F (16°C) and above 90°F (32°C) can kill the plant.
- Pineapples need 6 hours of daily sunlight. Provide partial shade in scorching noon.
- Add a fertilizer with an NPK ratio of 5-5-5, or 10-10-5 twice per month during spring and summer when the plant grows. Stop fertilizing during winter.
- Water adequately during planting and after adding fertilizers. Water regularly in between when the topsoil feels dry to the touch. Allow excess water to drain.
- Maintain humidity between 40–60 percent with a humidifier or a "pebble tray." It is a makeshift tray that

must be larger than the plant container. Place it underneath the container and fill it up with pebbles. Add clean water up to a level below the pebbles' tops. Water will evaporate to provide adequate humidity to the plant.

- Allow air circulation, using a small fan in the area.
- Remove any dead or decaying leaves.

### Harvesting

- At last, the fruit appears as a small bloom in the center of the leaves. It grows gradually, forming the pineapple.
- When the skin turns completely light yellow, the fruit is ready for harvesting.
- Cut the stalk bearing the fruit with a sharp knife in one go. The plant will bear fruit from the cut stalk in the next season.

## REGROWING STRAWBERRIES

Love strawberries? Grow as many plants as possible with a few store-bought berries. Enjoy them as they grow and mature to bear juicy red strawberries.

### *General Notes About Growing*

- Select a local variety of strawberries. Imported ones may not grow in your climate.
- The best time to grow strawberries is in early spring, after the last frost.
- They can be grown in a small container.
- Strawberries need 6-8 hours of direct sunlight. The amount and the size of the fruit depend on sunlight.
- There are 3 variants of strawberries: summer-bearing, spring-bearing, and all-season variants.

### *Preparation and Planting*

- Select a ripe fruit and gently scrape off the dark eyes on the skin. These eyes are strawberry seeds. Alternatively, make thin slices of the fruit skin with the seeds attached to them. Blending fresh strawberries with some water for a few seconds and straining the seeds from the mixture will also do.
- Fill a small 4" (10 cm) pot with a well-draining potting mixture and place the slices with the seeds in the soil, about 3–4 slices per pot; press gently on the soil.

- Expose the pot to bright sunlight.
- Water the soil regularly.
- Plants appear; when they send out multiple runners, it is time to transplant them in a separate container.
- Plant them 1/4" (6 mm) deep in well-draining soil at 1.5' (45 cm) apart. When planting them in rows, keep a 4' (120 cm) gap between the rows.
- Water after planting the strawberries. Use an all-purpose fertilizer to enrich the soil.

### Caring Instructions

- Water regularly, about 2" (5 cm) or less per day depending upon soil wetness.
- Ensure bright sunlight.
- Weed the soil regularly.
- If you are planting strawberries in a garden patch, do not place them with other vegetables to prevent a fungal infection of the roots.
- The plant lives for 4 years. Do not replant strawberries in the same spot within 2 years.
- Remove the first blossoms to get better crop production subsequently.

### Harvesting

- Fruit is ready for harvesting a month after blossoming.
- Select those berries with at least three-quarters of their surfaces red.

- Cut the berries from the stem. Do not pull them off; it may damage the plants.
- During the season, harvest every 3 days to ensure the ripening of the berries.

## REGROWING TOMATOES

These luscious red vegetables that double as fruit are power-houses of nutrition. Most of the time, when cooking with them, we discard the seeds. Instead of discarding them, use them to grow your own tomatoes.

### General Notes About Growing

- Tomatoes grow in a warm climate.
- The optimal soil temperature for seed germination is 70°F (21°C).
- Tomatoes love the sun. In the Northern hemisphere, 8–10 hours of direct sunlight is necessary; plant the seeds in late spring to early summer.
- In the Southern hemisphere, sow the seeds from fall through winter. Partial shade during midday will be required.
- Tomatoes take about 60–100 days to harvest.

### Preparation and Planting

- Collect the seeds from a ripe tomato and wash them in water.
- Soak them for 14 hours in lukewarm water.
- Pat dry and sow them in the soil as soon as possible.
- For indoor planting, select a date 6 weeks before the spring's last frost date. For outdoors, pick a date 2 weeks after that when the soil temperature is consistently above 55°F–60°F (13°C–16°C).

- For indoors, sow them 1/2" (13 mm) deep in small pots with drainage holes.
- Use a single seed for each pot.
- Use a good-quality potting mix containing peat moss, vermiculite, perlite, and sand. The soil should be moist but not soggy.
- Cover the soil with plastic wrap to retain moisture.
- Expose the pots to direct sunlight for 3 hours, increasing it every day until the plants get 6 hours of sunlight at a time.
- Check the soil; if it feels dry to the touch, add some water.
- Once 4 true leaves appear, transplant the plants to a larger container or plant them outdoors once the soil temperature is consistently above 60°F (16°C).
- For outdoors, plant the seedlings 2'–3' (60–90 cm) apart in 1' (30 cm) deep holes. Mix aged manure or compost with the soil.
- For containers, use well-draining fertile soil to plant a single plant per container.
- Expose the plants to 6–8 hours of sunlight.
- Add water immediately after potting.

### Caring Instructions

- During planting, use stakes or cages to support the plant, ward off diseases, and prevent the fruit from dropping to the ground.
- Water the plants well for the first few days, then about 1.2 gal (4.5 L) per sq ft (900 sq cm) weekly. Water near

the base in the early morning.

- Add 2" (5 cm) of mulch 5 weeks after transplanting to retain soil moisture and prevent infestations and weed growth.
- Add slow-release organic fertilizer or organic liquid fertilizer with seaweed or fish emulsion every two weeks once the plants are 1" (2.5 cm) in diameter.
- Avoid fast-release and heavy nitrogen-based fertilizers.
- Weed and prune the plants for better growth. Pinch off suckers—tiny stems and leaves between the main stem and the branches.
- Tie the stems loosely with rope or string.

### *Harvesting*

- Harvesting does not depend on the size of the tomato. Harvest when tomatoes are firm and deep red. However, some tomatoes may belong to a different subgroup and look yellow or mixed yellow-green-red when ripe. The best bet is to feel for firmness and pluck one to see if it tastes ripe and juicy.
- If the cold season starts and the tomatoes are not yet ripe, pull out the whole plant and remove loose dirt and leaves. Hang the plant upside down in a cool, dry place.
- Place the more mature green tomatoes in a paper bag with their stems and seal the bag loosely.
- Place the bags in cardboard boxes in a cool dark place.
- Check regularly for ripening.
- Do not leave green tomatoes on the windowsill for ripening as they will rot.

REGROWING WATERMELON

Love the watermelon you bought from the store? Maybe you thought how lovely it would have been to grow watermelons in your garden. Don't worry; you can grow them from store-bought fruit.

**General Notes About Growing**

- Store-bought fruit are usually hybrids, which means you may not get the same fruit from its seeds.
- Watermelons cannot thrive in very hot and humid conditions. In cooler regions, summer is the best time to grow them.
- An average temperature of 80°F (27°C) is suitable for growing watermelons.
- They need at least 3 months of good sunlight and water to grow, and the soil must be fertile.
- Watermelons are vines, and they require space to spread.

**Preparation and Planting**

- Collect the seeds of the watermelon and remove any trace of dirt with a soap-water solution.
- Pat dry.
- Spread the seeds on newspaper or paper towels to soak up the remaining moisture. Dry the seeds thoroughly for a week.

- In winter, you may store the seeds in an envelope inside an airtight container in a cool, dark place. Make a small packet of powdered milk and keep it with the seed envelope as it will absorb any remaining moisture. Keep the container in the refrigerator until spring.
- When the weather and the soil temperatures are right, take out the container; keep it outside for some time to allow it to warm up naturally.
- Watermelons do not like transplantation; plant them directly in raised beds that allow for excess water drainage. It will also prevent the leaching of nutrients into other areas of the garden.
- Plant the seeds 1″ (2.5 cm) deep in the ground when the soil temperature is 65°F (18°C).
- When planting multiple seeds, keep 1′ (30 cm) between them. Sowing more than you need will help you select the more robust ones.
- Once the seeds germinate, remove the weaker plants by cutting them off. Pulling them out may damage the roots of nearby plants.
- In case of limited space, watermelons can be grown on a trellis.

### Caring Instructions

- Water the soil regularly when it feels dry to the touch.
- Mulching prevents the growth of weeds and retains soil moisture.
- Feed the plants with compost or manure. Alternatively, you may use chicken manure pellets. Use a nitrogen-

based fertilizer during growth. Choose a potassium-heavy fertilizer during flowering and fruiting times.

- Once the vines are 6' (180 cm) in length, pinch off the tips to encourage branching.
- The plants grow male and female flowers that cross-pollinate with the help of insects. They can also be hand-pollinated early in the morning. Take some male flowers and strip off the petals. Rub the stamens against the pistils of the female flowers.

### *Harvesting*

- It is difficult to tell the ripe fruit from its appearance. Look at the curly tendril at the stem. Your fruit is probably ready once it is completely dry.
- Look at the colored patch on the bottom of the fruit. As the melon ripens, the patch changes color from green to yellow. The skin of the fruit toughens.
- Thump on the fruit. A ripe fruit gives a dull thud, while the unripe ones emit a higher-pitched note.
- When harvesting, leave 2" (5 cm) of the stem on the fruit.
- Watermelons stay at room temperature for a week and 2–3 weeks at 55°F (13°C).

With this, we end our chapter about regrowing fruit from store-bought varieties. In the next section, we will discuss regrowing herbs from the store-bought ones. Herbs are not only ornamental in the garden, they add value to our diet as well.

# 4

# FLAVORS ON DEMAND - REGROWING HERBS FROM GROCERY STORE ITEMS

We add herbs to soups, salads, beverages, and drinks to make them healthier and more flavorful. Regrow them in your garden from store-bought supplies and enjoy them all year round.

REGROWING BASIL

Basil has a wonderful aroma and strong medicinal uses. Growing new plants from store-bought basil is simple.

***General Notes About Growing***

- Basil loves warm temperatures above 75°F (24°C).
- It needs at least 6–8 hours of sunlight during the growing season.
- It loves moderate humidity.

***Preparation and Planting***

- Select healthy plants without any leaf rot or infestations.
- Cut the stems near the bottom to expose the flesh.
- Strip the lower leaves from the stems. Leave the top leaves behind to allow photosynthesis.
- Place the stem in a clean glass jar filled with chlorine-free water below its rim. The stem should be in the water, but the leaves must not touch the water's surface.
- Expose the plant to bright, indirect light.
- If the water becomes dirty, change it.
- Wait until the roots appear.
- Spray the leaves occasionally.
- Once the roots have grown, transfer the plant into a 3" (7.5 cm) pot filled with a good-quality potting mix.
- Spray after transplant, and then regularly. You may cover the soil surface to retain humidity.

- When the plant holds well to the soil, consider transplanting them outdoors.

### Caring Instructions

- Outdoor transplants must be gradually exposed to sunlight until the plant receives 6–8 hours of sunlight daily.
- Water basil at its base regularly and thoroughly depending upon soil conditions and the weather.
- A liquid plant-based fertilizer with an NPK ratio of 10-10-10 added every two weeks for outdoors and monthly for containers is sufficient.

### Harvesting

- Harvest the leaves once the plants are 6″ (15 cm) tall. With a clean pair of scissors, snip the leaves from the stems.
- Harvesting in the morning gives tastier leaves due to higher sugar concentration.
- Harvest regularly to encourage growth.

REGROWING BAY LAUREL

Bay leaves make a delightful addition to a lot of sweet and savory dishes. Regrowing them from store-bought leaves is possible.

### *General Notes About Growing*

- Growing bay leaves from store-bought ones may seem a little frustrating because there is a chance of failure, but the challenge makes it all the more rewarding.
- The plant grows up to 60′ (18 m) in height, but in containers, they can be trimmed to a height of 5′ (1.5 m).
- The optimal temperature for propagating bay laurel is 60°F (16°C).

### *Preparation and Planting*

- Select semi-hard branches with dark green leaves and stems. Dried leaves and branches are not good for propagating.
- At least 6″ (15 cm) of the stem with leaves is necessary for propagating the plant.
- Slice off the lower section of the stem with a clean knife. The section must be slanted, leaving a little skin like a "tail" from the main bark. This is called "heel cutting."

- Heel cutting improves chances of success as it includes the cambium layer from where the plants give out roots. It also has auxins that stimulate rooting.
- Plant it directly in a well-draining and moist potting mix with coco coir and perlite after removing all except for the few leaves at the top.
- You may use the rooting hormone to promote rooting.
- Insert half of the cutting inside the soil and press the soil around it gently.
- Water the plant to moisten the soil.
- Covering the pot with plastic retains moisture and humidity, promoting rooting.
- Support the plastic with 2 sticks placed into the soil, one on either side of the pot.
- Place the pot in an area that receives bright light but not directly.
- For the entire first month, keep the plastic cover on. Afterward, remove it for an hour and then gradually increase the duration of exposure to the atmosphere. This is called acclimating.
- The plant usually takes a couple of months to form new roots. You will know it by gently tugging the plant. A plant that has given out roots will resist being pulled.
- Plant multiple cuttings to increase the chances of successful attempts.
- At last, you can remove the plastic cover entirely.
- You may transplant the plants to your garden in the fall.
- Expose outdoor plants gradually to sunlight (hardening off), increasing by an hour every day until the plants get sunlight for 7 hours a day.

### Caring Instructions

- The bay laurel needs full sunlight for 7 hours a day.
- Well-draining, moist soil enriched with organic manure or compost is optimal for growth.
- An all-purpose fertilizer every two weeks from spring through fall ensures better growth.
- It is better to plant bay laurel indoors if the winter is harsh in your location; cover the roots with bubble wrap or burlap during the winter months.
- Prune dead or defective branches and leaves.
- Replant every 3 years, trim away a third of the roots and replace the top 2" (5 cm) of the soil with fresh, fertilizer-enriched soil.

### Harvesting

- Harvest the leaves of a mature plant at any time of the year.
- Harvesting is best done in the morning.
- Cut off the leaves at the stem to harvest.

## REGROWING CATNIP

Cats love this herb, and catnip-stuffed toys are in demand by cat lovers. Catnip has medicinal value and acts as a pesticide. Regrowing catnip from store-bought is possible.

### *General Notes About Growing*

- Catnip dies in winter but comes back to life in spring.
- They like sunny areas with partial shade.

### *Preparation and Planting*

- Remove the lower leaves from the stems of the store-bought herbs.
- Set them in a water-filled jug.
- Change the water when it turns milky.
- Roots sprout in a week.
- Transplant them in a pot with a potting mix.

### *Caring Instructions*

- Keep the plants in sunlight but avoid direct sun. Partial shade works well with herbs.
- Water when the soil feels dry to the touch.

## *Harvesting*

- Harvest when the growth is lush.
- Do not harvest more than a third of the plant.
- Snip off the leaves from the top, allowing the branches to grow.

## REGROWING CHIVES

Chives are used as garnishes in soups, salads, and beverages. They are nutritious and add flavor to the dishes. They can be grown from store-bought items.

### *General Notes About Growing*

- Chives grow well in colder climates.
- Plant them in early spring, 6–8 weeks before the last frost date.
- Chives need 6 hours of daily exposure to the sun. Give them partial shade during the hot noon hours.
- Soil temperature should be around 65°F (18°C).
- Adding compost to the top 8″ (20 cm) of soil ensures better growth.

### *Preparation and Planting*

- Select herbs that are 5″ (12.5 cm) long with bulbs.
- Plant the bulbs directly into moist but not soggy potting mix inside holes 4″ (10 cm) deep.
- Press the soil around the bulbs.
- Add water to moisten the soil.

### *Caring Instructions*

- Water when the soil feels dry to the touch. Chives do not like excess moisture.

- A liquid-based plant fertilizer every two weeks for outdoors and monthly for indoor plants is required.
- Herbs become less tasty when they produce flowers (bolting). Prevent this by snipping off the flowers.
- Divide the chives to ensure full growth potential for each plant.

### Harvesting

- Harvest chives when they are about 10″ (25 cm) in length.
- Cut the leaves to their bases about 2″ (5 cm) from the soil to allow regrowth from the cut surfaces.
- Cut them straight with a good pair of scissors or shears. Cutting at an angle causes the plant to dry up.
- Harvesting may be possible only once during the first year but more frequently afterward.
- In late fall, cut off all the leaves. Chives go into dormancy during winter.
- In spring, the chives will grow back from the cut ends.

## REGROWING CILANTRO

Cilantro is a popular herb used in different cuisines to enhance flavor. Regrow these interesting herbs from the store-bought samples.

### General Notes About Growing

- Cilantro can be grown anywhere: indoors or outdoors, in containers, pots, or in the garden.
- They thrive in 60°F–80°F (16°C–27°C).
- Cilantro should be planted in spring or fall. If they bolt during the summer, the leaves turn bitter.

### Preparation and Planting

- Choose fresh herbs with healthy leaves to regrow cilantro from the scraps.
- Remove leaves from the lower half of the stems.
- Place the stems in a glass of chlorine-free water.
- Leave near a windowsill so that it gets bright light indirectly.
- Change the water regularly.
- Roots appear from the cut ends.
- Once the roots are 3" (7.5 cm) in length, transplant the plants into the soil.
- Plant them directly into pots, trays, containers, or gardens using good quality potting mix.
- The soil should be well-draining and moist.
- Water immediately after planting.

- Expose to sunlight to ensure growth. Provide shade during hot noon times.
- Keep a gap of 6" (15 cm) between the plants.

### Caring Instructions

- Cilantro needs 6–8 hours of sunlight.
- Water when the soil feels dry to the touch.
- Add liquid-based plant fertilizers once a month for containers and every two weeks for outdoor plants.
- Mulching helps in water retention.
- Prune and trim the plants to encourage better growth.

### Harvesting

- Harvest the leaves once the growth has reached its peak.
- Snip off the leaves from the top of the herbs with a pair of scissors.
- To harvest both the small and large leaves, cut off the whole plant 2" (5 cm) from the soil.
- Use them fresh.
- Fresh stems can be wrapped in moist paper towels and refrigerated for a few days.

REGROWING DILL

Dill not only enhances the flavor of dishes but also increases milk production for lactating mothers. Regrowing dill from store-bought herbs is possible.

**General Notes About Growing**

- Dill is grown mid-spring through mid-summer.
- Dill needs warmth, sunlight, and fertile soil conditions to grow.

**Preparation and Planting**

- Choose fresh herbs with healthy leaves to regrow dill from the scraps.
- Make a clean cut at an angle on the stem just below a leaf node. The leaf node is a point from where the leaf grows.
- Trim the cutting by removing leaves from the lower two-thirds of the stem.
- Remove flower buds and large leaves from the stem to divert the plant's energy into making the roots.
- Place the cutting in a glass of water, making sure that no leaves touch the water's surface.
- Expose the cutting to bright indirect light. Ensure airflow and warmth.
- Change the water frequently to prevent the growth of microbes and fungi.
- Roots appear within 2–7 days.

- Transplant directly into the garden soil or a permanent container with drainage holes.
- Use well-draining, moist, and enriched soil for planting dill.
- Keep a gap of 6″ (15 cm) and plant them 1/2″ (13 mm) deep.

### Caring Instructions

- Water when the soil feels dry to the touch.
- Dill needs 6–8 hours of indirect sunlight.
- Use fertilizers sparingly.

### Harvesting

- Best time to harvest dill leaves is in mid-summer.
- Harvest in the morning or evening.
- Cut them at their stems.
- To harvest dill flowers, select the mature ones. Cut them at their stems.
- Put the flower in a paper bag and hang it upside down.
- Dried dill seeds will collect in the bag.
- Store the seeds in airtight containers for future use.

## REGROWING FENNEL

All parts of the fennel are edible. Fennel, with its strong aniseed flavor, is a hot favorite with people worldwide. Regrow fennel from the kitchen scraps following this simple technique.

### General Notes About Growing

- Fennel does not grow well from the fronds. Select the bulbs instead.
- Fennel loves cool weather conditions. Grow them in spring or in fall.

### Preparation and Planting

- Cut the bulb off with a clean, neat cut, keeping the roots intact.
- Place it in a glass half-filled with water.
- Keep it near a source of indirect light.
- Change water frequently.
- New roots appear in a few days.
- Transplant the fennel into well-draining, moist, and enriched soil at 6" (15 cm) apart.

### Caring Instructions

- Water when the soil feels dry to the touch.
- Fennel needs 6–8 hours of indirect sunlight.
- Use fertilizers sparingly.

## Harvesting

- Harvest when the plant is tall and has luxurious fronds.
- Harvest the fronds by cutting them off at the stems.
- To harvest the bulb, tug the plant and insert the scissors at the base of the plant. Cut at the base, leaving the roots intact.
- Fennel will regrow from the roots.

## REGROWING GINGER

Ginger is popular in cooking—both sweet and savory items. It has strong medicinal properties and it relieves dry cough and sore throat. Regrow this useful herb in your garden from store-bought ginger. Store-bought ginger does not have anti-sprout chemicals in them, so they are good for regrowing ginger plants.

### General Notes About Growing

- Ginger loves warm, humid weather.
- The plant needs indirect sunlight for at least 2–5 hours daily.
- They cannot tolerate strong wind or soggy soil.
- The best time to grow ginger is in spring.
- Grow ginger indoors on your kitchen counter or outdoors in the garden

### Preparation and Planting

- Select a healthy-looking and plump rhizome 6" (15 cm) long. It must have multiple nodes in it.
- Leaving the ginger indoors in a warm and humid area like on your kitchen counter for a couple of weeks allows the nodes to grow.
- The nodes swell and develop a light yellow to green tinge.

- Cut the ginger into smaller pieces, each with an "eye" or node.
- Allow the cut ends to recover for a few hours before planting.
- Plant the pieces in a well-draining, moist potting mix with their eyes facing up. Select a large container for indoor plants.
- Do not sow the pieces deep into the soil. Only the sides must be covered with soil, exposing the tops above the soil.

### Caring Instructions

- Water regularly and thoroughly but do not allow waterlogging.

- Add a little fertilizer like compost or aged manure once monthly.
- Expose the plants to indirect sunlight for at least 5 hours daily.
- Ginger does not thrive in the cold. Move the plants indoors and cover the soil with a few inches of mulch or burlap. Alternatively, you may choose to harvest.

### Harvesting

- Ginger is ready for harvesting once the plant grows to 3' (90 cm).
- Full maturity takes about 8–10 months when the ginger tastes better.
- Loosen the soil and tug gently to nudge one of the shoots out of the soil and break off a part of the ginger.
- Alternatively, dig out the whole plant and harvest the ginger root.
- Wash the ginger root before use.

## REGROWING LEMON BALM

Lemon balm, with its lemon flavor, is a popular herb for cooking or making beverages. Regrow lemon balm from the store-bought item.

### General Notes About Growing

- Lemon balm grows well in well-draining, loamy soil both indoors and outdoors.
- The container should be 8″ (20 cm) deep and wide.
- Plant outdoors in a raised bed. Lemon balm can be invasive and needs division.
- They need sunlight with partial shade to thrive.
- Grow lemon balm from store-bought pieces when the weather is cool.

### Preparation and Planting

- Select a healthy-looking stem with new shoots and leaves at its tip.
- Make a cutting at the base of the stem.
- Remove the lower leaves, preserving the new growth at the tip.
- Place the stem in a glass half-filled with water.
- Change water every 1 to 2 days and observe the stem for the growth of new roots.
- It takes about 4–6 weeks for the roots to grow.
- Once roots appear, plant the sapling in a well-draining, moist potting mix.

- Transplant lemon balm into the garden or container from early spring to early summer.

## Caring Instructions

- Lemon balm needs regular watering to keep the soil moist.
- Once grown, the plant can withstand mild drought.
- Lightly fertilize with aged compost during the growing season.
- Prune the herbs regularly.
- After flowering, split the plant in half to promote further plant growth.
- Remove dead flowers (deadheading) to prevent the scattering of seeds in the garden.

## Harvesting

- During the growing season, pinch off the leaves regularly to enhance further growth.
- The older, lower leaves are full of aroma.
- If you want to store dried leaves, collect them in the summer before the plant starts flowering.
- Reducing the plant by half in the fall promotes the growth of new leaves.
- To harvest the leaves and sprigs, use a sharp pair of scissors to snip them carefully from the stems.

## REGROWING LEMONGRASS

These ornamental yet sought-after lemony herbs belonging to the grass family are versatile and can be grown indoors or outdoors. Regrow them from store-bought lemongrass to add value to your garden.

### *General Notes About Growing*

- Lemongrass, once planted, requires minimal care.
- It is a perennial and grows throughout the year.
- In the garden, grow them in containers and move them indoors during harsh winters.
- Alternatively, you may re-pot the garden plant in the fall to bring it indoors.

### *Preparation and Planting*

- Grocery stores stalk fresh lemongrass. Select one of these white stalks to regrow the plant.
- Ensure the base of the stalk is healthy and free from mold.
- Cut off 4″ (10 cm) from the base. Use the rest in cooking.
- Place the cutting in a glass half-filled with chlorine-free water and keep it in a warm place like the kitchen windowsill.
- Change water frequently. At no point should the water evaporate or turn murky.
- Roots appear in 2–3 weeks.

- Plant the lemongrass in a pot with drainage holes.
- Use good quality potting mix, moist but not soggy.
- Once the plant has taken its hold in the soil and started to grow, transplant it to a 6" (15 cm) deep container, using a well-draining, fertile soil.
- Water the plant.

### Caring Instructions

- Lemongrass needs warmth and a sunny area with partial shade at noon.
- Water the plants regularly and adequately during the growing season; 1" (2.5 cm) per week per plant, or less after growth is adequate.
- Fertilize lightly once each month, using a seaweed or fish emulsion. Alternatively, use compost or aged manure.
- Divide when the clumps get crowded.
- Move outdoor plants indoors in the cold winter. Keep the container near a sunny area or under a grow light.

### Harvesting

- Harvest the mature lemongrass anytime.
- Harvest the leaves with a sharp pair of scissors.
- To harvest stem hearts, follow the plant back to the base and either crack or cut the whole stem at its base.
- Peel the outer sheath to use the white heart of the stem in cooking.

REGROWING MINT

Mint, a sweet-tasting and aromatic herb, is popular for cooking and preparing tasty beverages. Mint is actually grown from cuttings, and regrowing mint from store-bought mint is easy.

### General Notes About Growing

- Mint grows anywhere: indoors or outdoors, in containers, trays, pots, or in the garden.
- They grow well in moist, well-draining, fertile soil.
- Mint needs sunlight with partial shade to thrive.

### Preparation and Planting

- With sharp scissors, cut off mint stems about 3"–5" (7.5–10 cm) long.
- Remove leaves from the lower two-thirds of the stem. Let the upper leaves remain intact.
- Place the cutting in a glass half-filled with water.
- Expose to bright indirect light.
- Replace the water regularly.
- Plant in a well-draining potting mix when the roots are 3" (7.5 cm) long.
- Make holes in the soil with your finger to sow the saplings. You may plant several plants in the same container.

## Caring Instructions

- Allow indirect sunlight.
- Water to keep the soil moist but not wet.
- The plants can remain in the potting mix or can be transplanted in containers.
- For outdoor plants, a light mulch can check dehydration and weed infestation.

## Harvesting

- Mint is soon ready for harvest; harvest the leaves freely; young leaves are more flavorful.
- You can harvest two or three times in any growing season.
- Delay the growing season by pinching off the flowers or cutting the stems 1" (2.5 cm) from the ground.
- Snip off the leaves and sprigs; use a sharp pair of scissors to snip them off the stems.
- Mint can be used fresh or frozen.

## REGROWING OREGANO

Oregano, a Mediterranean herb, is widely used in cooking. It is simple to regrow them from store-bought oregano. You will only need a few healthy plants.

### General Notes About Growing

- Oregano tolerates poor soil and drought conditions.
- Grow it anywhere: indoors or outdoors, in containers, or in the garden.

### Preparation and Planting

- Select sprigs 6" (15 cm) long.
- Remove the leaves from the base, leaving 2" (5 cm) of a bared base.
- Place the stem in a glass with some chlorine-free water.
- Keep in indirect sunlight.
- Replenish and change the water regularly until the roots appear.
- Pot the plant as soon as possible using a well-draining, moist, fertile potting mix.

### Caring Instructions

- Oregano loves warm, humid weather.
- Keep the plants in indirect sunlight.
- Ensure soil moisture.

- Fertilize lightly using plant-based liquid fertilizer once a month.
- Sometimes, "transplant shock" can occur when the leaves of the young saplings turn yellow. Remove them to allow for new growth.

### Harvesting

- Harvest before the flowering season.
- Use sharp scissors to cut the stems with the leaves about 1" (2.5 cm) from the ground.
- Use them fresh or dried.

## REGROWING PARSLEY

Parsley is a Mediterranean herb. It is milder than cilantro and is widely used in cooking. Regrowing from store-bought parsley is easy. You will need a few healthy plants for successful regrowing.

### *General Notes About Growing*

- Parsley can be grown indoors or outdoors, in containers, or in the garden soil.
- It is a biennial; it dies after winter, once it flowers and seeds.
- Planting parsley in spring after the last frost will give you a supply of fresh garden herbs throughout the year.
- Parsley likes 6–8 hours of sunlight.

### *Preparation and Planting*

- You will need a 3″ (7.5 cm) stem with a few fresh leaves at the tip. Make a neat slanting cut with clean scissors.
- Avoid stems with flowers, rotten leaves, and huge leaves.
- Take several cuttings as the success rate is low.
- Place them in some water in a glass jar.
- Expose the plant to sunlight, ensuring air circulation.
- Change the water regularly until roots appear.
- Transfer the plants immediately to a well-draining, moist, enriched potting mix.

- If you are sowing multiple saplings in one container, plant them 9" (22.5 cm) apart.
- Water immediately.

### Caring Instructions

- Water thoroughly once the soil is dry.
- Use liquid-based plant fertilizer sparingly once a month for containers.
- Ensure 6–8 hours of sunlight.

### Harvesting

- Harvest once the growth is luxurious.
- Harvest the outer stems with leaves 1" (2.5 cm) from the base using sharp scissors. New stems appear from the center of the plant.

## REGROWING ROSEMARY

Rosemary, an evergreen Mediterranean herb, is well-known for its fragrance. Regrow this wonderful herb in your garden from store-bought pieces.

### *General Notes About Growing*

- Rosemary can grow 4' (1.2 m) in length and width.
- It grows in warm weather; in the cold, grow them indoors in containers.
- Grow rosemary in late spring to early summer.

### *Preparation and Planting*

- Rosemary is grown from the stem cuttings of grocery-bought herbs.
- Select several healthy-looking young plants with a good stem length of about 18" (45 cm).
- Ensure each stem has at least 2 nodes.
- Trim the lower 2" (5 cm) of the stem.
- Select a pot with drainage holes.
- Make your potting mix with 1 part perlite and 2 parts multi-purpose compost.
- Moisten the soil.
- You may dip the end of the stems in the rooting hormone to encourage rooting.
- Place them directly in the potting mix.
- Water immediately.

- You may choose to cover the soil with plastic wrap to retain moisture and soil temperature.
- Roots come out in 1–2 months. The soil must be kept moist during this time.
- You may transplant rosemary to a bigger container or the garden.

## Caring Instructions

- Rosemary needs 6–8 hours of sunlight.
- Water regularly and adequately when the soil feels dry to the touch.
- Use well-draining, enriched soil for growth.
- Prune rosemary regularly.

## Harvesting

- Harvest young stems for freshness.
- Do not harvest more than a third of the plant to allow regrowth.
- Use sharp scissors to harvest rosemary.
- Cut the branches as close to the main stem as possible.
- Use it fresh or dried.

## REGROWING SAGE

Sage, with its earthy flavor, is used in cooking and for medicinal purposes. Regrowing sage from store-bought herbs is possible.

### General Notes About Growing

- Grow sage in spring.
- Well-draining, sandy or loamy soil is good for sage.
- It needs 6–8 hours of sunlight with partial shade.
- Soil temperature is critical for growth and must be at 60°F–70°F (16°C–21°C).

### Preparation and Planting

- Grocery-bought plants must be used soon as they tend to wilt quickly.
- Select a few healthy, green stems of at least 4" (10 cm) in length—without flowers but with branches and leaves.
- Trim the leaves off the lower 2" (5 cm) of the stems.
- Make a neat slanting cut at their bases.
- To plant directly into the potting mix, use a rooting hormone to facilitate rooting.
- Alternatively, place the stems in a glass with some water and allow the roots to develop.
- Place the glass in indirect sunlight.
- The leaves turn yellow, they fall off, and new leaves appear. Roots form.

- Once the roots are 2″ (5 cm) long, transplant the herbs to a well-draining, moist potting mix.
- Ensure the soil temperature is optimal for growth.

## Caring Instructions

- Water the plants daily until growth is complete.
- Sage needs 6–8 hours of sunlight.
- Prune in spring.
- Replace aging plants after a few years.

## Harvesting

- Harvest lightly in the first year.
- Harvest fully in the fall, preparing the plants for winter dormancy.
- A plant yields 3 harvests each year.
- To harvest, pinch off the leaves from the plant.

## REGROWING TARRAGON

Tarragon, with its delicate flavor, is used as a garnish. Regrow tarragon from store-bought herbs.

### General Notes About Growing

- A perennial Mediterranean herb, tarragon loves warmth and sunlight.
- It grows well from stem cuttings.

### Preparation and Planting

- Take some healthy-looking tarragon and remove the leaves from the bottom 2" (5 cm) of the stems.
- Either use rooting hormone to plant the cuttings directly into potting mix or place the stem cuttings in a glass of water.
- Keep the glass near the windowsill for sunlight.
- Roots appear after a couple of weeks.
- Transplant the plants in a well-draining, moist, rich potting mix.

### Caring Instructions

- Tarragon needs a humid climate.
- Water the plants once the soil feels dry to the touch.

## *Harvesting*

- Snip the branches with leaves to harvest tarragon from a mature plant.
- Harvest them fully in the fall and store the dried leaves. The plant returns from dormancy in spring.

## REGROWING THYME

Thyme is used in cooking and aromatherapy. Regrow from store-bought thyme to get an assured herb supply for many years.

### General Notes About Growing

- Regrowing thyme from grocery-bought thyme is the quickest and easiest way to grow it in your garden.
- Store-bought herbs will produce a similar version. Since there are wide varieties, you may select the ones you prefer before planting them.
- Thyme requires a soil temperature of 60°F–70°F (16°C–21°C).

### Preparation and Planting

- Select 6" (15 cm) stems of healthy, young plants. Avoid the woody, hard ones.
- Remove the leaves from the bottom 2" (5 cm) of the stems.
- Cut the stems at a 45-degree angle.
- Pot them in a potting mix using rooting hormones.
- Keep the plants near sunlight.
- Add water to keep the soil moist.
- Once the plants are 12" (30 cm) long, you may transplant them in a bigger container or outdoors.

### Caring Instructions

- Thyme needs full sunlight.
- Soil should be well-draining and fertile.
- Water when the soil feels dry to the touch.
- Mulch during winter to retain soil moisture.

### Harvesting

- Harvest thyme using sharp scissors to snip off the center stem of a sprig directly above a node.
- Harvest a third of the plant every two weeks.
- Harvest the larger, more mature sprigs.

Yotam Ottolenghi, the celebrated restaurateur and food writer, believes that "herbs deserve to be used much more liberally."

He could not have been more right. Herbs are chock-full of nutrients and protect us naturally from various illnesses. Their addition to our daily diet boosts immunity, improves digestion, and uplifts mood. A cup of herbal tea like basil, echinacea, ginger, and elderberries cures coughs and colds. Lavender and mint reduce stress and anxiety and improve sleep.

Growing herbs from kitchen scraps and store-bought items is easy and does not require many resources. Most herbs are tenacious and, once taken to the soil, are most prolific.

With this, we come to the end of the chapter for regrowing herbs. But there are some other magics that we can still wield from our humble kitchen scraps and store-bought vegetables.

# 5

# BEYOND THE PRODUCE AISLE - REGROWING MUSHROOMS FROM THE SUPERMARKET

Mushrooms are increasingly gaining popularity worldwide, and there isn't a cuisine that does not include mushrooms in its repertoire.

It is neither animal nor plant. Mushrooms belong to a group of organisms called a fungus.

Mushrooms were traditionally used for their healing properties, and scientists have found them a powerhouse containing a vitamin called ergosterol.

Ergosterol is a precursor of vitamin D, the "sunshine vitamin." Vitamin D helps with our bones and teeth, produces hormones and cholesterol, and plays an important role in fostering immunity.

It is rarely found in vegetables, and mushrooms can be an important source of this vital vitamin in the vegan diet.

Low in calories and fats, mushrooms are rich in antioxidants and plant polyphenols that may have protective effects against many inflammatory diseases like heart and joint ailments and cancers, according to a report in Medical News Today.

Mushrooms, the chefs say, add a unique taste to food that they refer to as *umami*. It is due to the amino acid glutamate, which is also found in meat.

## REGROWING MUSHROOM FROM SCRAPS

Choose the type of mushroom you would like to regrow. The different varieties that you may choose from include oyster, portobello, shiitake, or white button mushrooms.

### *Mushroom Propagation*

Mushrooms are fungi. Unlike plants, they cannot synthesize their nutrition from air and sunlight. They depend on dead and decaying material to grow. Light hampers the germination of mushrooms.

- Select a cool, dark, damp place to grow your mushrooms. It can be the basement, a cupboard, or a shed.
- Mushroom propagation does not need soil, but it does need a suitable growing medium. Sawdust, wood chips, and straw are suitable mediums for cultivation.
- Mix these with some bran, like soy hulls, to improve the quality of the growth medium.
- The surrounding temperature should be around 70°F (21°C). You may use a heating pad.
- Once the spawning starts, maintain the temperature at 55°F–60F° (13°C–16°C).

### *Regrow Mushrooms from Store-Bought Mushrooms*

Cultivators grow mushrooms from spores. Spores form the mycelium (white tufts on the ends) on the growing medium. When we use store-bought mushrooms to propagate, we directly employ the mycelium on the mushrooms to propagate. We get the type of mushrooms we bought from the stores. Hence, regrowing mushrooms from store-bought ones is easier and faster.

**Step-by-step process: Take a "spore-print."**

- Carefully remove the stem from the mushroom. Look for any skirt that may be present. They are the veil-like structures at the stem cap junction. Snip them off.
- Next, we have to take the spore print.
- Remove the top of the mushroom to expose the gills on the undersurface.
- Lay the gill surface of the mushroom down on a piece of paper.
- Place a glass over it.
- Allow this to stand for 24 hours.
- Remove the glass and take out the mushroom carefully.
- You will notice a "gill pattern" on the paper. This is the spore print of the mushroom.
- If you do not want to cultivate the mushrooms immediately, keep the spore print in a sealed bag in a cool, dark place.
- Mixing the spores with the substrate medium will generate mycelium.

### Regrow Mushrooms from Ends (Store-Bought Mushrooms)

**Choose a healthy mushroom. Clean it thoroughly.**

- Use straw, shredded cardboard, or any moist cellulose material as the medium for spawning mushrooms.
- Soak the straw or other material for 1 or 2 days.
- Separate the stalks with their ends from the mushroom tops. It is where the mycelium lies.
- Cut the ends into smaller, 1/4″ (6 mm) pieces.
- Place some moist straw at the bottom of the medium and place the shredded cardboard or any other cellulose medium you choose as a substrate for growing the mushrooms.
- Lay the mushroom bits on this layer. Repeat layering with cardboard and mushroom pieces until the container is full. Cover the top with a paper lid.
- The ideal temperature for growth is 65°F–75°F (18°C–24°C).
- Finally, place plastic wrap on top of the box, and add holes to the plastic. These allow airflow but limit oxygen while allowing carbon dioxide to accumulate.
- You may also use a plastic container to bed the mushroom.
- Spray with water if the humidity is low.
- The mycelium is ready to bear fruit after 2 weeks.
- You can harvest the mushrooms in about 3 weeks.

**Mushrooms are susceptible to pests that can destroy crop production. These pests can be the following.**

- Cecid fly: They are transferred through the types of equipment used. Their larval forms feed on mycelium.
- Phorid fly: The creamy-white maggots of the phorid fly feed on mycelium. The adults have a hunchback look and hop actively.
- Sciarid fly: They are also called mushroom flies. The larval forms of these black gnats make the mushrooms brown and hard.
- Nematodes: Nematode infestation indicates a lack of hygiene.

**Methods to check for pest infestation:**

- Choose a healthy mushroom free from molds, mushy areas, or rot. Wash well before using them.
- Clean all implements you are using.
- Pasteurization of the substrate medium eliminates pest infestation that may come from the things used for cultivation. For straw, it means heating in water. Other tools and implements may be pasteurized by heating at 284°F (140°C) for 4 hours.
- Neem oil concentrate sprays diluted in water as per instructions or insecticidal soap in pyrethrin can check outside invasions.
- Spray these diluted pesticides twice a week.

*Harvesting Mushrooms*

- The mycelium bears fruit in about 15–30 days.
- Cut open the plastic after mycelium covers the entire surface.
- Pinheads of mushrooms grow within 2–3 days of cutting the plastic sheath.
- Stop watering a day before harvesting to facilitate the plucking of the mushrooms.
- Pluck the mushrooms, twisting them from their bases.
- Scrape the surface of the bed with a mesh of metal wire.
- Water the bed for the second harvest.
- You can collect 3 harvests from a bed.

Let us now see how to grow some of our tasty mushrooms in the garden.

### HOW TO REGROW KING OYSTER MUSHROOMS

King oyster mushrooms are well known for their umami that touches on licorice and seafood flavors. They have a chewy and meaty texture comparable to calamari.

King oysters are Mediterranean in origin but are popular worldwide. Can we regrow these "king" mushrooms from the kitchen scraps?

- Choose those king mushrooms that are packed in the original fluid-filled pack that ensures a sterile medium and the availability of the live mycelium.
- Slice the mushrooms carefully, keeping the mycelium intact.
- Sometimes, mycelium can be spotted on the top caps. You can slice these sections off for propagation.
- Layer these scraps of fungus on some straw beds in a cardboard box.
- You may supplement the nutrition with sterile coffee grounds or soy hulls. Sterilize the items in a pressure cooker for 90 minutes.
- If you do not have a cardboard box, you may use any paper cartons that groceries use to pack fruit such as cherries or apples.
- Ensure all your tools are sterilized using hot water that kills larval forms of pests and also keeps the environment damp.
- Keep on repeating the layers until the box is full.

- Wrap the box in a plastic cover and keep it in a damp, dark place.
- Spray with water to maintain humidity and encourage the growth of the mycelium.
- You will soon notice a silky white growth covering the plastic surface.
- King oysters are loved for their large stems. The growth of long fleshy stems depends on the availability of carbon dioxide that builds up when the plastic wrap is not opened prematurely.
- Over the next few days, the mycelial growth spreads rapidly, provided the room temperature and humidity are optimal.

### Regrowing Oyster Mushrooms

Oyster mushrooms are grown all over the world. They have subtle anise and seafood flavor with a meaty texture. These mushrooms can be easily grown again from kitchen scraps.

### General Notes for Growing

- You can use homemade mixes like coffee grounds and hay as substrates to grow oyster mushrooms. Shredded cardboard boxes are also good media for germinating the spores.
- Wash your hands well before the procedure.
- Substrates and the container must be sterilized by steaming in a pressure cooker to kill other pathogens that may hamper the growth of mycelia. Alternatively, use a microwave oven to sterilize the substrate.

- Cool them and squeeze out any water. They should be damp but not soggy.

### Grow Oysters from Stems

- Shred cardboard (substrate) into small pieces.
- Pour boiling water onto the pieces.
- Allow it to cool, then drain and squeeze out the water.
- Take a sterilized container and make some holes in it.
- Place some amount of substrate into the container.
- Using sterilized scissors, cut the oyster stems into small pieces and place them on a layer of the substrate.
- Cover this layer with another layer of a substrate.
- Layer the substrate and the pieces of oyster stems until the container is full.
- Close the container.
- Select a dark, humid area in your house to keep the container. It can be in the basement, bathroom, or store room.
- Wait for *spawning* to happen. The grain-mycelium mixture is called the spawn. You may use coffee grounds instead of cardboard and a glass jar instead of a container. The mouth of the jar must be covered with a paper towel to allow for optimal air circulation.
- Wash hands well.
- Cut the straw into small pieces.
- Heat the straw in water at 70°F–75°F (21°C–24°C) for an hour.
- Let it cool down. Squeeze. The straw should not drip.

- Pack the plastic bag with some straw, adding the mushroom spawns you grew earlier.
- Tie the mouth of the bag with a rubber band.
- Using a sterilized needle, punch small holes into the plastic bag.
- Keep the bag in an area with indirect light and a temperature of 59°F–68°F (15°C–20°C).
- Wait for the mycelium to develop and cover up the bag within 1–2 weeks.
- Spray with water, taking care the bag does not get soggy.
- Mushrooms form after about a month.
- Make larger holes in the plastic bag to allow for the rapid growth of mushrooms.

### How to Regrow Oyster Mushrooms with White Mold

Oysters can be grown on coffee grounds. However, coffee is notorious for its tendency to get moldy. Molds hamper the growth of mushrooms, which can endanger your crop. But before you decide to give up on your endeavor, try the following method.

- Carefully remove the moldy coffee grounds from the container where you are growing the oyster mushrooms.
- Put the grounds in a microwave-safe bowl and heat them for about 2 minutes.

## HOW TO REGROW PORTOBELLO MUSHROOMS

The brown portobello mushrooms are popular for their fantastic umami and meaty texture. They are loaded with heart-friendly minerals like potassium and have all the benefits of other mushrooms.

Can we grow portobellos from kitchen scraps? To be honest, it is a bit more challenging than regrowing the oysters, but not impossible.

How is it different from regrowing the oysters?

- You need a larger space to grow portobellos. So, a 4' (1.2 m) by 4' (1.2 m) plastic container or a large plastic bag is suitable for growing them.
- All the tools, ingredients, and equipment used must be sanitized in a pressure cooker or by boiling in water. You may microwave items that cannot be boiled.
- Prepare the growth medium with peat moss and newspaper shreds.
- Fill the container or bag with 6" (15 cm) of this material.
- Use straw or cardboard shreds as bedding materials.
- The straw must be moist but not dripping wet.
- Select healthy, plump portobellos. Remove the ends from the tops. The ends have the wooly white mycelial threads from which spawning takes place.
- Cut the ends into 1/4" (6 mm) pieces.
- Layer the container with alternate layers of straw or other cellulose-containing material and the pieces of the portobellos until the container is full.

- Keep it in a dark, humid place with a temperature range of 65°F–75°F (18°C–24°C).
- Cover the container with a plastic bag.
- Make small-sized holes in the plastic cover.
- Spray the bag when it feels dry.
- Mycelium forms in 2–4 weeks.

## HOW TO REGROW SHIITAKE MUSHROOMS

Shiitake is different from others in its strong woody and earthy flavor. Regrowing this nutritious mushroom from kitchen scraps is possible.

- Take a 5-gal (20-L) plastic bucket.
- Sanitize it with alcohol.
- In nature, shiitake grows on hardwood. In culture, preparing the substrate or the growth medium with wood pellets, wheat bran, and boiling water improves the chances of regrowing shiitake.
- For every 2 gal (8 L) of the container, you need 8 cups (2 L) of pellets, 2 cups (500 ml) of bran, and 1.5 gal (5.5 L) of water. Add the water after mixing the pellets and bran thoroughly.
- Shiitake mushrooms grow in a wide range of temperatures, from 41°F–86°F (5°C–30°C).
- Keep the medium in diffuse light in a damp place.

Regrowing vegetables, fruit, herbs, and mushrooms from grocery items and kitchen scraps is a wise method of reutilizing and recycling materials we discard as waste. It is a cost-effective way to replenish our diet and nutritious too.

However, if we spend a lot on fertilizers, soil, equipment, and other accessories, our attempt at subsistence farming loses its profitability. We must also consider practical ways to reduce our gardening expenses. In the next chapter, I will discuss how you can minimize gardening costs without hampering the quality of the produce.

# 6

# GARDENING FOR YOUR WALLET - TIPS TO SAVE MONEY WHILE TENDING YOUR GARDEN

A 16-fluid-ounce (approximately 500 ml) bottle of good-quality liquid plant fertilizer costs nearly $15. And that is not the only expenditure you need to make while gardening. There are other overhead expenses like preparing the area and enriching the soil, as well as the cost of mulch, insecticides, and pesticides. We have to consider the equipment we need to buy, the source of water, and a myriad of similar problems.

## LET US GO THE NATURAL WAY

Do you know that you can prepare good quality compost from kitchen waste and scores of other items we use every day? Going natural is an insightful and shrewd approach to reducing most gardening expenses. It streamlines our efforts, maintains the compatibility of the environment, and helps us to save more money.

### Why Should You Make Your Own Fertilizer?

Why do plants need fertilizer at all? They make food from sunlight and air, utilizing carbon dioxide in a process called photosynthesis.

How does fertilizer help in photosynthesis?

The thing is, plants need nutrients like minerals from the soil for their health and growth. Crop production suffers when the soil is depleted of these nutrients. In nature, constant decay and decomposition of organisms and plants replenish the soil with these essential nutrients. Everything is maintained harmoniously in the circle of life.

In our home setting, we have to provide this extra nourishment through fertilizer. Fertilizer provides the essential nutrients and minerals which are absorbed through the root systems to maintain the growth and health of plants.

But you may say that you are using fresh soil from the garden to plant. How can that be depleted? The truth is, garden soil gets depleted of nutrients due to overuse, watering, or simply due to its inferior ability to support the growth of a particular fruit, vegetable, or mushroom.

Fertilizers can be chemical or organic. When we give ourselves the option of making our fertilizer, we have the choice to make organic fertilizer for our use at home instead of using store-bought chemical ones. In what ways do homemade fertilizers boost soil and plant growth?

- They *improve* the carbon content of the soil and replenish it with organic nutrients. When using organic fertilizer, you essentially create a *soil improver.*
- They put back nutrients into the soil and maintain the fertility of the soil.
- They reduce our dependency on costly chemical fertilizers which are based on fossil fuels.
- They facilitate biodiversity and the biological activities of soil.
- The crops are full of vitality and rich in nutrients.
- The yield of crop production is better.
- Chemical fertilizers may overload the soil. With organic fertilizer, you can never go wrong. They release nutrients slowly, and this is just what is needed by many plants like herbs.
- Organic fertilizer also makes the plants more tough and resilient. If water is a scarce resource for you, using organic fertilizer will require less of this resource for your plants.
- Organic fertilizer reduces waste by reducing the leaching of nutrients.

Making our own plant fertilizer is an effective, eco-friendly, and sustainable way to regrow them. Indeed, it is an extension of what we were attempting to do in our home all along. Examples of such fertilizers include banana peel fertilizers, eggshell fertilizers, and ones made from coffee grounds. Do you know that weeds make good compost? Do you have a fish tank? If you do, you are already in possession of a potential source of fertilizer. The water of the fish tank is just perfect for your herbs.

The next section will discuss how we can DIY our own fertilizer at home.

### Make Organic Fertilizer

Simple, everyday items make the best quality fertilizer. And making fertilizer from kitchen scraps, tea bags, nutshells, yard waste, grass cuttings and leaves, used newspaper, cardboard, untreated wood chips, straw, hair, or pet fur is not difficult and does not require any special technique. A good fertilizer has a combination of "greens" and "browns" mixed together with an adequate quantity of water.

What do the "greens" and "browns" provide? The three most essential minerals that plants need are nitrogen, phosphorus, and potassium, or NPK, where K stands for potassium (kalium is the Latin name for potassium). Plants need other minerals like magnesium and calcium, but by far, the triad NPK forms the backbone of any fertilizer for plants.

In commercially available packages, their proportion in a particular fertilizer is given in a ratio expressed as 5-1-1 or 4-1-1. Therefore, if a package indicates an NPK ratio of 10-5-5, it means it has 10 lb (4.5 kg) of nitrogen, 5 lb (2.25 kg) of phosphorus, and 5 lb (2.25 kg) of potassium.

What do these minerals do?

Nitrogen improves plant growth and increases crop production.

Phosphorus increases the bulk of fruit and vegetables and helps herbs to thrive.

Potassium is a soil "conditioner," and makes plants more resistant to insects and pests. It maintains plant hydration and helps in plant growth.

Now, when we are purchasing fertilizer from stores, we are assured of its NPK component. But at home, how do we ensure our vegetables, fruit, and herbs get adequate amounts of each of these nutrients?

The following ingredients are sources of these three essential soil nutrients, and including them to make your home-grown fertilizer will ensure its quality.

- Nitrogen: Coffee grounds, grass clippings, plant cuttings, aged manure
- Phosphorus: Chicken or fish bones, crushed eggshells
- Potassium: Banana, orange, and lemon peels; beet, spinach, and tomato scraps

How to make fertilizer from these sources? We cannot mix them in any proportion and use them in the soil. We have to be careful when we are trying to mimic nature. There are procedures to make compost from scratch. And given below are 13 methods of how you can make organic compost with these ingredients at home.

- Coffee grounds and "green" manure: Collect fresh grass clippings and leaves from your backyard. Mix equal portions of dried coffee grounds, grass clippings, and leaves. Mix them thoroughly. Add adequate water (enough to make all the dry items turn into a rough paste) to make the compost. Coffee grounds are not only a source of nitrogen for the soil but also improve the soil by returning carbon to it.

You can use coffee grounds even if they are moldy. The mold may actually help in the composting process.

- Compost tea fertilizer: If you are in the habit of drinking tea, do not throw away the tea bags or the tea leaves. Rinse them well and keep them in a container or bucket; add water or rainwater, exposing them to sunlight and moisture. In a month's time, tea leaves turn into good compost. Use tea compost with humates to help the plants absorb nutrients. Tea compost also checks weed growth. Tea increases the acidity of the soil and supplies oxygen.
- Bone meal: Use chicken or fish bones to make an organic bone meal at home. Crush the bones, completely turning them into a powder in a grinder. Alternatively, boil the bones and cut them into small pieces, and then pulverize them. Mix them with soil.
- Ash fertilizer: Do not discard wood ash from your fireplace or the wood fire barbecue or pizza oven you have on your lawn. Ash is a good source of carbon, and you can return it to the soil. Add 2" (5 cm) of ash to your

garden bed and mix it up with soil. Use this enriched soil as a potting mix. You may also use coal ash.

Ash has calcium carbonate and potassium; it also reduces the acidity of the soil. Therefore, do not use ash for plants that need acidic soil for growth, like parsley, potatoes, or sweet potatoes.

- Banana peels: Heat the banana peels in a microwave until they dry up. The process is complete when you cannot bend the peels anymore—they lose their flexibility and crack. Take care not to burn them. Pulverize dehydrated banana peels into a fine powder. You can mix the powder with some water or add it directly to the soil.
- Eggshell fertilizer: Wash the eggshells well to remove any traces of the egg. You have to completely dry the shells. The best way to dehydrate eggshells is by heating them in the microwave. Heat 6–8 shells at a time, taking care that they do not burn. Take them out and pulverize them in a grinder or food processor. Store in an airtight container and use as a topdressing, or mix with soil to enrich it.

Eggshells supply calcium and phosphorus to the soil making the root systems strong. Eggshell fertilizer is especially good for root veggies and tubers.

- Weed fertilizer: How do you dispose of weeds? If you usually throw them away, stop, as this is a good way to give back to the soil what is due to it. Collect the weeds and, over time, fill a large container with them. Steep them in water and expose them to sunlight. Stir occasionally. Strain the water after 2 to 3 weeks. Use this water to water your plants.

- Epsom salt fertilizer: Mix a handful of Epsom salt, a rich source of magnesium, with dirt. Add this to planting holes. You may also use the mix as the topdressing for the soil. For this use, sprinkle the salt around the base of the plant, keeping a rim of 4" (10 cm) from the stem.

- Coffee grounds fertilizer: Instead of mixing coffee grounds with leaves and stems, dry heat them or leave them on a paper towel to dry up. Make a powder and use it around the base of the plants.

- Powder milk fertilizer: Although the idea seems a little preposterous at the outset, research says powder milk can increase the NPK ratio of the soil considerably. It also enhances chlorophyll (green pigment) production by the leaves, making them more nutritious. Mix 1 part milk powder with 4 parts water and use it as a fungicidal and antiviral spray.

- Epsom salt spray: Add 1 Tbs (15 ml) of Epsom salt to 1 gal (4 L) of water and feed the plants with magnesium for larger fruit and vegetables.

- Fish tank water: Fish tank water has all the essential nutrients from the fish droppings, fish food, and other organic remnants. Therefore, next time when you are changing the water of your fish tank, instead of throwing it away, use it to fertilize the plants.

- Blackstrap molasses: Add 1 Tbs (15 ml) of blackstrap molasses to 1 gal (4 L) of water and spray the plants. This solution supplies calcium, potassium, magnesium, and iron.

**_Handy Gardening Tip: Make Your Own Mulch!_**

Mulch is like an elixir for your soil and plant health. You don't necessarily need to buy it from shops. If you have access to leaves, you can do it from the comfort of your own home by following these steps:

1. Leaf mulch is a terrific all-purpose mulch for the garden, and many houses have trees and plants with a lot of foliage. In the fall, rake up the leaves that have fallen. Alternatively, collect the ones that have been cut off from plants.
2. As a precaution, leaves from walnut and eucalyptus trees might impede the growth of other plants, so avoid using them in your mulch.
3. Pile up your leaves. If you don't have access to a rake or leaf blower, you can simply collect them in a makeshift box until you have enough for the quantity of mulch you want to make.
4. If you have a lawnmower, the next step will be to shred the leaves into dime-sized pieces. If you don't have one, you can use hedge trimmers to get them to a small enough size. There's no rush—you want to ensure that you're getting a good end product.

5. Leaves are ready for the garden once they've been shredded.

6. There are a variety of ways to store excess mulch, including perforated (ventilated) barrels, giant bags with air holes, and covering it with a tarp. Mulch ferments and releases high pH toxins when kept in poor or no ventilation conditions. Mulch kept in an aired bag will last for 4–6 months, but no longer.

7. The longer you store mulch, the more you risk losing essential nutrients. On the soil, however, it keeps well for 5–6 years.

### Saving Money on Pest Control

Preventing pests is more cost-effective than treating infestations. Here are a few methods that can economically control pest infestations.

- Encourage natural methods of pest control: birds, such as cardinals, eat slugs, cabbage worms, whiteflies, and other pests. Honey bees and ladybugs feed on various larval forms of pests. Microscopic organisms in the soil, like some friendly nematodes, are natural pesticides.
- Use natural fertilizer like a fish water emulsion as fertilizer instead of chemical fertilizers.
- Planting trees in their proper location depending on their need for sunlight, water, and air prevents plant stress.
- Some strong-scented herbs that deter bugs from other plants are calendula, coriander, chives, and thyme. Plant

them among the fruit and vegetables to keep a natural pest-free garden.

- Crop rotation prevents pest infestation.
- Bugs have a higher chance of invading monocrops. Grow insect-attracting and bug-repelling herbs like thyme, catnip, and mint among the vegetables and fruit.
- A floating row cover for young saplings may protect them from the bugs. Alternatively, cover them with inverted yogurt tubs.
- Permanent pathways are a natural habitat for helpful insects. A temporary path that breaks down and needs to be formed each year destroys their habitat.
- A few pests or bugs can be safely ignored.
- Companion plants check infestation and increase soil nutrients. For every variety of vegetables and fruit, there is a companion plant. For instance, basil repels flies and mosquitoes and increases the yield of tomatoes.
- If there is an outbreak of pests, find out if it is the larva of a beneficial or harmless insect.
- Every incident is a learning experience, and so is pest control. Utilize this opportunity to reflect on the soil composition. It may lack some essential mineral that makes the plants prone to infestation.

### Irrigation System: How to Reduce Your Water Bill

One of the most arduous tasks of gardening, no doubt, is watering your plants. And when you are planning on homesteading, you are plagued by what will happen to the plants if you miss watering them for a week or two.

Watering comes with a price tag too, and it may add up to a considerable amount of money for an entire season.

This section will discuss how to help plants thrive on minimal water and how to water them in a more cost-effective way.

- Invest in a water meter to have an idea of how much water you need for the plants and what the cost is.
- Make mulch from the yard scraps. A mix of wood chips, straw, organic substances, and grass clippings can go into the mulch. Mulching reduces weed growth. Weeds compete for soil nutrients. Mulching retains soil moisture and protects the roots from extreme variations in weather conditions. It provides shade for the soil diminishing soil loss due to wind erosion and leaching.
- Instead of using chemical fertilizers, use compost. Make your own compost from kitchen scraps and yard waste. Unlike chemical fertilizers, compost is an organic substance that does not make the plants or the soil thirsty. It prevents soil crusting, which is the hardening up of soil layers, making it difficult for water to permeate it. If you are concerned about feeding the plants in warm summers, use compost without hesitation. Its high water-retaining capacity relieves stressful conditions for the plants.
- Watering is best done in the morning. It will be used up during the day. Plants do not make food at night. Excess

water on the leaves at night may encourage fungal disease. If you have only the evenings to spare, water near the base of the plants and not the tops.

- If possible, choose a drip irrigation system to water your plants. It delivers a small quantity of water near the plant stems and roots.

- Most herbs and plants need infrequent watering once they are grown. But watering sporadically and excessively can kill the plants. Check if the soil feels dry. Water deeply and slowly for about 15 minutes, allowing the water to permeate the soil. Deep watering encourages a strong root system.

- Before you choose a plant to grow, consider its water requirement, weather tolerance, and requirements for space and sunlight. Planning and organization are the most crucial steps for any endeavor, and gardening is no different. Native plants require much less water. Usually, rainwater is sufficient for them, and watering is only required during dry spells.
- Harvesting rainwater is the best way to build up your own water bank. Rainwater is free from chlorine and can be easily collected in barrels or containers to be used whenever required. In the US, two states, Colorado and Utah, have current regulations on harvesting rainwater; the rest of the states actively encourage it.

### Saving Money on Gardening Tools

What are some other areas where costs can be significantly reduced? Besides water, plants in a garden need care. Weeding, pruning, trimming, providing the vines with supports, and removing dead leaves and flower heads are only a few of the jobs entailed.

But hiring help or a professional gardener is not an option in an ordinary homestead. The cost is prohibitive. The truth is, although gardening seems to be a lot of added tasks, once we plan and organize our daily routine, it becomes a part of our daily lifestyle. We can also engage our family members and teach our children the basics of a healthful and natural existence that is closer to the soil. Our incentives are the bountiful, nutritious, and garden-fresh produce that we may serve to our family and community.

Gardening is a very good exercise, and an hour of working in the garden burns 300–400 calories. It is uplifting and calming, and in time, the plants become our friends. They greet us in the morning and cheer us up with their produce. We get rewarded healthily for all our efforts.

Besides this, gardening seemingly means purchasing a lot of tools and equipment like pots, containers, ropes, stakes, baskets, trowels, shears, spades, etc. While some may be necessary, most are not.

There are other areas and ideas on how you can improvise on what you have at hand and use them for your garden.

Use a 1-gal (4-L) milk jug for the following purposes:

- Regrowing the seeds of grocery-bought fruit and vegetables or from stem cuttings is by itself cost-effective. Once your plants produce fruit and vegetables, you can repeat the cycle by collecting their seeds and stem cuttings. To sow the seeds, slice off the top of the milk jug and punch a few holes in the bottom. Use this as a seed-starting tray instead of purchasing one from the store. Fill it with a potting mix. Make holes and rows with your finger and sow the seeds.
- In harsh cold winters, make your own "greenhouse." Slice off the bottom of the jug and use the top to cover the plants. Leave the lid off or on according to the need

for air circulation and maintenance of the temperature.
Remove the cover in hot, sunny weather.

- Cut the sides of the milk jug near the handle to make a
  spoon for measuring out fertilizer.
- Turn the jug into a dispenser for liquid fertilizer by
  drilling a few tiny holes in the lid. The handle allows
  you to easily hold the jug while watering.
- A cold frame protects plants from the medium cold and
  drier winds of late fall and early spring, lengthening the
  growing season. To maintain the temperature within
  the frame, use some water-filled milk jugs inside it. Let
  the water-filled jugs warm up in the sun during the day
  and, at night, use them to maintain the temperature
  inside the frame.

Similarly, we can use yogurt or ice cream tubs for various
gardening purposes.

Used yogurt tubs:

- Protect young plants from cutworms that attack them
  at night by using a yogurt container. Slice off its bottom
  and thrust it an inch (2.5 cm) into the ground on top of
  the plant.
- Used yogurt cups also work well for disbursing
  granular fertilizers or soil.
- Turn them into pots for some herbs. A yogurt or ice
  cream tub must be at least 3" (7.5 cm) deep. Drill some
  tiny holes at the bottom and fill them up with a potting
  mix. Keep the lid as it may still come to good use. You

can use the lid to make a water catcher below the improvised pot. Get creative and paint the pots.

Have any used and worn towels? Do not throw them out yet. We may find some use for them in our garden.

Used towels, sheets, and blankets:

- Use them to tie up plants that are heavily laden with fruit and vegetables. The softness of used cotton does not injure the plants or their produce.
- You need tarps to collect the dirt as you dig a hole in the soil. Instead of purchasing one, use an old vinyl tablecloth to contain the dirt. The area remains clean, and you can return the topsoil to the ground after the completion of your task. Spread it out while making compost.
- Use one as a makeshift wheelbarrow to transfer heavy items like a bag of fertilizer around your garden.
- Use the blanket as a shield to protect the plants from frost. Secure the edges of the blanket all around the plant so that cold air cannot enter from underneath.

Used newspapers:

- Newspapers are the key component of "lasagna gardening." Clip the grass close to the ground. Spread about six or more layers of newspapers and pile them up with compost, soil, and mulch. The mass inhibits the growth of weeds and grasses in that area. In a few months, the newspaper layers turn into soil. Use this bed to plant the greens.
- Shredded newspapers can be added to your compost pile. It adds to the "brown" component of the compost and replenishes carbon to balance out the nitrogen "greens."
- Make biodegradable paper pots with used newspapers.

With a little improvisation, it is possible to turn many old and unused products into useful gardening tools.

- Old baskets: Place a piece of paper on the bottom and use it to collect the harvest.
- Dish pans: Use them to store potting materials. They can also serve as a portable workbench.
- Used jars of jams and jellies: These are versatile containers. Use them to store seeds and flowers, keep jams and preserves, or simply for holding stem cuttings until rooting occurs.
- Used chopsticks: Use them as stakes and support to hold saplings until their stems become strong. Use them to support any plastic wrap you may apply to make

your mini greenhouse. Do not expose a covered plant to direct sunlight.

- Egg cartons: Can be used for establishing seedlings as well as for direct planting. The cardboard will simply break down once planted.

- Shower caddy: Use one to hold your small gardening tools.
- Cardboard: Shredded cardboard is a good ingredient for compost. It is also used as a substrate for mushroom cultivation.

### Saving Money on Garden Soil

Soil is a resource. For gardening, we need a lot of it. We also need to improve soil quality by adding fertilizer and mulch. Large and medium-sized containers must be filled with a large quantity of soil. This increases their weight and the cost of maintenance. However, such problems can be easily solved and we can also cut back on the cost of soil by using fillers.

Soil fillers are unused milk jars and other such lightweight items with which we can fill up the space of large or medium-sized containers. They become lighter, and plants grown in such environments can thrive because reducing the bulk of soil actually helps to maintain soil moisture. This especially helps small plants with delicate root structures. They cannot absorb water efficiently, and in big containers, soil water remains unused and collects at the bottom, making the soil wet and swampy.

- Choose some lightweight objects that may make good fillers. Close the lids and flaps of the cartons. We do not want water and soil to enter them.
- Place the fillers in the bottom of the containers, ensuring they do not block the drainage holes.
- Pour soil into the container to fill it up.
- Select which plants you want to grow in a container with fillers. Annuals need 12″ (30 cm) of soil. Perennials need 12″–18″ (30–45 cm). Shrubs need 18″–24″ (45–60 cm) of soil. Trees will need a soil depth of 24″–35″ (60–90 cm).

What are some materials that can be used as fillers?

- Plastic jugs
- Milk cartons

- Plastic bottles
- Plastic bags filled with some packaging materials
- Polystyrene packaging of peanuts, cereals, etc.

All these items are part of our garbage, and using them as fillers reduces the load on the landfill system.

Wash the milk cartons, dry them, and close the flaps before using them. Avoid plastics with BPA to prevent soil toxicity.

### Money-Saving Landscaping Tips

Everybody loves a beautifully adorned garden laden with colorful fruit, vegetables, flowers, and a manicured lawn with a tastefully decorated garden path. But even when you do not have the luxury of owning a patch, does landscaping your humble garden have to be a costly affair?

By landscaping, we assume we must rid our garden of weeds completely. But not all weeds are harmful; in fact, some, like wild violets, add a diversion and a different dimension to your garden.

Who has the heart to pluck out the cheerful clovers? They are considered lucky, and if you spot them in your garden, let them stay. They bear beautiful flowers and are good nitrogen-fixers for the soil.

Similarly, do not go overboard whenever you identify a hole or a spot in a plant. Oftentimes, nature cures itself. And allowing natural agents like bees, butterflies, and ladybugs in your garden can keep them free from pests and fungal infestations.

If you are bothered by the overgrowth of grasses on your lawn and want to reduce its size, try the lasagna method of spreading out layers of newspapers on the lawn. Pile them up with compost, mulch, and soil so that the papers stay in place.

In time, the newspapers decay, adding carbon to the soil, and while it is there, it will prevent the growth of grass and weeds. Grow plants like perennials, some vegetables, or herbs in this area.

Use natural "spillers," "fillers," and "thrillers" to landscape the containers. The thrillers like rosemary and parsley announce their presence by form and color. The fillers like sage and chervil fill up the spaces between. Choose the spillers, like peppermint geranium which cascades over the container's edge, giving them spectacular opulence.

Choose plants that are easy to grow when resources like soil, water, and labor are scarce. Growing such plants can also be a rewarding experience.

If you love a small pond or waterfall in your garden, choose from one of the many DIY options.

Make your own garden paths with leftover items. Color them to give a nice effect. Creativity knows no bounds, and your garden is an area where you can unleash your imagination.

### Planting Calendar

We can increase the chances of successfully regrowing a plant when we tune our cultivation to nature's calendar. Often, despite our best efforts, our attempts to regrow plants fail, leaving us wondering the reasons why. In most, if not all of these instances, carefully studying the planting calendar can ensure that our efforts get the desired results.

The planting calendar is an easy-to-understand but detailed guide that tells us the optimal time to plant vegetables, fruit, herbs, and mushrooms. The best website to consult is https://gilmour.com/planting-calendar. It helps you to locate your zone, choose the plants accordingly, and provides guides for exploring the calendar further.

# CONCLUSION

Regrowing vegetables, fruit, herbs, and mushrooms from kitchen scraps and grocery-bought items is a sensible, economical, and productive way to utilize things we otherwise discard. There is a far-reaching consequence of this action which is not limited to our homes and community but society at large.

It is a sustainable way of living where we replenish carbon in the soil, reduce the use of fossil-based chemical fertilizers, and mitigate the impact of solid waste on the ecosystem in small ways.

The return we get makes us happy and fulfilled. For who does not like the taste of garden-fresh, organic produce? Essentially, regrowing your own produce teaches you that organic production need not burn a hole in your pocket. We just need to have the know-how and the keys to regrowing our food—the success is then ours to enjoy.

If you have enjoyed reading this book, please do not forget to leave a review on Amazon.

# A SPECIAL GIFT TO MY READERS

Included with your purchase of this book is your free copy of
Your Homestead Planner

Follow the link below to receive your free copy:
www.kellyreedauthor.com
Or by accessing the QR code:

You can also join our Facebook community
**Homestead Living & Self Sufficiency,**
or contact me directly via kelly@kellyreedauthor.com

# REFERENCES

*10 Easy Ways to Save Water in Your Yard and Garden.* (n.d.). Love Your Landscape. https://www.loveyourlandscape.org/expert-advice/water-smart-landscaping/water-saving-tips/

12 Steps to Preventing Garden Pests Naturally. (2023). *Tenth Acre Farm.* https://www.tenthacrefarm.com/preventing-garden-pests/

*A Guide to Growing Your Own Hazelnuts.* (2014, November 13). GrowVeg. https://www.growveg.com/guides/a-guide-to-growing-your-own-hazelnuts/

*About FigNut.com - FigNut.* (2021, March 15). FigNut. https://fignut.com/harvest-oranges/a

*After Eating a Watermelon, Can You Plant the Seeds?* (2020, November 17). Home Guides | SF Gate. https://homeguides.sfgate.com/after-eating-watermelon-can-plant-seeds-50035.html

Albert, S. (2022). How to Plant, Grow, and Harvest Lemon Balm. *Harvest to Table.* https://harvesttotable.com/how_to_grow_lemon_balm/

Aurther. (2020, October 22). *How to Grow Lemongrass from Cuttings or Stalks - GreensGuru.* GreensGuru. https://www.greensguru.com/how-to-grow-lemongrass-from-cuttings/

Badgett, B. (2021, July 27). Learn How To Grow An Orange Tree. *Gardening Know How.* https://www.gardeningknowhow.com/edible/fruits/oranges/growing-an-orange-tree.htm

Badgett, B. (2022, December 12). Picking Celery In Your Garden. *Gardening Know How.* https://www.gardeningknowhow.com/edible/vegetables/celery/harvesting-celery.htm

Beaulieu, D. (2021). 5 Tips for Landscaping on a Budget. *The Spruce.* https://www.thespruce.com/landscaping-on-a-budget-2131962

*Blackberries.* (n.d.). Almanac.com. https://www.almanac.com/plant/blackberries

Bovshow, S. (2015). How to Grow Kiwi From Store Bought Kiwi Fruit! *The Foodie Gardener.&lt;sup&gt;TM.* &lt;span&gt;https://foodiegardener.com/how-to-grow-kiwi-from-store-bought-kiwi-fruit/

Brown, B. (2022). Plant Care 101: How to Care for Avocado Trees.

*FastGrowingTrees.com.* https://www.fast-growing-trees.com/pages/plant-care-avocado-trees

*Brussels Sprouts.* (n.d.). Almanac.com. https://www.almanac.com/plant/brussels-sprouts#

*Cabbage.* (n.d.). Almanac.com. https://www.almanac.com/plant/cabbage

*Can I Plant Pumpkin Seeds From a Store Bought Pumpkin? - Plan Your Patch.* (n.d.). https://planyourpatch.com/can-i-plant-pumpkin-seeds-from-a-store-bought-pumpkin/

*Can You Grow Cantaloupe From Store Bought Fruit?* (n.d.). https://planyourpatch.com/can-you-grow-cantaloupe-from-store-bought-fruit/

*Can You Grow Grapes From A Store Bought Bunch? - Plan Your Patch.* (n.d.). https://planyourpatch.com/can-you-grow-grapes-from-a-store-bought-bunch/

*Can You Plant a Mango Seed Bought From the Grocery Store?* (2020, November 17). Home Guides | SF Gate. https://homeguides.sfgate.com/can-plant-mango-seed-bought-grocery-store-57604.html

Caroline. (2022, December 27). How To Grow Portobello Mushrooms From Store Bought - Gardening Dream. *Gardening Dream.* https://www.gardeningdream.com/how-to-grow-portobello-mushrooms-from-store-bought/

Carroll, J. (2023, January 7). Reasons For White Cucumbers: Why Cucumber Fruit Turns White. *Gardening Know How.* https://www.gardeningknowhow.com/edible/vegetables/cucumber/white-cucumber-fruit.htm

*Carrots.* (n.d.). Almanac.com. https://www.almanac.com/plant/carrots

Carter, H. (2022). Lemon Tree Guide: How to Grow &#038; Care For Lemon Trees. *GardenBeast.* https://gardenbeast.com/lemon-tree-guide/

*Cauliflower.* (n.d.). Almanac.com. https://www.almanac.com/plant/cauliflower

*Checking Out on Plastics III.* (n.d.). https://checkingoutonplastics.org/

Coyle-Levy, C. (2021, November 26). How to Root and Grow an Avocado Tree from a Store-Bought Avocado - A Natural Curiosity. *A Natural Curiosity.* https://anaturalcuriosity.org/how-to-root-and-grow-an-avocado-tree-from-a-store-bought-avocado/

Daniel. (2021, July 3). How To Grow Blackberries From Cuttings? Here's The Answer! *Plantophiles.* https://plantophiles.com/gardening/grow-blackberries-from-cuttings/

David, L. (2022, September 30). Learn How to Lower Your Gardening Water

Bill With These Easy Tips. *Better Homes & Gardens*. https://www.bhg.com/gardening/how-to-garden/reduce-water-costs-gardening/

Dell, C. (2023). Growing Oregano From Cuttings: Tips for Propagating Oregano. *Garden Basics*. https://www.homesteadgardenspa.com/blog/growing-oregano-from-cuttings/

Dyer, M. H., & Dyer, M. H. (2022, January 4). Growing Mint From Cuttings: How To Root Mint Stem Cuttings. *Gardening Know How*. https://www.gardeningknowhow.com/edible/herbs/mint/growing-mint-from-cuttings.htm

*Eggplants*. (n.d.). Almanac.com. https://www.almanac.com/plant/eggplants

*Food Recycler Composting Alternative | FoodCycler*. (n.d.). Foodcycler-production. https://www.foodcycler.com/post/homemade-fertilizer-13-organic-recipes-for-your-garden

Freedman, G. (2020, December 1). Can You Grow Carrots from Scraps? Here's What You Need to Know. *EatingWell*. https://www.eatingwell.com/article/7874487/growing-carrots-from-scraps/

Gallagher, D. (2021). Grow Your Own Cilantro from Seeds or Cuttings With This Easy Guide. *Backyard Boss*. https://www.backyardboss.net/how-to-grow-cilantro/

*Garden Vegetables—More Healthy Than Vegetables From the Market? | Winchester Hospital*. (n.d.). https://www.winchesterhospital.org/health-library/article?id=13932

Garden, Z. (2022). How to Tell if Dragon Fruits Are Ripe & Ready For Harvest? *Zenyr Garden*. https://zenyrgarden.com/how-to-tell-if-dragon-fruits-are-ripe-ready-for-harvest/

Gardener, M. (2020, July 7). How to Grow Turnips from Scraps in (Practical Steps). *GardeningBank*. https://gardeningbank.com/how-to-grow-turnips-from-scraps/

GardeningChannel. (2020). Can we grow okra from fresh seeds? *Gardening Channel*. https://www.gardeningchannel.com/grow-okra-from-fresh-seeds/

George, L. (2018, June 29). *All you need to know about growing pumpkin in your kitchen garden*. https://www.thehindu.com/life-and-style/food/on-pumpkins-and-other-cucurbits/article24280131.ece

Go, G. (2014, May 7). 7 Surprising Financial Benefits of Gardening. *US News & World Report*. https://money.usnews.com/money/blogs/my-money/2014/05/07/7-surprising-financial-benefits-of-gardening

Godefroy, A. (2022). Grow Your Own Avocado From Scraps | Blog — Urban Growth. *Urban Growth.* https://urbangrowth.london/2020/04/24/love-guacamole-grow-your-own-avocado-from-scraps/

Gonzales, B. (2016). The Benefits of Regrowing Fruits and Veggies from Scraps. *Mrs Greens World.* https://www.mrsgreensworld.com/regrowing-fruits-and-vegetables-from-scraps/

Grant, A. (2021). Gardening How to. *Gardening Know How.* https://www.gardeningknowhow.com

Greaves, V. (2020, February 25). How To Regrow Celery From Scraps. *Allrecipes.* https://www.allrecipes.com/article/regrow-celery-from-scraps/

Greg, & Greg. (2022). Cost Of Starting The Garden. Is It Worth It? | Homestead Crowd. *Homestead Crowd | Homesteading, Gardening, Raising Animals Tips.* https://homesteadcrowd.com/Cost-of-Starting-the-Garden/

*Grow an orange tree from a pip!* (n.d.). http://www.margamcountrypark.co.uk/2575

*Growing Cilantro from Refrigerated Cuttings.* (2020, November 17). Home Guides | SF Gate. https://homeguides.sfgate.com/growing-cilantro-refrigerated-cuttings-88005.html

*Growing Guide Apples.* (n.d.). Almanac.com. https://www.almanac.com/plant/apples

*Guidelines for Mango Tree Care.* (2021, July 13). Home Guides | SF Gate. https://homeguides.sfgate.com/guidelines-mango-tree-care-54609.html

Home, C. F. (2019). How To Grow Lemongrass From Kitchen Scraps | Crafty For Home. *Crafty for Home.* https://craftyforhome.com/2019/01/03/how-to-grow-lemongrass-from-kitchen-scraps/

*How do I know when a watermelon is ready to harvest?* (n.d.). Horticulture and Home Pest News. https://hortnews.extension.iastate.edu/faq/how-do-i-know-when-watermelon-ready-harvest

*How Long Does It Take to Get Fruit From a Seed-Grown Guava Tree?* (2020, November 17). Home Guides | SF Gate. https://homeguides.sfgate.com/long-fruit-seedgrown-guava-tree-57484.html

*How to Care for Ginger Plants.* (2020, September 3). Garden Guides. https://www.gardenguides.com/109832-care-ginger-plants.html

*How to Grow.* (2020, November 8). MasterClass. https://www.masterclass.com

*How to Grow a Coconut Tree from a Store Bought Coconut?* (2022, August 29). The Mama Pirate. https://themamapirate.com/how-to-grow-a-coconut-tree-from-a-store-bought-coconut/

*How to Grow a Lemon Tree From Grocery Store Lemons.* (2020, November 17). Home Guides | SF Gate. https://homeguides.sfgate.com/grow-lemon-tree-grocery-store-lemons-26685.html

How to Grow a Lemon Tree in Pot | Care and Growing Lemon Tree. (2023). *Balcony Garden Web.* https://balconygardenweb.com/how-to-grow-lemon-tree-in-pot-complete-growing-guide/

How to Grow Avocado from Seed. (2023). *A Piece of Rainbow.* https://www.apieceofrainbow.com/how-to-grow-avocado-from-seed-2-easy-ways/

*How to Grow Blackberries From Cuttings.* (2020, November 17). Home Guides | SF Gate. https://homeguides.sfgate.com/grow-blackberries-cuttings-48501.html

*How To Grow Blueberries | Care and Maintenance| joe gardener®.* (2018, November 1). Joe Gardener® | Organic Gardening Like a Pro. https://joegardener.com/podcast/how-to-grow-blueberries/

*How to grow eggplant from store bought?* (2023, March 31). The Mama Pirate. https://themamapirate.com/how-to-grow-eggplant-from-store-bought/

*How To Grow Papaya: Growing Papaya From Seeds.* (n.d.). https://www.tropicalpermaculture.com/growing-papaya.html

*How to Grow Seeds from Store-Bought Apples.* (2020, November 17). Home Guides | SF Gate. https://homeguides.sfgate.com/grow-seeds-store bought-apples-53725.html

*How To Grow Strawberries From Scraps? Step by Step Guide.* (n.d.). GardenSynthesis. https://gardensynthesis.com/how-to-grow-strawberries-from-scraps/

*How to Know When a Papaya on a Tree Is Ready to Be Picked.* (2023, March 28). Garden Guides. https://www.gardenguides.com/13426671-how-to-know-when-a-papaya-on-a-tree-is-ready-to-be-picked.html

*How to Maintain Your Peach Tree.* (2020, November 17). Home Guides | SF Gate. https://homeguides.sfgate.com/maintain-peach-tree-54618.html

*How to Plant a Peach Seed from the Grocery Store.* (2020, November 17). Home Guides | SF Gate. https://homeguides.sfgate.com/plant-peach-seed-grocery-store-57929.html

*How To: Regrow Lemon Balm from Cuttings.* (n.d.). 17 Apart. https://www.17apart.com/2013/08/how-to-regrow-lemon-balm-from-cuttings.html

How to Regrow Onions from Onion Scraps Easily. (2023). *A Piece of Rainbow.* https://www.apieceofrainbow.com/regrow-onions-from-scraps/

*How to Save Seeds - Seed Savers Exchange.* (n.d.). https://www.seedsavers.org/

how-to-save-seeds

*How to Take Care of Asparagus Plants.* (2020, November 17). Home Guides | SF Gate. https://homeguides.sfgate.com/care-asparagus-plants-40859.html

Iannotti, M. (2022). How to Grow Sweet Potatoes. *The Spruce.* https://www.thes pruce.com/how-to-grow-sweet-potatoes-in-the-home-garden-1403479

Idris. (2022). Learn Gardening, Composting, And Waste Management. *Webgardener.* https://www.webgardner.com

Igra, J. (2023). Bok Choy Plant: Growing Tips and Care Guide. *Igra World.* https://www.igra-world.com/how-to-grow-bok-choy/

Instructables. (2018). Grow Onions From Discarded Onion Bottoms. *Instructables.* https://www.instructables.com/Grow-Onions-from-Discarded-Onion-Bottoms/

Jagdish. (2019). How to grow. *Gardening Tips.* https://gardeningtips.in/grow ing-mung-beans-planting-care-harvesting

Javed, S. (2021, September 29). Popular fruit and vegetables covered in a 'cocktail of pesticides', study finds. *The Independent.* https://www.indepen dent.co.uk/life-style/food-and-drink/fruit-vegetables-pesticides-food-study-b1929040.html

Joan Clark. (2023, February 23). *Lettuce Plant Care - The Easy-Growing Lettuce Guide.* Tips Bulletin. https://www.tipsbulletin.com/how-to-plant-lettuce/

Karen. (2023). How to Grow Bean Sprouts (DIY). *The Art of Doing Stuff.* https://www.theartofdoingstuff.com/how-to-grow-your-own-mung-bean-sprouts/

Kellogggarden. (2021, February 15). Growing Cilantro: Planting & Growing Tips. *Kellogg Garden Organics&lt;sup&gt;TM.* &lt;span&gt;https://www. kellogggarden.com/blog/gardening/herb-gardening/growing-cilantro-planting-and-care-tips/

Knerl, L. (2022). The Cost Effectiveness of Growing a Garden. *Investopedia.* https://www.investopedia.com/financial-edge/0312/the-true-cost-of-growing-a-garden.aspx

Kring, L. (2023). How to Grow and Care for Bay Laurel Trees. *Gardener's Path.* https://gardenerspath.com/plants/herbs/bay-laurel/

Link, K. (2021, March 31). *Can Supermarkets Reduce Single-Use Plastic Waste? - FoodPrint.* FoodPrint. https://foodprint.org/blog/plastic-waste/

Lofgren, K. (2023). How to Regrow Lettuce from Kitchen Scraps. *Gardener's Path.* https://gardenerspath.com/how-to/regrow-lettuce-scraps/

Lovefoodies. (2021). How To Re Grow Bok Choy. An easy way to recycle off cuts and regrow to save money! *Lovefoodies.* https://lovefoodies.com/how-to-re-grow-bok-choy/

Ly, L. (2023, April 2). *How to Propagate Lemongrass from Store-Bought Stalks.* Garden Betty. https://www.gardenbetty.com/how-to-propagate-lemongrass/

Manhart, T. (2023, March 18). How To Grow A Banana Tree with A Store Bought Banana - Gardening Dream. *Gardening Dream.* https://www.gardeningdream.com/how-to-grow-a-banana-tree-with-a-store-bought-banana/#Soak_the_Seeds_in_Warm_Water

Mark. (2017, March 16). *Grow your Own Mushrooms from Store Bought | Five Gallon Ideas.* Five Gallon Ideas. http://fivegallonideas.com/grow-mushrooms-grocery-store-mycelium/

McIntosh, J. (2022). How to Grow and Care for Lemongrass. *The Spruce.* https://www.thespruce.com/lemongrass-plant-profile-4686088

Miller, L. (2021, April 26). Planting Bok Choy: How To Grow Bok Choy. *Gardening Know How.* https://www.gardeningknowhow.com/edible/vegetables/bok-choy/planting-bok-choy.htm#:~:text=apart%20and%20mulch%20to%20keep,sooner%20than%20the%20standard%20size

*Mint.* (n.d.). Almanac.com. https://www.almanac.com/plant/mint#:

*More Than 90 Percent of Americans Have Pesticides or Their Byproducts in Their Bodies | The Nation.* (2019, March 22). The Nation. https://www.thenation.com/article/archive/pesticides-farmworkers-agriculture/

Myers, V. R. (2022). How to Grow and Care for a Banana Tree. *The Spruce.* https://www.thespruce.com/banana-tree-growing-profile-3269353

NimeshPeiris. (2021, September 9). How To Grow Cucumber From Scraps: [For 2 Month Harvest !!]. *Find Gardening.* https://findgardening.com/how-to-grow-cucumber-from-scraps-for-2-month-harvest/#Harvest_cucumbers

*Okra.* (n.d.). Almanac.com. https://www.almanac.com/plant/okra

*Onions.* (n.d.). Love the Garden. https://www.lovethegarden.com/uk-en/growing-guide/how-grow-onions

Oolya. (2021, April 22). How To Plant And Care For Celery. *Best Landscape Ideas.* https://bestlandscapeideas.com/how-to-plant-and-care-for-celery/

*Peach Growing Guide.* (n.d.). Tui | When to Plant, Feed and Harvest. https://tuigarden.co.nz/how-to-guide/peach-growing-guide/

*Planting, Growing, and Harvesting Blackberries.* (n.d.). Almanac.com. https:// www.almanac.com/plant/blackberries

PreparednessMama. (2021, May 6). *8 Tips to Grow Grocery Store Ginger at Home.* PreparednessMama. https://preparednessmama.com/grow-grocery-store-ginger/

Purnell, J. (2022, June 7). *Pricing Guide: How Much Do Raised Garden Beds Cost? - Lawnstarter.* Lawnstarter. https://lawnstarter.wpengine.com/blog/cost/ raised-garden-beds-price/

*Radishes.* (n.d.). Almanac.com. https://www.almanac.com/plant/radishes

*Re-grow sweet potatoes from the supermarket.* (n.d.). Brisbane City Council. https://www.brisbane.qld.gov.au/clean-and-green/green-home-and-community/clean-and-green-blog/re-grow-sweet-potatoes-from-the-supermarket

*Research Guides: Pineapples Grown at Home: Home.* (n.d.). https://libguides.nybg. org/pineapple

Reuters. (2016). How Gardening Could Save You $600 on Groceries. *Money.* https://money.com/gardening-grocery-savings/

Rhoades, H., & Rhoades, H. (2022, November 15). How To Harvest Broccoli – When To Pick Broccoli. *Gardening Know How.* https://www. gardeningknowhow.com/edible/vegetables/broccoli/harvest-broccoli.htm

Saleem, I. (2021, April 22). Articles how to. *Slick Garden.* https:// slickgarden.com/

Schrader, H. (2020). Don't throw the leftover durian seeds. Soak them in the water and they grow up in the soil. *The Plant Aide.* https://www.theplan taide.com/articles/dont-throw-the-leftover-durian-seeds-soak-them-in-the-water-and-they-grow-up-in-the-soil.html

Shelly. (2021, November 7). *How To Regrow Parsley - Seniorcare2share.* Seniorcare2share. https://www.seniorcare2share.com/how-to-regrow-parsley/

Sidhu, A. (2022). How to Grow and Care for Chestnuts. *Gardener's Path.* https://gardenerspath.com/plants/nut-trees/grow-chestnuts/#Harvesting

Spengler, T., & Spengler, T. (2022, November 23). How To Root Catnip Cuttings – Can You Grow Catnip From Cuttings. *Gardening Know How.* https://www.gardeningknowhow.com/edible/herbs/catnip/how-to-root-catnip-cuttings.htm#:

*Spinach.* (n.d.). Almanac.com. https://www.almanac.com/plant/spinach

Staff, H. D. H. (2022, March 27). *How to Plant, Grow, and Care for Your Coconut Tree*. Happy DIY Home. https://happydiyhome.com/coconut-tree/

Stark Bro's Nurseries & Orchards Co. (n.d.). *How to Tell When Pears Are Ready to Harvest*. https://www.starkbros.com/growing-guide/article/pears-ready-to-harvest#:

Stephens, J. (2022). Growing Mushrooms from Stems (Solved & Explained!) - [2023]. *Total Gardener*. https://totalgardener.com/growing-mushrooms-from-stems/

Steve. (2022, December 20). Can you grow store bought chestnuts? - Garden Super Power. *Garden Super Power*. https://gardensuperpower.com/can-you-grow-store-bought-chestnuts/

Takahashi, A. (2021). How to Regrow. *Gardenisms*. https://gardenisms.com

Taylor, M. (2021). 23 DIY Garden Tools You Can Make from Household Items. *Better Homes & Gardens*. https://www.bhg.com/gardening/yard/tools/no-cost-garden-tools/

*The Advantages of Home Gardens*. (2021, February 16). Home Guides | SF Gate. https://homeguides.sfgate.com/advantages-home-gardens-39103.html

*The Boar*. (n.d.). https://theboar.org/2020/06/environmental-benefits-growing-fruits-vegetables/

The Millennial Gardener. (2020, February 29). *Avocado Won't Fruit? How To Pollinate An Avocado Tree For Self Fertility* [Video]. YouTube. https://www.youtube.com/watch?v=8jdMMjZjI6g

*Tips For Growing Dill From Cuttings*. (2021, February 2). Easily Grow Food. https://easilygrowfood.com/tips-for-growing-dill-from-cuttings/

*Tomatoes*. (n.d.). Almanac.com. https://www.almanac.com/plant/tomatoes#:

"TOP 25 SELF SUFFICIENT QUOTES (of 138)." A-Z Quotes. Accessed October 26, 2023. https://www.azquotes.com/quotes/topics/self-sufficient.html.

*Tricks of the Trade: How to Save Money on Garden Soil*. (n.d.). Houzz. https://www.houzz.com.au/magazine/tricks-of-the-trade-how-to-save-money-on-garden-soil-stsetivw-vs~106098341

Vanderlinden, C. (2022, September 12). How and When to Harvest Asparagus. *The Spruce*. https://www.thespruce.com/growing-vegetables-4127744

Vanorio, A. (2019). Growing Hazelnuts: Your Complete Guide to Planting, Growing and Harvesting Hazelnuts. *Morning Chores*. https://morningchores.com/growing-hazelnuts/

VanZile, J. (2021). How to Grow and Care for an Avocado Plant Indoors. *The Spruce*. https://www.thespruce.com/grow-avocados-indoors-1902590

Veronica.Regly. (2022). How Much Does A Vegetable Garden Cost? *Mini Urban Farm*. https://miniurbanfarm.com/Vegetable-Garden-Costs/

W, R. (2020). Planting a mango seed. *Naples Botanical Garden*. https://www.naplesgarden.org/kitchen-scrap-gardening-series-planting-a-mango-seed/

*When To Harvest Lemongrass For Tea: Lemongrass*. (n.d.). https://www.growkitchenherbs.com/herb/lemongrass/when-to-harvest-lemongrass-for-tea

*When to pick avocados - Science-Based Solutions for Ventura County's Communities, Farms and Environment*. (n.d.). https://ceventura.ucanr.edu/Com_Ag/Subtropical/Avocado_Handbook/Harvesting/When_to_pick_avocados_/

wikiHow. (2023). How to Grow Parsley from Cuttings: 13 Steps (with Pictures). *wikiHow*. https://www.wikihow.com/Grow-Parsley-from-Cuttings

*Will a Radish Top Regrow?* (2020, November 17). Home Guides | SF Gate. https://homeguides.sfgate.com/radish-top-regrow-98007.html

Will, M. J. (2021a). How to Grow Mango from Seed (Easy Method). *Empress of Dirt*. https://empressofdirt.net/grow-mango-seed/

Will, M. J. (2021b). How to Grow An Apple Tree From Seed (Easy Tutorial). *Empress of Dirt*. https://empressofdirt.net/grow-apple-seed/

Woodstream, W. (2020). Growing Mushrooms: How to Deal with Mushroom Pests. *www.saferbrand.com*. https://www.saferbrand.com/articles/mushroom-pests

## INSPIRE A NEW READER!

Whether it's to save money or to step further towards their dream of self-sufficiency, there are many people out there looking for the same guidance you were, and this is your chance to help them find it!

Simply by sharing your honest opinion of this book and a little about your own experience, you'll show new readers where they can find all the information they're looking for.

# LET'S HEAR FROM YOU!

Thank you so much for your support. It makes an incredible difference.

# INDEX